MW00678133

# THE EVOLUTION OF
# PROFESSIONAL
# FOOTBALL

# THE EVOLUTION OF
# PROFESSIONAL
# FOOTBALL

## AN ALMANAC (1920 TO 2015)

## STERLING MILLER

MILL CITY PRESS | MINNEAPOLIS, MN

Copyright © 2015 by Sterling Miller

Mill City Press, Inc.
322 First Avenue N, 5th floor
Minneapolis, MN 55401
612.455.2293
www.millcitypublishing.com

All rights reserved. No part of this publication may be reproduced, stored in a retrieval system, or transmitted, in any form or by any means, electronic, mechanical, photocopying, recording, or otherwise, without the prior written permission of the author.

ISBN-13: 978-1-63413-737-9
LCCN: 2015917842

Cover Design by  Alan Pranke
Typeset by Emily Keenan

*Printed in the United States of America*

# CONTENTS

# INTRODUCTION

**I grew up in York, Nebraska,** a small town with a population a little over 5,000 people. My first football memory is getting a Tudor Electric Football game on Christmas Day 1970. The game, from Sears, was based on the January 1970 Super Bowl and featured figures painted in the colors of the Kansas City Chiefs and the Minnesota Vikings. My brother Paul and I played this game for hours, watching the little men spin around in aimless circles and hoping against hope that they would somehow magically straighten-out and head into the end zone with the felt football in tow. A week later I watched the Nebraska Cornhuskers beat LSU in the 1971 Orange Bowl when No. 14 Jerry Tagge lunged over the Tiger line, holding the ball out with two hands, to score the winning touchdown late in the fourth quarter. The win gave Nebraska a share of the 1970 National Title and an eight-year old boy from York, Nebraska was hooked on football.

My obsession was almost total. In the pre-internet/pre-24-hour a day multi-sport TV channels, this meant I watched every game I could (and these were the days of one college game per week and limited NFL games). I could only get to halftime on *Monday Night Football* because of bedtime. I read every book I could find on football, exhausting the local library and my elementary school shelves. My mom got me a subscription to *Pro Football Weekly*, the bible of football news (and which, sadly, went out of business in 2013). I religiously watched *This Week in Pro Football* with Pat Summerall and Tom Brookshire and was utterly fascinated by the wall of half-NFL team helmets that made up the back drop for the show – and wishing I could somehow duplicate that wall of helmets at my house. Like most 8 to 10-year old kids from a state or town without a NFL franchise, I picked my favorite team based on the helmet logo. Am not proud of it, but dammit, that's just the way it was. I even went as far as to draw a Detroit Lions "lion" on an old white helmet we kept in the "sports trash can"[1] (when the Lions were my favorite team for about two weeks).

At school I had my Baltimore Colts and Green Bay Packers three-ring binder notebooks and I used to trace the single-bar facemask helmet on the front cover so I could experiment with creating new logos for different teams (none of which were ever adopted by any team). We annoyed our teachers with daily "finger-flick" or paper football games, using index fingers and thumbs as goal posts and folded notebook paper to create a small triangular "football" that you knocked back and forth on a desk top, scoring a touchdown if you got the tip of the "ball" over the edge of the desk without it falling off (and if it did fall off your opponent got a field goal try). In addition to electric football, my brother and I played endless hours of Cadaco Foto-Electric National Pro Football Hall of Fame game (which I still own) where you used cards to pick an offensive play and a defensive coverage, laid them on top of each other on the game board, and then slowly pulled out a cardboard sleeve to reveal the results of the play through the magic of a 40 watt light bulb (on which my brother and I burned ourselves numerous times). I treasured my collection of NFL mini ("gum-ball") helmets that rested on four yellow-goalposts, moving the helmets around weekly to show the standings of each division -- just in case someone needed that valuable information. I still have those helmets and goal posts. I lusted after an Oakland Raiders helmet that sat on a shelf in the basement floor of the local J.C. Penny, wishing time and time again that my mom would somehow read my mind and buy it for me (though for some reason never thinking of the more straightforward approach of simply asking for it as a birthday or Christmas gift). And if Joe Namath endorsed it, I had to own it -- shirts, shoes, Brut and popcorn popper.

Above all, I remember my love of football statistics. Every Christmas I got the *World Almanac Book of Facts* in my stocking (yes, I was a weird kid). The first thing I would look up were the standings of the NFL and college conferences, fascinated by the neat columns setting out things like divisions, teams, wins, loses, and ties, and playoff/bowl game results. I kept stats during our neighborhood sandlot football games (and am proud to report that I once rushed for over 3,000 yards in single season – but I am not sure if our measurements would hold up to real NFL scrutiny). What our

---

1        I am not sure about you, but most families I knew growing up had an old trash can in the garage where they kept the footballs, baseballs, basketballs, bats, gloves, and whatever other sports equipment they had lying around.

Neighborhood Football League (my own play on "NFL") lacked in talent, we more than made up for in pages of Big Chief tablet paper setting out my well-kept passing and rushing statistics.

Which brings me to the purpose of this book. I am still a football fanatic. While I do not spend quite as much time watching every football game on television (which is virtually impossible given the fact that just about every college or NFL football game is on TV now), I do have an extensive collection of football memorabilia, books, magazines, buttons, helmets, and record books. Despite my extensive collection, I was looking for a straight-forward book that showed the evolution of the NFL year-by-year via the standings of the teams – showing teams joining and leaving the league, relocating to different cities, or changing names. I couldn't find one. You can easily find books that contain this information but with a lot of clutter and extraneous information. You can definitely find it all online. But I wanted an honest-to-God book that you could hold in your hands and easily figure out how the 1934 NFL differed from the 1975 NFL.

So, I decided to write it myself. This book starts in 1920 at the formation of the National Football League and goes through the most current season (2014) and Super Bowl XLIX (January 2015). I decided to focus my book on the NFL and any leagues that ultimately merged into the NFL, i.e., the AAFC and the AFL. Which means this book will ignore the World Football League, the USFL, XFL, CFL, NFL Europe and any other professional football leagues that did not ultimately become part of the NFL. Not that those leagues are not interesting or important (well, the XFL isn't), but trying to work all of the extra information into my book would detract from its purpose – simple, clean, and easy to find what you want to find.

The book goes year-by-year setting out the standings for that year, along with the playoff results (if any), and the winners of notable awards, e.g., Most Valuable Player. I used the Associated Press awards for simplicity. Other media organizations named award winners over the years (e.g., UPI, *Sporting News*, etc.) but I found the AP to be the most consistent and straight forward to follow. Also, relying on the results of only one media organization allowed me to keep the book as streamlined as possible, a key objective of mine. The book also tells you when new teams joined the league and when (especially in the first 20 years of the NFL) teams left the league and when they relocated or changed their names. I also show the numerous realignments of conferences and divisions.

There is not a lot of narrative in this book but there is a good amount of text and a lot of footnotes (and who doesn't like footnotes?). I have also included the results of things like the Playoff Bowl, the Pro Bowl, the annual Hall of Fame game and other facts and figures along these lines. My sources were varied, including NFL.com, Wikipedia, newspapers, several football-related encyclopedias and a number of official NFL record books.

I enjoyed researching and writing this book very much, reading about the pioneers of the league, the interesting towns and nicknames of franchises long since gone (Oorang Indians anyone?). I especially enjoyed the writing process when I got to the time frame when I first became aware of football, recalling games I watched and players I idolized, bringing up memories of a lot of snowy afternoons in York, Nebraska huddled up on the couch with my brother, eating tomato soup and grilled cheese sandwiches, each of us picking a team to root for against the other (yes, usually based on helmet logo – go "B E N G A L S"!).

While my daughters Maren and Zoe do not share my love for football, I can say that they definitely learned some "new words" if they happened to wander into the media room during a particular bad stretch of play by my beloved Cornhuskers. I want to thank my wife Inger for her patience and encouragement as I researched and wrote this book. Her tolerance of my football addiction (and need to create something like this) is amazing and very, very much appreciated. As my friends say, when I married her I "out-kicked my coverage" by a good bit.

I hope you enjoy the book.

Sterling Miller
July 2015

# 1920 - 1929

## 1920 – American Professional Football Association

| Team | Win | Lost | Tie | Pct. |
|------|-----|------|-----|------|
| Akron Pros | 6 | 0 | 3 | 1.000 |
| Decatur Staleys | 10 | 1 | 2 | .909 |
| Buffalo All-Americans | 9 | 1 | 1 | .900 |
| Chicago Cardinals | 6 | 2 | 1 | .750 |
| Rock Island Independents | 6 | 2 | 1 | .750 |
| Dayton Triangles | 5 | 2 | 2 | .714 |
| Rochester Jeffersons | 6 | 3 | 2 | .667 |
| Canton Bulldogs | 7 | 4 | 2 | .636 |
| Detroit Heralds | 2 | 3 | 3 | .400 |
| Cleveland Panthers/Tigers | 2 | 4 | 2 | .333 |
| Chicago Tigers | 2 | 5 | 1 | .286 |
| Hammond Pros | 2 | 5 | 0 | .286 |
| Columbus Panhandles | 2 | 6 | 2 | .250 |
| Muncie Flyers | 0 | 1 | 0 | .000 |

**Champion: Akron Pros**

---

**The National Football League** was born in 1920 after a meeting held at an automobile dealership in Canton, Ohio. The original name of the NFL was the American Professional Football Association, which was changed to the National Football League several years later. In the early days of the NFL there were no set number of games played per team. The league champion was generally determined by the best winning percentage and ties were not included as part of the calculation. At the league meeting in Akron, Ohio on April 30, 1921, the Akron Pros were awarded the 1920 league title by a vote of the teams (one vote per team). The Decatur Staleys and Buffalo All-Americans protested because they each won more games than Akron and neither had lost to Akron (they tied). The Decatur Staleys would become the Chicago Bears in 1921. The Bears and the Arizona Cardinals (originally the Chicago Cardinals) are the two oldest NFL franchises, both there at the formation of the league.

# 1921 – American Professional Football Association

| Team | Win | Lost | Tie | Pct. |
|------|-----|------|-----|------|
| Chicago Staleys (Bears) | 9 | 1 | 1 | .900 |
| Buffalo All-Americans | 9 | 1 | 1 | .900 |
| Akron Pros | 8 | 3 | 1 | .727 |
| Canton Bulldogs | 5 | 2 | 3 | .714 |
| Rock Island Independents | 4 | 2 | 1 | .667 |
| Evansville Crimson Giants | 3 | 2 | 0 | .600 |
| Green Bay Packers | 3 | 2 | 1 | .600 |
| Dayton Triangles | 4 | 4 | 1 | .500 |
| Chicago Cardinals | 3 | 3 | 2 | .500 |
| Rochester Jeffersons | 2 | 3 | 0 | .400 |
| Cleveland Indians | 3 | 5 | 0 | .375 |
| Washington Senators | 1 | 2 | 0 | .333 |
| Cincinnati Celts | 1 | 3 | 0 | .250 |
| Hammond Pros | 1 | 3 | 1 | .250 |
| Minneapolis Marines | 1 | 3 | 0 | .250 |
| Detroit Panthers/Tigers | 1 | 5 | 1 | .167 |
| Columbus Panhandles | 1 | 8 | 0 | .111 |
| Louisville Brecks | 0 | 2 | 0 | .000 |
| Muncie Flyers | 0 | 2 | 0 | .000 |
| New York Giants | 0 | 2 | 0 | .000 |
| Tonawanda Kardex | 0 | 1 | 0 | .000 |

**Champion: Chicago Staleys (Bears)**

**Teams dropping out:** Detroit Heralds and Chicago Panthers/Tigers.

**Teams joining:** Green Bay Packers, Evansville Crimson Giants, Washington Senators, Cincinnati Celts, Detroit Panthers/Tigers, Louisville Brecks, New York (Brinkley) Giants, and Tonawanda Kardex (Tonawanda, NY).

The Cleveland Panthers/Tigers changed their name to the Indians. The Chicago Staleys won the league title over the Buffalo All-Americans by vote of the league members. There was controversy over whether a second game played between the two teams (Buffalo won the first game) should count in the standings or was it an exhibition, as was common at the time. The league decided it should count and that the latter game played between teams playing multiple times should be given more weight in the event of a tie. Since Chicago defeated Buffalo in the second game – played a week later – the league awarded Chicago the title. It is interesting to see the number of teams that adopted the same nickname as the local major league baseball team, e.g., the Washington Senators. This happened a number of times during the first 20 years of the NFL. Whether it was just a way to cash in on the popularity of baseball or simply lack of imagination, it's difficult to see anything like that happening today without massive litigation.

# 1922 – National Football League

| Team | Win | Lost | Tie | Pct. |
|---|---|---|---|---|
| Canton Bulldogs | 10 | 0 | 2 | 1.000 |
| Chicago Bears | 9 | 3 | 0 | .750 |
| Chicago Cardinals | 8 | 3 | 0 | .727 |
| Toledo Maroons | 5 | 2 | 2 | .714 |
| Rock Island Independents | 4 | 2 | 1 | .667 |
| Racine Legion | 6 | 4 | 1 | .600 |
| Dayton Triangles | 4 | 3 | 1 | .571 |
| Green Bay Packers | 4 | 3 | 3 | .571 |
| Buffalo All-Americans | 5 | 4 | 1 | .556 |
| Akron Pros | 3 | 5 | 2 | .375 |
| Milwaukee Badgers | 2 | 4 | 3 | .333 |
| Oorang Indians | 2 | 6 | 0 | .250 |
| Minneapolis Marines | 1 | 3 | 0 | .250 |
| Louisville Brecks | 1 | 3 | 0 | .250 |
| Rochester Jeffersons | 0 | 4 | 1 | .000 |
| Hammond Pros | 0 | 5 | 1 | .000 |
| Evansville Crimson Giants | 0 | 3 | 0 | .000 |
| Columbus Panhandles | 0 | 8 | 0 | .000 |

**Champion: Canton Bulldogs**

**Teams dropping out:** Cleveland Indians, Washington Senators, Cincinnati Celts, Detroit Panthers/Tigers, Muncie Flyers, New York Giants, and Tonawanda Kardex.

**Teams joining:** Toledo Maroons, Racine Legion, Milwaukee Badgers, and Oorang Indians.

———

The American Professional Football Association changed its name to National Football League in June 1922. The Staleys changed their name to the Chicago Bears. The Oorang Indians were based in Marion, Ohio.

## 1923 – National Football League

| Team | Win | Lost | Tie | Pct. |
|------|-----|------|-----|------|
| Canton Bulldogs | 11 | 0 | 1 | 1.000 |
| Chicago Bears | 9 | 2 | 1 | .818 |
| Green Bay Packers | 7 | 2 | 1 | .778 |
| Milwaukee Badgers | 7 | 2 | 3 | .778 |
| Cleveland Indians | 3 | 1 | 3 | .770 |
| Chicago Cardinals | 8 | 4 | 0 | .667 |
| Duluth Kelleys | 4 | 3 | 0 | .571 |
| Columbus Tigers | 5 | 4 | 1 | .556 |
| Buffalo All Americans | 4 | 4 | 3 | .500 |
| Racine Legion | 4 | 4 | 2 | .500 |
| Toledo Maroons | 3 | 3 | 2 | .500 |
| Rock Island Independents | 2 | 3 | 3 | .400 |
| Minneapolis Marines | 2 | 5 | 2 | .286 |
| St. Louis All-Stars | 1 | 4 | 2 | .200 |
| Hammond Pros | 1 | 5 | 1 | .167 |
| Dayton Triangles | 1 | 6 | 1 | .143 |
| Akron Pros | 1 | 6 | 0 | .143 |
| Oorang Indians | 1 | 10 | 0 | .091 |
| Rochester Jeffersons | 0 | 4 | 0 | .000 |
| Louisville Brecks | 0 | 3 | 0 | .000 |

**Champion: Canton Bulldogs**

**Teams dropping out:** Evansville Crimson Giants.

**Teams joining:** Duluth Kelleys and St. Louis All-Stars.

———————

The Columbus Panhandlers changed their name to the Columbus Tigers.

# 1924 – National Football League

| Team | Win | Lost | Tie | Pct. |
|------|-----|------|-----|------|
| Cleveland Bulldogs | 7 | 1 | 1 | .875 |
| Chicago Bears | 6 | 1 | 4 | .857 |
| Frankford Yellow Jackets | 11 | 2 | 1 | .846 |
| Duluth Kelleys | 5 | 1 | 1 | .833 |
| Rock Island Independents | 5 | 2 | 2 | .714 |
| Green Bay Packers | 7 | 4 | 0 | .636 |
| Racine Legion | 4 | 3 | 3 | .571 |
| Chicago Cardinals | 5 | 4 | 1 | .556 |
| Buffalo Bisons | 6 | 5 | 0 | .545 |
| Columbus Tigers | 4 | 4 | 0 | .500 |
| Hammond Pros | 2 | 2 | 1 | .500 |
| Milwaukee Badgers | 5 | 8 | 0 | .385 |
| Akron Pros | 2 | 6 | 0 | .250 |
| Dayton Triangles | 2 | 6 | 0 | .250 |
| Kansas City Cowboys/Blues | 2 | 7 | 0 | .222 |
| Kenosha Maroons | 0 | 4 | 1 | .000 |
| Minneapolis Marines | 0 | 6 | 0 | .000 |
| Rochester Jeffersons | 0 | 7 | 0 | .000 |

**Champion: Cleveland Bulldogs**

**Teams dropping out:** Louisville Brecks, St. Louis All-Stars, Oorang Indians, and Toledo Maroons.

**Teams joining:** Frankford Yellow Jackets (Frankford, PA), Kansas City Cowboys/Blues, and Kenosha Maroons (Kenosha, IL).

––––––––––––

The owners of the defunct Cleveland Indians football team bought the name and players from the Canton Bulldogs and moved the franchise to Cleveland. The Buffalo All-Americans changed their name to the Buffalo Bisons.

## 1925 – National Football League

| Team | Win | Lost | Tie | Pct. |
|------|-----|------|-----|------|
| Chicago Cardinals | 11 | 2 | 1 | .846 |
| Pottsville Maroons | 10 | 2 | 0 | .833 |
| Detroit Panthers | 8 | 2 | 2 | .800 |
| New York Giants | 8 | 4 | 0 | .667 |
| Akron Pros/Indians | 4 | 2 | 2 | .667 |
| Frankford Yellow Jackets | 13 | 7 | 0 | .650 |
| Chicago Bears | 9 | 5 | 3 | .643 |
| Rock Island Independents | 5 | 3 | 3 | .625 |
| Green Bay Packers | 8 | 5 | 0 | .615 |
| Providence Steam Roller | 6 | 5 | 1 | .545 |
| Canton Bulldogs | 4 | 4 | 0 | .500 |
| Cleveland Bulldogs | 5 | 8 | 1 | .385 |
| Kansas City Cowboys | 2 | 5 | 1 | .286 |
| Hammond Pros | 1 | 4 | 0 | .200 |
| Buffalo Bisons | 1 | 6 | 2 | .143 |
| Duluth Kelleys | 0 | 3 | 0 | .000 |
| Rochester Jeffersons | 0 | 6 | 1 | .000 |
| Milwaukee Badgers | 0 | 6 | 0 | .000 |
| Dayton Triangles | 0 | 7 | 1 | .000 |
| Columbus Tigers | 0 | 9 | 0 | .000 |

**Champion: Chicago Cardinals**

**Teams dropping out:** Kenosha Maroons, Racine Legion, and Minneapolis Marines.

**Teams joining:** Pottsville Maroons, Detroit Panthers, New York Giants, Providence Steam Roller, and Canton Bulldogs.

———

There was another disputed league title in 1925. The Pottsville Maroons were declared ineligible to play for the title when they scheduled an unsanctioned game against Notre Dame. The Maroons claimed the Commissioner had given them permission to play the game over the telephone (a claim the Commissioner denied and was contrary to a letter he had sent to the Maroons warning them not to play the game), and that the Cardinals had scheduled extra games against inferior teams to pad their record. The Commissioner sided with the Cardinals and there was no joy in Pottsville in

1925. On a side note, it was after reading the story of the 1925 Pottsville Maroons (captured so well in David Fleming's book, *Breaker Boys: The Story of the Pottsville and the Stolen 1925 Championship*) and the various now defunct NFL franchises he writes about that inspired this book.

The 1925 season was also important because of the arrival of Harold "Red" Grange, the "Galloping Ghost." After a stellar college career, Grange did what many thought unthinkable and agreed to play professional football, signing with the Chicago Bears of the nascent NFL. Many considered professional football a shady enterprise and far below the dignity of the college version. Grange's arrival changed that. After signing, he and the team embarked on a 19-game, 67-day barnstorming tour of America that ultimately legitimized the NFL in the eyes of the nation. His appearances drew huge crowds, sometimes over 70,000 when most teams struggled to get over 20,000 on the best of days. The games with Grange saved many NFL teams from financial ruin and with enough money to carry over into the next season. During the season, Grange and Coach Halas met with President Coolidge at the White House. They were introduced as "Mr. Halas and Mr. Grange of the Chicago Bears" to which the non-sport savvy President replied, "Glad to meet you. I always did like animal acts."

## 1926 – National Football League

| Team | Win | Lost | Tie | Pct. |
|---|---|---|---|---|
| Frankford Yellow Jackets | 14 | 1 | 2 | .933 |
| Chicago Bears | 12 | 1 | 3 | .923 |
| Pottsville Maroons | 10 | 2 | 2 | .833 |
| Kansas City Cowboys | 8 | 3 | 0 | .727 |
| Green Bay Packers | 7 | 3 | 3 | .700 |
| Los Angeles Buccaneers | 6 | 3 | 1 | .667 |
| New York Giants | 8 | 4 | 1 | .667 |
| Duluth Eskimos | 6 | 5 | 3 | .545 |
| Buffalo Rangers | 4 | 4 | 2 | .500 |
| Chicago Cardinals | 5 | 6 | 1 | .455 |
| Providence Steam Roller | 5 | 7 | 1 | .417 |
| Detroit Panthers | 4 | 6 | 2 | .400 |
| Hartford Blues | 3 | 7 | 0 | .300 |
| Brooklyn Lions | 3 | 8 | 0 | .273 |
| Milwaukee Badgers | 2 | 7 | 0 | .222 |
| Akron Indians | 1 | 4 | 3 | .200 |
| Dayton Triangles | 1 | 4 | 1 | .200 |
| Racine Tornadoes | 1 | 4 | 0 | .200 |
| Columbus Tigers | 1 | 6 | 0 | .143 |
| Canton Bulldogs | 1 | 9 | 3 | .100 |
| Hammond Pros | 0 | 4 | 0 | .000 |
| Louisville Colonels | 0 | 4 | 0 | .000 |

**Champion: Frankford Yellow Jackets**

**Teams dropping out:** Rock Island Independents (left to join a rival league), Rochester Jeffersons (suspended operations), and Cleveland Bulldogs (suspended operations).

**Teams joining:** Brooklyn Lions, Hartford Blues, Los Angeles Buccaneers, Louisville Colonels, and Racine Tornadoes.

———————

The Duluth Kelleys changed their name to the Duluth Eskimos. The Buffalo Bisons changed their name to the Buffalo Rangers. The Akron Pros changed their name to the Akron Indians.

# 1927 – National Football League

| Team | Win | Lost | Tie | Pct. |
|---|---|---|---|---|
| New York Giants | 11 | 1 | 1 | .917 |
| Green Bay Packers | 7 | 2 | 1 | .778 |
| Chicago Bears | 9 | 3 | 2 | .750 |
| Cleveland Bulldogs | 8 | 4 | 1 | .667 |
| Providence Steam Roller | 8 | 5 | 1 | .615 |
| New York Yankees | 7 | 8 | 1 | .467 |
| Frankford Yellow Jackets | 6 | 9 | 3 | .400 |
| Pottsville Maroons | 5 | 8 | 0 | .385 |
| Chicago Cardinals | 3 | 7 | 1 | .300 |
| Dayton Triangles | 1 | 6 | 1 | .143 |
| Duluth Eskimos | 1 | 8 | 0 | .111 |
| Buffalo Bisons | 0 | 5 | 0 | .000 |

**Champion: New York Giants**

**Teams dropping out:** Kansas City Cowboys, Los Angeles Buccaneers, Detroit Panthers, Hartford Blues, Brooklyn Lions, Canton Bulldogs, Milwaukee Badgers, Akron Indians, Racine Tornadoes, Columbus Tigers, Hammond Pros, and Louisville Colonels.

**Teams joining:** New York Yankees (joined from a rival league) and Cleveland Bulldogs (returned).

---

The Buffalo Rangers changed their name back to the Buffalo Bisons, but folded mid-season.

## 1928 – National Football League

| Team | Win | Lost | Tie | Pct. |
|---|---|---|---|---|
| Providence Steam Roller | 8 | 1 | 2 | .889 |
| Frankford Yellow Jackets | 11 | 3 | 2 | .786 |
| Detroit Wolverines | 7 | 2 | 1 | .778 |
| Green Bay Packers | 6 | 4 | 3 | .600 |
| Chicago Bears | 7 | 5 | 1 | .583 |
| New York Giants | 4 | 7 | 2 | .364 |
| New York Yankees | 4 | 8 | 1 | .333 |
| Pottsville Maroons | 2 | 8 | 0 | .200 |
| Chicago Cardinals | 1 | 5 | 0 | .167 |
| Dayton Triangles | 0 | 7 | 0 | .000 |

**Champion: Providence Steam Roller**

**Teams dropping out:** Cleveland Bulldogs, Duluth Eskimos, and Buffalo Bisons.

**Teams joining:** Detroit Wolverines.

---

1928 was the last year a team not still in existence today won the NFL title.

# 1929 – National Football League

| Team | Win | Lost | Tie | Pct. |
|------|-----|------|-----|------|
| Green Bay Packers | 12 | 0 | 1 | 1.000 |
| New York Giants | 13 | 1 | 1 | .929 |
| Frankford Yellow Jackets | 10 | 4 | 5 | .714 |
| Chicago Cardinals | 6 | 6 | 1 | .500 |
| Boston Bulldogs | 4 | 4 | 0 | .500 |
| Staten Island Stapletons | 3 | 4 | 3 | .429 |
| Providence Steam Roller | 4 | 6 | 2 | .400 |
| Orange Tornadoes | 3 | 5 | 4 | .375 |
| Chicago Bears | 4 | 9 | 2 | .308 |
| Buffalo Bisons | 1 | 7 | 1 | .125 |
| Minneapolis Red Jackets | 1 | 9 | 0 | .100 |
| Dayton Triangles | 0 | 6 | 0 | .000 |

**Champion: Green Bay Packers**

**Teams dropping out:** Detroit Wolverines and New York Yankees.

**Teams joining:** Staten Island Stapletons, Orange Tornadoes (Orange, NJ), Minneapolis Red Jackets, and Buffalo Bisons (returning).

––––––––––

The Pottsville Maroons relocated to Boston and changed their name to the Boston Bulldogs. Running back Ernie Nevers of the Chicago Cardinals rushed for six touchdowns during one game, a 40-0 win over cross-town rivals the Chicago Bears, a record that still stands today. Nevers also kicked all four extra-points and is the only player to score 40 points in a single game.

# 1930-1939

## 1930 – National Football League

| Team | Win | Lost | Tie | Pct. |
|---|---|---|---|---|
| Green Bay Packers | 10 | 3 | 1 | .769 |
| New York Giants | 13 | 4 | 0 | .765 |
| Chicago Bears | 9 | 4 | 1 | .692 |
| Brooklyn Dodgers | 7 | 4 | 1 | .636 |
| Providence Steam Roller | 6 | 4 | 1 | .600 |
| Staten Island Stapletons | 5 | 5 | 2 | .500 |
| Chicago Cardinals | 5 | 6 | 2 | .455 |
| Portsmouth Spartans | 5 | 6 | 3 | .455 |
| Frankford Yellow Jackets | 4 | 13 | 1 | .235 |
| Minneapolis Red Jackets | 1 | 7 | 1 | .125 |
| Newark Tornadoes | 1 | 10 | 1 | .091 |

**Champion: Green Bay Packers**

**Teams dropping out:** Buffalo Bisons and Boston Bulldogs.

**Teams joining:** Portsmouth Spartans (Ohio).

––––––––––

**The Dayton Triangles relocated** to Brooklyn and changed their name to the Brooklyn Dodgers. The new Portsmouth Spartans franchise would move to Detroit in 1934 and become the Detroit Lions. The Orange Tornadoes relocated to Newark, NJ.

## 1931 – National Football League

| Team | Win | Lost | Tie | Pct. |
|------|-----|------|-----|------|
| Green Bay Packers | 12 | 2 | 0 | .857 |
| Portsmouth Spartans | 11 | 3 | 0 | .786 |
| Chicago Bears | 8 | 5 | 0 | .615 |
| Chicago Cardinals | 5 | 4 | 0 | .556 |
| New York Giants | 7 | 6 | 1 | .538 |
| Providence Steam Roller | 4 | 4 | 3 | .500 |
| Staten Island Stapletons | 4 | 6 | 1 | .400 |
| Cleveland Indians | 2 | 8 | 0 | .200 |
| Brooklyn Dodgers | 2 | 12 | 0 | .143 |
| Frankford Yellow Jackets | 1 | 6 | 1 | .143 |

**Champion: Green Bay Packers**

**Teaming dropping out:** Newark Tornadoes and Minneapolis Red Jackets.

**Teams joining:** Cleveland Indians.

————————

The Frankford Yellow Jackets folded at mid-season.

# 1932 – National Football League

| Team | Win | Lost | Tie | Pct. |
|---|---|---|---|---|
| Chicago Bears | 7 | 1 | 6 | .875 |
| Green Bay Packers | 10 | 3 | 1 | .769 |
| Portsmouth Spartans | 6 | 2 | 4 | .750 |
| Boston Braves | 4 | 4 | 2 | .500 |
| New York Giants | 4 | 6 | 2 | .400 |
| Brooklyn Dodgers | 3 | 9 | 0 | .250 |
| Chicago Cardinals | 2 | 6 | 2 | .250 |
| Staten Island Stapletons | 2 | 7 | 3 | .222 |

**Champion: Chicago Bears**

**Teams dropping out:** Providence Steam Rollers, Cleveland Indians, and Frankford Yellow Jackets.

**Teams joining:** Boston Braves.

---

The Chicago Bears defeated the Portsmouth Spartans in a post-season playoff to break the tie for the championship. The game was played indoors on a shortened field inside Chicago Stadium due to severe weather. The results of that game (a Bears' win and a Spartans' loss) were added to the season results which dropped the Spartans to third place behind the Green Bay Packers. The newly formed Boston Braves would relocate to Washington, D.C. in 1937 and become the Washington Redskins. The Great Depression began taking its toll on the league and 1932 saw it ebb to its lowest number of teams at eight.

# 1933 – National Football League

## Eastern Division

| Team | Win | Lost | Tie |
|------|-----|------|-----|
| New York Giants | 11 | 3 | 0 |
| Brooklyn Dodgers | 5 | 4 | 1 |
| Boston Redskins | 5 | 5 | 2 |
| Philadelphia Eagles | 3 | 5 | 1 |
| Pittsburgh Pirates | 3 | 6 | 2 |

## Western Division

| Team | Win | Lost | Tie |
|------|-----|------|-----|
| Chicago Bears | 10 | 2 | 1 |
| Portsmouth Spartans | 6 | 5 | 0 |
| Green Bay Packers | 5 | 7 | 1 |
| Cincinnati Reds | 3 | 6 | 1 |
| Chicago Cardinals | 1 | 9 | 1 |

**Champion: Chicago Bears defeat the New York Giants in Chicago, 23-21.**

**Teams dropping out:** Staten Island Stapletons.
**Teams joining:** Cincinnati Reds, Philadelphia Eagles, and Pittsburgh Pirates.

---

In 1933, the NFL split into the Eastern and Western divisions with the winners of each division playing for the league title (with the location of the game alternating between the divisions, i.e., the Western Division hosted the first championship game despite a lessor record than the Eastern Division winner). Many consider 1933 the beginning of the NFL as we know it today. Changes were made in the rules to encourage the forward pass and open up the offenses. The Boston Braves changed their name to the Boston Redskins. In 2015, a federal court invalidated the "Redskins" federal trademark due to it being offensive to Native Americans. The Redskins announced they will appeal. While it will be interesting to see what happens, the effect of losing the federal trademark will not force the Redskins to change their nickname as they will still have common law trademark rights and there is no law preventing the team from using the "Redskins" name even if no federal trademark protection exists. If the decision is upheld, it will make it easier for "knock-off" merchandise to use the Redskins name and logo.

## 1934 – National Football League

### Eastern Division

| Team | Win | Lost | Tie |
| --- | --- | --- | --- |
| New York Giants | 8 | 5 | 0 |
| Boston Redskins | 6 | 6 | 0 |
| Brooklyn Dodgers | 4 | 7 | 0 |
| Philadelphia Eagles | 4 | 7 | 0 |
| Pittsburgh Pirates | 2 | 10 | 0 |

### Western Division

| Team | Win | Lost | Tie |
| --- | --- | --- | --- |
| Chicago Bears | 13 | 0 | 0 |
| Detroit Lions | 10 | 3 | 0 |
| Green Bay Packers | 7 | 6 | 0 |
| Chicago Cardinals | 5 | 6 | 0 |
| Cincinnati Reds/ St. Louis Gunners | 1 | 10 | 0 |

**Champion:  New York Giants defeat the Chicago Bears in New York, 30-13.**

The Cincinnati Reds team folded after a 0-8 start and their place in the league was taken by the St. Louis Gunners. The Gunners were formed out of local rookies and castoffs from other NFL teams and went 1-2 over the last three games of the 1934 season. The Portsmouth Spartans relocated to Detroit before the start of the season and changed their name to the Detroit Lions.

# 1935 – National Football League

## Eastern Division

| Team | Win | Lost | Tie |
|------|-----|------|-----|
| New York Giants | 9 | 3 | 0 |
| Brooklyn Dodgers | 5 | 6 | 1 |
| Pittsburgh Pirates | 4 | 8 | 0 |
| Boston Redskins | 2 | 8 | 1 |
| Philadelphia Eagles | 2 | 9 | 0 |

## Western Division

| Team | Win | Lost | Tie |
|------|-----|------|-----|
| Detroit Lions | 7 | 3 | 2 |
| Green Bay Packers | 8 | 4 | 0 |
| Chicago Bears | 6 | 4 | 2 |
| Chicago Cardinals | 6 | 4 | 2 |

**Champion: Detroit Lions defeat the New York Giants in Detroit, 26-7.**

**Teams dropping out:** St. Louis Gunners.

**Teams joining:** None.

The St. Louis Gunners folded before the start of the season and the league dropped to nine teams. 1935 was the first year each team played the same number of games, in this case 12 (other than for a weather cancelation of the game between the Boston Redskins and Philadelphia Eagles).

## 1936 – National Football League

### Eastern Division

| Team | Win | Lost | Tie |
|---|---|---|---|
| Boston Redskins | 7 | 5 | 0 |
| Pittsburgh Pirates | 6 | 6 | 0 |
| New York Giants | 5 | 6 | 1 |
| Brooklyn Dodgers | 3 | 8 | 1 |
| Philadelphia Eagles | 1 | 11 | 0 |

### Western Division

| Team | Win | Lost | Tie |
|---|---|---|---|
| Green Bay Packers | 10 | 1 | 1 |
| Chicago Bears | 9 | 3 | 0 |
| Detroit Lions | 8 | 4 | 0 |
| Chicago Cardinals | 3 | 8 | 1 |

**Champion: Green Bay Packers defeat the Boston Redskins in New York, 21-6.**

**Teaming dropping out:** None.

**Teams joining:** None.

---

Boston Redskins owner, George Marshall, raised tickets prices for the championship game without notice. In the face of anger from fans and local press, Marshall simply moved the championship game to New York City thus depriving the hometown fans of the game being played in Boston. The next year he moved the franchise to Washington, D.C.

# 1937 – National Football League

## Eastern Division

| Team | Win | Lost | Tie |
| --- | --- | --- | --- |
| Washington Redskins | 8 | 3 | 0 |
| New York Giants | 6 | 3 | 2 |
| Pittsburgh Pirates | 4 | 7 | 0 |
| Brooklyn Dodgers | 3 | 7 | 1 |
| Philadelphia Eagles | 2 | 8 | 1 |

## Western Division

| Team | Win | Lost | Tie |
| --- | --- | --- | --- |
| Chicago Bears | 9 | 1 | 1 |
| Green Bay Packers | 7 | 4 | 0 |
| Detroit Lions | 7 | 4 | 0 |
| Chicago Cardinals | 5 | 5 | 1 |
| Cleveland Rams | 1 | 10 | 0 |

**Champion: Washington Redskins defeat the Chicago Bears in Chicago, 28-21.**

Teams dropping out: None.

Teams joining: Cleveland Rams.

––––––––––

The Boston Redskins relocated to Washington, D.C. The league dropped to an 11 game schedule, down from 12 games. Additionally, with the relocation of the Boston franchise and the addition of the Cleveland Rams, the league reached a new level of stability with no changes in teams until World War II.

## 1938 – National Football League

### Eastern Division

| Team | Win | Lost | Tie |
|------|-----|------|-----|
| New York Giants | 8 | 2 | 1 |
| Washington Redskins | 6 | 3 | 2 |
| Brooklyn Dodgers | 4 | 4 | 3 |
| Philadelphia Eagles | 5 | 6 | 0 |
| Pittsburgh Pirates | 2 | 9 | 0 |

### Western Division

| Team | Win | Lost | Tie |
|------|-----|------|-----|
| Green Bay Packers | 8 | 3 | 0 |
| Detroit Lions | 7 | 4 | 0 |
| Chicago Bears | 6 | 5 | 0 |
| Cleveland Rams | 4 | 7 | 0 |
| Chicago Cardinals | 2 | 9 | 0 |

**Champion: New York Giants defeat the Green Bay Packers in New York, 23-17.**

### Season Awards

*Most Valuable Player*          Mel Hein, Center, New York Giants

---

In 1938 the NFL created the "Joe F. Carr Most Valuable Player Award." Joe Carr was the President of the NFL from 1921 – 1939. The first award went to Mel Hein of the New York Giants. There is much confusion about NFL MVP awards given the number of organizations handing out some type of "MVP award" over the years. This book will use the Joe F. Carr award through the 1946 season and then, to the extent awarded, use the Associated Press awards for MVP, Rookie of the Year, Offensive Player of the Year, Defensive Player of the Year, etc.

# 1939 – National Football League

## Eastern Division

| Team | Win | Lost | Tie |
|---|---|---|---|
| New York Giants | 9 | 1 | 1 |
| Washington Redskins | 8 | 2 | 1 |
| Brooklyn Dodgers | 4 | 6 | 1 |
| Philadelphia Eagles | 1 | 9 | 1 |
| Pittsburgh Pirates | 1 | 9 | 1 |

## Western Division

| Team | Win | Lost | Tie |
|---|---|---|---|
| Green Bay Packers | 9 | 2 | 0 |
| Chicago Bears | 8 | 3 | 0 |
| Detroit Lions | 6 | 5 | 0 |
| Cleveland Rams | 5 | 5 | 1 |
| Chicago Cardinals | 1 | 10 | 0 |

**Champion: Green Bay Packers defeat the New York Giants in Milwaukee, 27-0.**

## Season Awards

*Most Valuable Player*                Parker Hall, Halfback, Cleveland Rams

---

The Green Bay Packers 27-0 defeat of the New York Giants was the first shutout in an NFL championship game. The Brooklyn Dodgers vs. Philadelphia Eagles game on October 22, 1939 was the first televised NFL football game. NBC televised the game and it was only available to viewers in New York and Albany. The Dodgers won the game, 23-14. Regular television broadcasts of NFL games did not begin until 1951.

# 1940-1949

## 1940 – National Football League

### Eastern Division

| Team | Win | Lost | Tie |
|------|-----|------|-----|
| Washington Redskins | 9 | 2 | 0 |
| Brooklyn Dodgers | 8 | 3 | 0 |
| New York Giants | 6 | 4 | 1 |
| Pittsburgh Pirates | 2 | 7 | 2 |
| Philadelphia Eagles | 1 | 10 | 0 |

### Western Division

| Team | Win | Lost | Tie |
|------|-----|------|-----|
| Chicago Bears | 8 | 3 | 0 |
| Green Bay Packers | 6 | 4 | 1 |
| Detroit Lions | 5 | 5 | 1 |
| Cleveland Rams | 4 | 6 | 1 |
| Chicago Cardinals | 2 | 7 | 2 |

**Champion:  Chicago Bears defeat the Washington Redskins in Washington, 73-0.**

### Season Awards

*Most Valuable Player*          Ace Parker, Halfback, Brooklyn Dodgers

---

**The Chicago Bears' 73-0 win** over the Washington Redskins remains the largest point differential for any NFL championship or playoff game.

# 1941 – National Football League

## Eastern Division

| Team | Win | Lost | Tie |
|------|-----|------|-----|
| New York Giants | 8 | 3 | 0 |
| Brooklyn Dodgers | 7 | 4 | 0 |
| Washington Redskins | 6 | 5 | 0 |
| Philadelphia Eagles | 2 | 8 | 1 |
| Pittsburgh Steelers | 1 | 9 | 1 |

## Western Division

| Team | Win | Lost | Tie |
|------|-----|------|-----|
| Chicago Bears | 10 | 1 | 0 |
| Green Bay Packers | 10 | 1 | 0 |
| Detroit Lions | 4 | 6 | 1 |
| Chicago Cardinals | 3 | 7 | 1 |
| Cleveland Rams | 2 | 9 | 0 |

**Champion: Chicago Bears defeat the New York Giants in Chicago, 37-9.**

## Season Awards

*Most Valuable Player*                Don Hutson, Wide Receiver, Green Bay Packers

---

The Chicago Bears defeated the Green Bay Packers in a playoff game for the Western Division title, 33-14. Leading up to the 1941 season, the league enacted rules to create a playoff when a division race was tied and "sudden death" to determine the winner of playoff games. The Pittsburgh Pirates changed their name to the Pittsburgh Steelers, after the steel manufacturing industry so important to Pittsburgh at the time.

# 1942 – National Football League

## Eastern Division

| Team | Win | Lost | Tie |
|------|-----|------|-----|
| Washington Redskins | 10 | 1 | 0 |
| Pittsburgh Steelers | 7 | 4 | 0 |
| New York Giants | 5 | 5 | 1 |
| Brooklyn Dodgers | 3 | 8 | 0 |
| Philadelphia Eagles | 2 | 9 | 0 |

## Western Division

| Team | Win | Lost | Tie |
|------|-----|------|-----|
| Chicago Bears | 11 | 0 | 0 |
| Green Bay Packers | 8 | 2 | 1 |
| Cleveland Rams | 5 | 6 | 0 |
| Chicago Cardinals | 3 | 8 | 0 |
| Detroit Lions | 0 | 11 | 0 |

**Champion: Washington Redskins defeat the Chicago Bears in Washington, 14-6.**

## Season Awards

*Most Valuable Player*          Don Hutson, Wide Receiver, Green Bay Packers

---

In an interesting dichotomy, the 1942 Chicago Bears went undefeated in the regular season and the 1942 Detroit Lions lost all of their games. Both teams were in the Western Division.

# 1943 – National Football League

## Eastern Division

| Team | Win | Lost | Tie |
|---|---|---|---|
| Washington Redskins | 6 | 3 | 1 |
| New York Giants | 6 | 3 | 1 |
| Philadelphia Eagles-Pittsburgh Steelers | 5 | 4 | 1 |
| Brooklyn Dodgers | 2 | 8 | 0 |

## Western Division

| Team | Win | Lost | Tie |
|---|---|---|---|
| Chicago Bears | 8 | 1 | 1 |
| Green Bay Packers | 7 | 2 | 1 |
| Detroit Lions | 3 | 6 | 1 |
| Chicago Cardinals | 0 | 10 | 0 |
| Cleveland Rams | - | - | - |

**Champion:  Chicago Bears defeat the Washington Redskins in Chicago, 41-21.**

## Season Awards

*Most Valuable Player*                    Sid Luckman, Quarterback, Chicago Bears

---

The wearing of helmets by all players became mandatory beginning with the 1943 season.  For financial reasons and manpower reasons due to World War II, the Philadelphia and Pittsburgh franchises merged for the 1943 season (called the "Steagles" by fans).  Due to hardship created by the war, the league played one fewer game, 10, than it had in the past several years and the Cleveland franchise was allowed to suspend operations for the 1943 season.

## 1944 – National Football League

### Eastern Division

| Team | Win | Lost | Tie |
|------|-----|------|-----|
| New York Giants | 8 | 1 | 1 |
| Philadelphia Eagles | 7 | 1 | 2 |
| Washington Redskins | 6 | 3 | 1 |
| Boston Yanks | 2 | 8 | 0 |
| Brooklyn Tigers | 0 | 10 | 0 |

### Western Division

| Team | Win | Lost | Tie |
|------|-----|------|-----|
| Green Bay Packers | 8 | 2 | 0 |
| Chicago Bears | 6 | 3 | 1 |
| Detroit Lions | 6 | 3 | 1 |
| Cleveland Rams | 4 | 6 | 0 |
| Chicago Cardinals-Pittsburgh Steelers | 0 | 10 | 0 |

**Champion:  Green Bay Packers defeat the New York Giants in New York, 14-7.**

### Season Awards

*Most Valuable Player*          Frank Sinkwich, Halfback, Detroit Lions

---

The Boston Yanks joined the league as a new franchise. The Cleveland Rams were able to restart operations. The Brooklyn Dodgers changed their name to the Brooklyn Tigers. Similar to its merger with the Philadelphia franchise in 1943, and due to the same financial and manpower reasons, the Pittsburgh Steelers merged with the Chicago Cardinals for the 1944 season (and played in the Western Division).

# 1945 – National Football League

## Eastern Division

| Team | Win | Lost | Tie |
|---|---|---|---|
| Washington Redskins | 8 | 2 | 0 |
| Philadelphia Eagles | 7 | 3 | 0 |
| New York Giants | 3 | 6 | 1 |
| Boston Yanks | 3 | 6 | 1 |
| Pittsburgh Steelers | 2 | 8 | 0 |

## Western Division

| Team | Win | Lost | Tie |
|---|---|---|---|
| Cleveland Rams | 9 | 1 | 0 |
| Detroit Lions | 7 | 3 | 0 |
| Green Bay Packers | 6 | 4 | 0 |
| Chicago Bears | 3 | 7 | 0 |
| Chicago Cardinals | 1 | 9 | 0 |

**Champion: Cleveland Rams defeat the Washington Redskins in Cleveland, 15-14.**

## Season Awards

*Most Valuable Player*              Bob Waterfield, Quarterback, Cleveland Rams

---

The Brooklyn Tigers were merged into the Boston Yanks at the start of the 1945 season. The Pittsburgh Steelers were able to sustain operations as a separate team.

## 1946 – National Football League

### Eastern Division

| Team | Win | Lost | Tie |
|------|-----|------|-----|
| New York Giants | 7 | 3 | 1 |
| Philadelphia Eagles | 6 | 5 | 0 |
| Washington Redskins | 5 | 5 | 1 |
| Pittsburgh Steelers | 5 | 5 | 1 |
| Boston Yanks | 2 | 8 | 1 |

### Western Division

| Team | Win | Lost | Tie |
|------|-----|------|-----|
| Chicago Bears | 8 | 2 | 1 |
| Los Angeles Rams | 6 | 4 | 1 |
| Green Bay Packers | 6 | 5 | 0 |
| Chicago Cardinals | 6 | 5 | 0 |
| Detroit Lions | 1 | 10 | 0 |

**Champion: Chicago Bears defeat the New York Giants in New York, 24-14.**

### Season Awards

*Most Valuable Player*      Bill Dudley, Halfback, Pittsburgh Steelers

―――――――――

The Cleveland Rams moved to Los Angeles prior to the start of the 1946 NFL season. The league went back to an 11 game schedule.

# 1946 – All American Football Conference

## Eastern Division

| Team | Win | Lost | Tie |
| --- | --- | --- | --- |
| New York Yankees | 10 | 3 | 1 |
| Brooklyn Dodgers | 3 | 10 | 1 |
| Buffalo Bisons | 3 | 10 | 1 |
| Miami Seahawks | 3 | 11 | 0 |

## Western Division

| Team | Win | Lost | Tie |
| --- | --- | --- | --- |
| Cleveland Browns | 12 | 2 | 0 |
| San Francisco 49ers | 9 | 5 | 0 |
| Los Angeles Dons | 7 | 5 | 2 |
| Chicago Rockets | 5 | 6 | 3 |

**Champion: Cleveland Browns defeat the New York Yankees in Cleveland, 14-9.**

## Season Awards

*Most Valuable Player*                Glen Dobbs, Halfback, Brooklyn Dodgers

---

Due to the post-war popularity of football and the NFL's refusal to expand, a new league was set up to compete with the NFL. The All American Football Conference had eight teams and played a 14 game regular season schedule. The AAFC competed directly with the NFL in New York, Chicago, and Los Angeles. Like the NFL, the winners of each division played each other in the championship game. Like the NFL, the location of the championship game rotated between the divisions regardless of which team had the better record. The Brooklyn Tigers franchise moved from the NFL to the AAFC after sitting out the 1945 NFL season. The team was renamed the New York Yankees. The Yankees took back the players they had merged into the NFL Boston Yanks franchise for the 1945 season. The AAFC began play with a new team in Brooklyn, named (of course) the Brooklyn Dodgers.

## 1947 – National Football League

### Eastern Division

| Team | Win | Lost | Tie |
|---|---|---|---|
| Philadelphia Eagles | 8 | 4 | 0 |
| Pittsburgh Steelers | 8 | 4 | 0 |
| Boston Yanks | 4 | 7 | 1 |
| Washington Redskins | 4 | 8 | 0 |
| New York Giants | 2 | 8 | 2 |

### Western Division

| Team | Win | Lost | Tie |
|---|---|---|---|
| Chicago Cardinals | 9 | 3 | 0 |
| Chicago Bears | 8 | 4 | 0 |
| Green Bay Packers | 6 | 5 | 1 |
| Los Angeles Rams | 6 | 6 | 0 |
| Detroit Lions | 3 | 9 | 0 |

**Champion: Chicago Cardinals defeat the Philadelphia Eagles in Chicago, 28-21.**

### Season Awards

*Most Valuable Player*          No Selection

---

The Philadelphia Eagles defeated the Pittsburgh Steelers in a playoff game for the Eastern Division title, 21-0. The NFL moved to a 12 game schedule for the 1947 season.

# 1947 – All American Football Conference

## Eastern Division

| Team | Win | Lost | Tie |
|------|-----|------|-----|
| New York Yankees | 11 | 2 | 1 |
| Buffalo Bills | 8 | 4 | 2 |
| Brooklyn Dodgers | 3 | 10 | 1 |
| Baltimore Colts | 2 | 11 | 1 |

## Western Division

| Team | Win | Lost | Tie |
|------|-----|------|-----|
| Cleveland Browns | 12 | 1 | 1 |
| San Francisco 49ers | 8 | 4 | 2 |
| Los Angeles Dons | 7 | 7 | 0 |
| Chicago Rockets | 1 | 13 | 0 |

**Champion: Cleveland Browns defeat the New York Yankees in New York, 14-3.**

## Season Awards

*Most Valuable Player*          Otto Graham, Quarterback, Cleveland Browns

---

The Buffalo Bisons changed their name from the Buffalo Bisons to the Buffalo Bills (not to be confused with the AFL Buffalo Bills established in 1960). The Miami Seahawks relocated to Baltimore and changed their name to the Baltimore Colts (not to be confused with the later day incarnation of the NFL's Baltimore Colts).

## 1948 – National Football League

### Eastern Division

| Team | Win | Lost | Tie |
|------|-----|------|-----|
| Philadelphia Eagles | 9 | 2 | 1 |
| Washington Redskins | 7 | 5 | 0 |
| New York Giants | 4 | 8 | 0 |
| Pittsburgh Steelers | 4 | 8 | 0 |
| Boston Yanks | 3 | 9 | 0 |

### Western Division

| Team | Win | Lost | Tie |
|------|-----|------|-----|
| Chicago Cardinals | 11 | 1 | 0 |
| Chicago Bears | 10 | 2 | 0 |
| Los Angeles Rams | 6 | 5 | 1 |
| Green Bay Packers | 3 | 9 | 0 |
| Detroit Lions | 2 | 10 | 0 |

**Champion: Philadelphia Eagles defeated the Chicago Cardinals in Philadelphia, 7-0.**

### Season Awards

*Most Valuable Player*        No Selection

---

In 1948, the Los Angeles Rams became the first NFL team to use helmet emblems by painting ram "horns" on the sides of their helmets. Over the next decade virtually all NFL teams adopted helmet logos with some holdouts waiting until the early 1960's before adding a helmet logo, e.g., the Green Bay Packers and Pittsburgh Steelers. The Steelers are the only NFL team that sports their logo on only one side of their helmet. At first, this was to be temporary as the Steelers were not sure they would like the look of the now famous "steel" logo on what was then an all-gold helmet. They decided to test it on one side of the helmet during the 1962 season. The Steelers and their fans liked the unique look so much they kept it.

# 1948 – All American Football Conference

## Eastern Division

| Team | Win | Lost | Tie |
|------|-----|------|-----|
| Buffalo Bills | 7 | 7 | 0 |
| Baltimore Colts | 7 | 7 | 0 |
| New York Yankees | 6 | 8 | 0 |
| Brooklyn Dodgers | 2 | 12 | 0 |

## Western Division

| Team | Win | Lost | Tie |
|------|-----|------|-----|
| Cleveland Browns | 14 | 0 | 0 |
| San Francisco 49ers | 12 | 2 | 0 |
| Los Angeles Dons | 7 | 7 | 0 |
| Chicago Rockets | 1 | 13 | 0 |

**Champion: Cleveland Browns defeat the Buffalo Bills in Cleveland, 49-7.**

## Season Awards

*Most Valuable Player*          Otto Graham, Quarterback, Cleveland Browns and
                                Frankie Albert, Quarterback, San Francisco 49ers

---

The Buffalo Bills beat the Baltimore Colts in a playoff game for the Eastern Division title, 28-17.

## 1949 – National Football League

### Eastern Division

| Team | Win | Lost | Tie |
|---|---|---|---|
| Philadelphia Eagles | 11 | 1 | 0 |
| Pittsburgh Steelers | 6 | 5 | 1 |
| New York Giants | 6 | 6 | 0 |
| Washington Redskins | 4 | 7 | 1 |
| New York Bulldogs | 1 | 10 | 1 |

### Western Division

| Team | Win | Lost | Tie |
|---|---|---|---|
| Los Angeles Rams | 8 | 2 | 2 |
| Chicago Bears | 9 | 3 | 0 |
| Chicago Cardinals | 6 | 5 | 1 |
| Detroit Lions | 4 | 8 | 0 |
| Green Bay Packers | 2 | 10 | 0 |

**Champion: Philadelphia Eagles defeated the Los Angeles Rams in Los Angeles, 14-0.**

### Season Awards

*Most Valuable Player*          No selection

---

The Boston Yanks relocated to New York and changed their name to the New York Bulldogs.

## 1949 – All American Football Conference

| Team | Win | Lost | Tie |
|------|-----|------|-----|
| Cleveland Browns | 9 | 1 | 2 |
| San Francisco 49ers | 9 | 3 | 0 |
| New York Yankees | 8 | 4 | 0 |
| Buffalo Bills | 5 | 5 | 2 |
| Chicago Hornets | 4 | 8 | 0 |
| Los Angeles Dons | 4 | 8 | 0 |
| Baltimore Colts | 1 | 11 | 0 |

**Playoffs:**     Cleveland Browns defeat the Buffalo Bills, 31-21
San Francisco 49ers defeat the New York Yankees, 17-7

**Champion:**     **Cleveland Browns defeat the San Francisco 49ers in Cleveland, 21-7.**

## Season Awards
*Most Valuable Player*          No selection

---

Both the NFL and the AAFC were struggling, especially financially as the two leagues engaged in a high-priced battle for talent. To stop the bleeding, the AAFC and NFL announced that the AAFC would merge into the NFL beginning with the 1950 season. Due to financial issues, the AAFC was not broken into divisions in 1949. Instead, there was one conference and the first-and fourth-place teams and second- and third-place teams played each other to determine the two teams for the championship game. The league also went to a 12 game schedule, down from 14. Before the season started, the Chicago Rockets changed their name to the Chicago Hornets.

# 1950-1959

## 1950 – National Football League

### American (Eastern) Conference

| Team | Win | Lost | Tie |
|------|-----|------|-----|
| Cleveland Browns | 10 | 2 | 0 |
| New York Giants | 10 | 2 | 0 |
| Philadelphia Eagles | 6 | 6 | 0 |
| Pittsburgh Steelers | 6 | 6 | 0 |
| Chicago Cardinals | 5 | 7 | 0 |
| Washington Redskins | 3 | 9 | 0 |

### National (Western) Conference

| Team | Win | Lost | Tie |
|------|-----|------|-----|
| Los Angeles Rams | 9 | 3 | 0 |
| Chicago Bears | 9 | 3 | 0 |
| New York Yanks | 7 | 5 | 0 |
| Detroit Lions | 6 | 6 | 0 |
| Green Bay Packers | 3 | 9 | 0 |
| San Francisco 49ers | 3 | 9 | 0 |
| Baltimore Colts | 1 | 11 | 0 |

**Champion: Cleveland Browns defeat the Los Angeles Rams in Cleveland, 30-28.**

### Season Awards

*Most Valuable Player*          No Selection

---

**The AAFC merged into the NFL** prior to the 1950 season. Only three AAFC teams were accepted by the NFL: the Cleveland Browns, the San Francisco 49ers, and the Baltimore Colts. The Los Angeles Dons were merged into the Los Angeles Rams. The remaining AAFC teams folded and their players were dispersed to other NFL teams either directly or via a special draft. The NFL then realigned its teams into two different conferences, moving the Chicago Cardinals to the American (Eastern) Conference and the New York Yanks (formerly the New York Bulldogs) to the National (Western) Conference. With demise of the AAFC's New York Yankees, the New York Bulldogs were able to change their name back to the New York Yanks. There were ties for first place in both the National and American Conferences, leading to an unprecedented four team playoff. The Cleveland Browns defeated the New York Giants, 8-3; and the Los Angeles Rams defeated the Chicago Bears, 24-14 to set up the championship game between the Browns and Rams. The Browns proved they were for real by defeating the Rams, 30-28 for the NFL title. The Los Angeles Rams became the first NFL team to have all of their games (home and away) televised for the 1950 season. The NFL began permitting free substitution starting with the 1950 season, meaning any or all players could be substituted after each play. This rule led to the establishment of specialized players for offense, defense, and special teams.

# 1951 – National Football League

## American (Eastern) Conference

| Team | Win | Lost | Tie |
|------|-----|------|-----|
| Cleveland Browns | 11 | 1 | 0 |
| New York Giants | 9 | 2 | 1 |
| Washington Redskins | 5 | 7 | 0 |
| Pittsburgh Steelers | 4 | 7 | 1 |
| Philadelphia Eagles | 4 | 8 | 0 |
| Chicago Cardinals | 3 | 9 | 0 |

## National (Western) Conference

| Team | Win | Lost | Tie |
|------|-----|------|-----|
| Los Angeles Rams | 8 | 4 | 0 |
| Detroit Lions | 7 | 4 | 1 |
| San Francisco 49ers | 7 | 4 | 1 |
| Chicago Bears | 7 | 5 | 0 |
| Green Bay Packers | 3 | 9 | 0 |
| New York Yanks | 1 | 9 | 2 |

**Champion: Los Angeles Rams defeat the Cleveland Browns in Los Angeles, 24-17.**

## Season Awards

*Most Valuable Player*          No Selection

---

The 1951 championship game between the Los Angeles Rams and Cleveland Browns was the first to be televised nationally. It was broadcast on the DeMont Television Network for the price of $75,000. The Baltimore Colts franchise (from the old AAFC) went under before the start of the 1951 season. The Colts players were spread among the remaining teams as part of the 1951 collegiate draft. The demise of the Colts led to the league having a balanced 12 team league (six in each conference), which made scheduling easier.

# 1952 – National Football League

## American (Eastern) Conference

| Team | Win | Lost | Tie |
|------|-----|------|-----|
| Cleveland Browns | 8 | 4 | 0 |
| New York Giants | 7 | 5 | 0 |
| Philadelphia Eagles | 7 | 5 | 0 |
| Pittsburgh Steelers | 5 | 7 | 0 |
| Chicago Cardinals | 4 | 8 | 0 |
| Washington Redskins | 4 | 8 | 0 |

## National (Western) Conference

| Team | Win | Lost | Tie |
|------|-----|------|-----|
| Detroit Lions | 9 | 3 | 0 |
| Los Angeles Rams | 9 | 3 | 0 |
| San Francisco 49ers | 7 | 5 | 0 |
| Green Bay Packers | 6 | 6 | 0 |
| Chicago Bears | 5 | 7 | 0 |
| Dallas Texans | 1 | 11 | 0 |

**Champion: Detroit Lions defeat the Cleveland Browns in Cleveland, 17-7.**

## Season Awards

*Most Valuable Player*          No Selection

---

The Detroit Lions defeated the Los Angeles Rams, 31-21, in a playoff for the National Conference title and the right to play the Cleveland Browns in the championship game. New York Yanks owner, Ted Collins, sold his franchise back to the league before the start of the 1952 season. The league then sold the team to a group of investors from Dallas, Texas who renamed the Yanks the Dallas Texans. The team was a flop in Dallas and the owners turned the team back over to the league mid-season. The league operated the Texans as a "road" team for the rest of the season.

## 1953 – National Football League

### Eastern Conference

| Team | Win | Lost | Tie |
|---|---|---|---|
| Cleveland Browns | 11 | 1 | 0 |
| Philadelphia Eagles | 7 | 4 | 1 |
| Washington Redskins | 6 | 5 | 1 |
| Pittsburgh Steelers | 6 | 6 | 0 |
| New York Giants | 3 | 9 | 0 |
| Chicago Cardinals | 1 | 10 | 1 |

### Western Conference

| Team | Win | Lost | Tie |
|---|---|---|---|
| Detroit Lions | 10 | 2 | 0 |
| San Francisco 49ers | 9 | 3 | 0 |
| Los Angeles Rams | 8 | 3 | 1 |
| Chicago Bears | 3 | 8 | 1 |
| Baltimore Colts | 3 | 9 | 0 |
| Green Bay Packers | 2 | 9 | 1 |

**Champion: Detroit Lions defeat the Cleveland Browns in Detroit, 17-16.**

### Season Awards

*Most Valuable Player*      No Selection

---

In 1953 the American and National Conferences were renamed the Eastern and Western Conferences respectively. Prior to the start of the season, the Dallas Texans franchise was sold to new owners in Baltimore and renamed the Baltimore Colts. 1953 became the first year the NFL played football with franchises that are all still in existence today under their current nicknames.

# 1954 – National Football League

## Eastern Conference

| Team | Win | Lost | Tie |
|------|-----|------|-----|
| Cleveland Browns | 9 | 3 | 0 |
| Philadelphia Eagles | 7 | 4 | 1 |
| New York Giants | 7 | 5 | 0 |
| Pittsburgh Steelers | 5 | 7 | 0 |
| Washington Redskins | 3 | 9 | 0 |
| Chicago Cardinals | 2 | 10 | 0 |

## Western Conference

| Team | Win | Lost | Tie |
|------|-----|------|-----|
| Detroit Lions | 9 | 2 | 1 |
| Chicago Bears | 8 | 4 | 0 |
| San Francisco 49ers | 7 | 4 | 1 |
| Los Angeles Rams | 6 | 5 | 1 |
| Green Bay Packers | 4 | 8 | 0 |
| Baltimore Colts | 3 | 9 | 0 |

**Champion: Cleveland Browns defeat the Detroit Lions in Cleveland, 56-10.**

## Season Awards

*Most Valuable Player*          No Selection

---

In 1954, the Cleveland Browns and Detroit Lions played for the NFL title for the third time in five seasons. They would play again in 1957. It would be the last time the Lions played for a league title. Cleveland played one more time in 1964.

## 1955 – National Football League

## Eastern Conference

| Team | Win | Lost | Tie |
|------|-----|------|-----|
| Cleveland Browns | 9 | 2 | 1 |
| Washington Redskins | 8 | 4 | 0 |
| New York Giants | 6 | 5 | 1 |
| Chicago Cardinals | 4 | 7 | 1 |
| Philadelphia Eagles | 4 | 7 | 1 |
| Pittsburgh Steelers | 4 | 8 | 0 |

## Western Conference

| Team | Win | Lost | Tie |
|------|-----|------|-----|
| Los Angeles Rams | 8 | 3 | 1 |
| Chicago Bears | 8 | 4 | 0 |
| Green Bay Packers | 6 | 6 | 0 |
| Baltimore Colts | 5 | 6 | 1 |
| San Francisco 49ers | 4 | 8 | 0 |
| Detroit Lions | 3 | 9 | 0 |

**Champion: Cleveland Browns defeat the Los Angeles Rams in Los Angeles, 38-14.**

## Season Awards

*Most Valuable Player*    No Selection

---

In 1955, facemasks became mandatory for all NFL players. Players could, however, apply to the Commissioner for special permission to play without one, which several did – playing without facemasks for several more years.

# 1956 – National Football League

## Eastern Conference

| Team | Win | Lost | Tie |
|------|-----|------|-----|
| New York Giants | 8 | 3 | 1 |
| Chicago Cardinals | 7 | 5 | 0 |
| Washington Redskins | 6 | 6 | 0 |
| Cleveland Browns | 5 | 7 | 0 |
| Pittsburgh Steelers | 5 | 7 | 0 |
| Philadelphia Eagles | 3 | 8 | 1 |

## Western Conference

| Team | Win | Lost | Tie |
|------|-----|------|-----|
| Chicago Bears | 9 | 2 | 1 |
| Detroit Lions | 9 | 3 | 0 |
| San Francisco 49ers | 5 | 6 | 1 |
| Baltimore Colts | 5 | 7 | 0 |
| Green Bay Packers | 4 | 8 | 0 |
| Los Angeles Rams | 4 | 8 | 0 |

**Champion: New York Giants defeat the Chicago Bears in New York, 47-7.**

## Season Awards

*Most Valuable Player*          No Selection

---

In 1956, CBS became the first television network to televise some NFL regular season games nationally.

## 1957 – National Football League

## Eastern Conference

| Team | Win | Lost | Tie |
| --- | --- | --- | --- |
| Cleveland Browns | 9 | 2 | 1 |
| New York Giants | 7 | 5 | 0 |
| Pittsburgh Steelers | 6 | 6 | 0 |
| Washington Redskins | 5 | 6 | 1 |
| Philadelphia Eagles | 4 | 8 | 0 |
| Chicago Cardinals | 3 | 9 | 0 |

## Western Conference

| Team | Win | Lost | Tie |
| --- | --- | --- | --- |
| Detroit Lions | 8 | 4 | 0 |
| San Francisco 49ers | 8 | 4 | 0 |
| Baltimore Colts | 7 | 5 | 0 |
| Los Angeles Rams | 6 | 6 | 0 |
| Chicago Bears | 5 | 7 | 0 |
| Green Bay Packers | 3 | 9 | 0 |

**Champion: Detroit Lions defeat the Cleveland Browns in Detroit, 59-14.**

## Season Awards[1]

*Most Valuable Player*        Jim Brown, Running Back, Cleveland Browns
*Coach of the Year*        George Wilson, Detroit Lions

---

The Detroit Lions defeated the San Francisco 49ers, 31-27, in a playoff game for the Western Conference title and the right to play the Cleveland Browns in the championship game. 1957 was the first year the league required the home team to wear dark jerseys and the visiting team to wear light colored jerseys (usually white). Prior to 1957 teams could wear whatever color jersey they preferred, even if it clashed with the opponent's jersey color.

---

1        For ease of reference, this book will use the Associated Press (AP) award winners. 1957 marked the first year the AP awarded MVP and Coach of the Year awards for the NFL. Other news services gave (and give) similar awards.

# 1958 – National Football League

## Eastern Conference

| Team | Win | Lost | Tie |
|---|---|---|---|
| New York Giants | 9 | 3 | 0 |
| Cleveland Browns | 9 | 3 | 0 |
| Pittsburgh Steelers | 7 | 4 | 1 |
| Washington Redskins | 4 | 7 | 1 |
| Chicago Cardinals | 2 | 9 | 1 |
| Philadelphia Eagles | 2 | 9 | 1 |

## Western Conference

| Team | Win | Lost | Tie |
|---|---|---|---|
| Baltimore Colts | 9 | 3 | 0 |
| Chicago Bears | 8 | 4 | 0 |
| Los Angeles Rams | 8 | 4 | 0 |
| San Francisco 49ers | 6 | 6 | 0 |
| Detroit Lions | 4 | 7 | 1 |
| Green Bay Packers | 1 | 10 | 1 |

**Champion: Baltimore Colts defeat the New York Giants in New York, 23-17.**

## Season Awards

*Most Valuable Players*        Jim Brown, Running Back, Cleveland Browns
*Coach of the Year*        Weeb Eubank, Baltimore Colts

———————

The New York Giants defeated the Cleveland Browns, 10-0, in a playoff game for the Eastern Conference title and the right to play the Baltimore Colts in the championship game. The Baltimore Colts won the title in the first "sudden-death" overtime NFL championship game. The excitement of this title game, broadcast nationally, directly led to the upsurge in popularity of the NFL across the United States as the game of football fit perfectly within the growing medium of television.

# 1959 – National Football League

## Eastern Conference

| Team | Win | Lost | Tie |
|------|-----|------|-----|
| New York Giants | 10 | 2 | 0 |
| Cleveland Browns | 7 | 5 | 0 |
| Philadelphia Eagles | 7 | 5 | 0 |
| Pittsburgh Steelers | 6 | 5 | 1 |
| Washington Redskins | 3 | 9 | 0 |
| Chicago Cardinals | 2 | 10 | 0 |

## Western Conference

| Team | Win | Lost | Tie |
|------|-----|------|-----|
| Baltimore Colts | 9 | 3 | 0 |
| Chicago Bears | 8 | 4 | 0 |
| Green Bay Packers | 7 | 5 | 0 |
| San Francisco 49ers | 7 | 5 | 0 |
| Detroit Lions | 3 | 8 | 1 |
| Los Angeles Rams | 2 | 10 | 0 |

**Champion: Baltimore Colts defeat the New York Giants in Baltimore, 31-16.**

## Season Awards

*Most Valuable Player*     Johnny Unitas, Quarterback, Baltimore Colts

*Coach of the Year*     Vince Lombardi, Green Bay Packers

---

Bert Bell, Commissioner of the league since 1945, passed away during the 1959 season, after suffering a heart attack at an Eagles game. A one-time coach and owner, he implemented a proactive anti-gambling policy, negotiated a merger with the AAFC, and created a league schedule that emphasized key late season match ups to appeal to fans. He introduced the policy of blacking out local television broadcasts of the home contests within a 75-mile area to protect ticket receipts. He also helped create the draft and the process whereby the teams with the worst records would have first crack at the best players, a move that helped establish competitive parity.

# 1960-1969

## 1960 – National Football League

### Eastern Conference

| Team | Win | Lost | Tie |
|---|---|---|---|
| Philadelphia Eagles | 10 | 2 | 0 |
| Cleveland Browns | 8 | 3 | 1 |
| New York Giants | 6 | 4 | 2 |
| St. Louis Cardinals | 6 | 5 | 1 |
| Pittsburgh Steelers | 5 | 6 | 1 |
| Washington Redskins | 1 | 9 | 2 |

### Western Conference

| Team | Win | Lost | Tie |
|---|---|---|---|
| Green Bay Packers | 8 | 4 | 0 |
| Detroit Lions | 7 | 5 | 0 |
| San Francisco 49ers | 7 | 5 | 0 |
| Baltimore Colts | 6 | 6 | 0 |
| Chicago Bears | 5 | 6 | 1 |
| Los Angeles Rams | 4 | 7 | 1 |
| Dallas Cowboys | 0 | 11 | 1 |

**Champion: Philadelphia Eagles defeat the Green Bay Packers in Philadelphia, 17-13.**

**Playoff Bowl:** Detroit Lions defeat the Cleveland Browns in Miami, 17-16.

### Season Awards

| | |
|---|---|
| *Most Valuable Player* | Norm Van Brocklin, Quarterback, Philadelphia Eagles |
| *Coach of the Year* | Buck Shaw, Philadelphia Eagles |

---

**Prior to the start of the 1960 season**, the Chicago Cardinals relocated to St. Louis to become the St. Louis Cardinals. This would be the last NFL franchise to move until 1982 when the Oakland Raiders moved to Los Angeles. 1960 also provided the first pure NFL expansion team since the Boston Yanks in 1944. The Dallas Cowboys were added in part to combat the new upstart American Football League which also placed a franchise in Dallas. In light of the AFL, the NFL also announced a franchise for Minnesota that would begin play in 1961 (after convincing the owners to jump from the AFL to the NFL). The NFL created the Playoff Bowl (Officially the Bert Bell Benefit Bowl) in 1960 as a game for third place between the runners up of the Eastern and Western Conferences. It was played in Miami after the NFL Championship game and proceeds benefitted the players' pension fund. After Bert Bell's passing, Pete Rozelle was named Commissioner in 1960.

1960 was also the year of one of the most famous tackles in NFL history. On November 20, Eagles linebacker Chuck Bednarik laid out New York Giant's running back Frank Gifford with a devastating hit. Gifford was knocked out of the game and missed the entire 1961 season as well recovering from his injuries. Bednarik was the last of the full-time 60-minute players, playing both linebacker and center in a Hall of Fame career. Both Bednarik and Gifford passed away in 2015.

## 1960 –American Football League

### Eastern Division

| Team | Win | Lost | Tie |
|---|---|---|---|
| Houston Oilers | 10 | 4 | 0 |
| New York Titans | 7 | 7 | 0 |
| Buffalo Bills | 5 | 8 | 1 |
| Boston Patriots | 5 | 9 | 0 |

### Western Division

| Team | Win | Lost | Tie |
|---|---|---|---|
| Los Angeles Chargers | 10 | 4 | 0 |
| Dallas Texans | 8 | 6 | 0 |
| Oakland Raiders | 6 | 8 | 0 |
| Denver Broncos | 4 | 9 | 1 |

**Champion: Houston Oilers defeat the Los Angeles Chargers in Houston, 24-16.**

### Season Awards

*Most Valuable Player*     No award

---

In 1960, the American Football League came into being in part due to frustration around the inability to obtain NFL franchises for certain cities (e.g., Dallas and Houston). The AFL went head-to-head with the NFL in New York, Los Angeles, San Francisco-Oakland Bay area, and Dallas. The AFL adopted a 14 game schedule (vs. 12 games played by the NFL) and added a two-point conversion option after touchdowns, along with other innovations designed to appeal to fans. The Oakland franchise was originally awarded to Minneapolis-St. Paul. The NFL, sensing the threat posed by the AFL, offered the Minneapolis-St. Paul owners a NFL franchise instead, which they accepted. The Minnesota franchise would begin NFL play in 1961. The AFL was able to place a team in Oakland just before the season started.

# 1961 – National Football League

## Eastern Conference

| Team | Win | Lost | Tie |
|------|-----|------|-----|
| New York Giants | 10 | 3 | 1 |
| Philadelphia Eagles | 10 | 4 | 0 |
| Cleveland Browns | 8 | 5 | 1 |
| St. Louis Cardinals | 7 | 7 | 0 |
| Pittsburgh Steelers | 6 | 8 | 0 |
| Dallas Cowboys | 4 | 9 | 1 |
| Washington Redskins | 1 | 12 | 1 |

## Western Conference

| Team | Win | Lost | Tie |
|------|-----|------|-----|
| Green Bay Packers | 11 | 3 | 0 |
| Detroit Lions | 8 | 5 | 1 |
| Baltimore Colts | 8 | 6 | 0 |
| Chicago Bears | 8 | 6 | 0 |
| San Francisco 49ers | 7 | 6 | 1 |
| Los Angeles Rams | 4 | 10 | 0 |
| Minnesota Vikings | 3 | 11 | 0 |

**Champion: Green Bay Packers defeat the New York Giants in Green Bay, 37-0.**

**Playoff Bowl:** Detroit Lions defeat the Philadelphia Eagles in Miami, 38-10.

## Season Awards

| | |
|---|---|
| *Most Valuable Player* | Paul Horning, Running Back, Green Bay Packers |
| *Coach of the Year* | Allie Sherman, New York Giants |

---

The NFL moved to a 14 game schedule in 1961 to compete with the AFL schedule. As agreed in 1960, the NFL added the Minneapolis-St. Paul franchise in 1961, expanding the league to 14 teams. This was the first NFL franchise to use the name of a state vs. a specific city. The league placed the Vikings in the Western Conference. Dallas moved from Western Conference to Eastern Conference to accommodate the Vikings joining the league.

# 1961 –American Football League

## Eastern Division

| Team | Win | Lost | Tie |
|------|-----|------|-----|
| Houston Oilers | 10 | 3 | 1 |
| Boston Patriots | 9 | 4 | 1 |
| New York Titans | 7 | 7 | 0 |
| Buffalo Bills | 6 | 8 | 0 |

## Western Division

| Team | Win | Lost | Tie |
|------|-----|------|-----|
| Los Angeles Chargers | 12 | 2 | 0 |
| Dallas Texans | 6 | 8 | 0 |
| Denver Broncos | 3 | 11 | 0 |
| Oakland Raiders | 2 | 12 | 0 |

**Champion: San Diego Chargers defeat the Houston Oilers in San Diego, 10-3.**

## Season Awards

*Most Valuable Player*          George Blanda, Quarterback, Houston Oilers

———

The Chargers moved from Los Angeles to San Diego before the start of the 1961 season.

# 1962 – National Football League

## Eastern Conference

| Team | Win | Lost | Tie |
|------|-----|------|-----|
| New York Giants | 12 | 2 | 0 |
| Pittsburgh Steelers | 9 | 5 | 0 |
| Cleveland Browns | 7 | 6 | 1 |
| Washington Redskins | 5 | 7 | 2 |
| Dallas Cowboys | 5 | 8 | 1 |
| St. Louis Cardinals | 4 | 9 | 1 |
| Philadelphia Eagles | 3 | 10 | 1 |

## Western Conference

| Team | Win | Lost | Tie |
|------|-----|------|-----|
| Green Bay Packers | 13 | 1 | 0 |
| Detroit Lions | 11 | 3 | 0 |
| Chicago Bears | 9 | 5 | 0 |
| Baltimore Colts | 7 | 7 | 0 |
| San Francisco 49ers | 6 | 8 | 0 |
| Minnesota Vikings | 2 | 11 | 1 |
| Los Angeles Rams | 1 | 12 | 1 |

**Champion: Green Bay Packers defeat the New York Giants in New York, 16-7.**

**Playoff Bowl:** Detroit Lions defeat the Pittsburgh Steelers in Miami, 17-10.

## Season Awards

| | |
|---|---|
| *Most Valuable Player* | Jim Taylor, Running Back, Green Bay Packers |
| *Coach of the Year* | Allie Sherman, New York Giants |

In 1962, the NFL made grabbing a player's facemask illegal. 1962 also marked the beginning of NFL Films which began when Ed Sabol bid $5,000 to film the 1962 NFL championship game between the Green Bay Packers and the New York Giants. NFL Films became an institution and an innovator in film-making, both in terms of sporting events and film-making generally (and can be thanked for bringing us John "The Voice" Facenda, coining the phrase "frozen tundra," and the creation of the "football follies" blooper reels).

# 1962 –American Football League

## Eastern Division

| Team | Win | Lost | Tie |
|------|-----|------|-----|
| Houston Oilers | 11 | 3 | 0 |
| Boston Patriots | 9 | 4 | 1 |
| Buffalo Bills | 7 | 6 | 1 |
| New York Titans | 5 | 9 | 0 |

## Western Division

| Team | Win | Lost | Tie |
|------|-----|------|-----|
| Dallas Texans | 11 | 3 | 0 |
| Denver Broncos | 7 | 7 | 0 |
| San Diego Chargers | 4 | 10 | 0 |
| Oakland Raiders | 1 | 13 | 0 |

**Champion: Dallas Texans defeat the Houston Oilers in Houston, 20-17.**

## Season Awards

*Most Valuable Player*        Cookie Gilchrist, Full Back, Buffalo Bills

---

The Dallas Texans won the AFL championship in the second overtime period on a Tommy Brooker field goal at the 2:54 mark. This remains the longest championship game played in professional football.

# 1963 – National Football League

## Eastern Conference

| Team | Win | Lost | Tie |
|------|-----|------|-----|
| New York Giants | 11 | 3 | 0 |
| Cleveland Browns | 10 | 4 | 0 |
| St. Louis Cardinals | 9 | 5 | 0 |
| Pittsburgh Steelers | 7 | 4 | 3 |
| Dallas Cowboys | 4 | 10 | 0 |
| Washington Redskins | 3 | 11 | 0 |
| Philadelphia Eagles | 2 | 10 | 2 |

## Western Conference

| Team | Win | Lost | Tie |
|------|-----|------|-----|
| Chicago Bears | 11 | 1 | 2 |
| Green Bay Packers | 11 | 2 | 1 |
| Baltimore Colts | 8 | 6 | 0 |
| Detroit Lions | 5 | 8 | 1 |
| Minnesota Vikings | 5 | 8 | 1 |
| Los Angeles Rams | 5 | 9 | 0 |
| San Francisco 49ers | 2 | 12 | 0 |

**Champion:  Chicago Bears defeat the New York Giants in Chicago, 14-10.**

**Playoff Bowl:** Green Bay Packers defeat the Cleveland Browns in Miami, 40-23.

## Season Awards

*Most Valuable Player*          Y.A. Tittle, Quarterback, New York Giants
*Coach of the Year*             George Halas, Chicago Bears

---

Two days after the November 22, 1963 assassination of President Kennedy in Dallas, the NFL played its full slate of games.  None of the games were televised as CBS (which had the exclusive contract for NFL games) broadcast only news about the assassination and funeral.  The AFL canceled its games for that weekend.  There is still debate as to whether the NFL should have canceled its games as well.  Prior to the season starting, the NFL opened its Hall of Fame in Canton, Ohio - the birthplace of the NFL - in 1963 with 17 charter enshrines (see the Appendix for list of all Hall of Fame members).

## 1963 –American Football League

### Eastern Division

| Team | Win | Lost | Tie |
|------|-----|------|-----|
| Boston Patriots | 7 | 6 | 1 |
| Buffalo Bills | 7 | 6 | 1 |
| Houston Oilers | 6 | 8 | 0 |
| New York Jets | 5 | 8 | 1 |

### Western Division

| Team | Win | Lost | Tie |
|------|-----|------|-----|
| San Diego Chargers | 11 | 3 | 0 |
| Oakland Raiders | 10 | 4 | 0 |
| Kansas City Chiefs | 5 | 7 | 2 |
| Denver Broncos | 2 | 11 | 1 |

**Champion: San Diego Chargers defeat the Boston Patriots in San Diego, 51-10.**

### Season Awards

*Most Valuable Player*          Tobin Rote, Quarterback, San Diego Chargers

---

The Boston Patriots defeated the Buffalo Bills, 26-8, in a playoff game to decide the Eastern Conference title. Under new owners, the New York Titans changed their name to the New York Jets. They also changed their uniform colors from blue and gold to green and white. The Dallas Texans moved to Kansas City before the start of the 1963 season and changed their name to the Kansas City Chiefs. The only places the NFL went head-to-head with the AFL in 1963 were in New York (Jets/Giants) and the San Francisco Bay Area (49ers/Raiders).

# 1964 – National Football League

## Eastern Conference

| Team | Win | Lost | Tie |
|------|-----|------|-----|
| Cleveland Browns | 10 | 3 | 1 |
| St. Louis Cardinals | 9 | 3 | 2 |
| Philadelphia Eagles | 6 | 8 | 0 |
| Washington Redskins | 6 | 8 | 0 |
| Dallas Cowboys | 5 | 8 | 1 |
| Pittsburgh Steelers | 5 | 9 | 0 |
| New York Giants | 2 | 10 | 2 |

## Western Conference

| Team | Win | Lost | Tie |
|------|-----|------|-----|
| Baltimore Colts | 12 | 2 | 0 |
| Green Bay Packers | 8 | 5 | 1 |
| Minnesota Vikings | 8 | 5 | 1 |
| Detroit Lions | 7 | 5 | 2 |
| Los Angeles Rams | 5 | 7 | 2 |
| Chicago Bears | 5 | 9 | 0 |
| San Francisco 49ers | 4 | 10 | 0 |

**Champion: Cleveland Browns defeat the Baltimore Colts in Cleveland, 27-0.**

**Playoff Bowl:** St. Louis Cardinals defeat the Green Bay Packers in Miami, 24-17.

## Season Awards

*Most Valuable Player*          Johnny Unitas, Quarterback, Baltimore Colts
*Coach of the Year*             Don Shula, Baltimore Colts

———————

Since 1957, the NFL required the home team to wear their dark-colored jerseys, leaving the white-colored jerseys for the away team. In 1964, the NFL changed this policy and allowed the home team to use their white-colored jerseys at home. A number of teams took advantage of this change but only the Dallas Cowboys have continuously used white as their home jersey (except if forced to do otherwise as the "home" team in the Super Bowl).

## 1964 –American Football League

### Eastern Division

| Team | Win | Lost | Tie |
|------|-----|------|-----|
| Buffalo Bills | 12 | 2 | 0 |
| Boston Patriots | 10 | 3 | 1 |
| New York Jets | 5 | 8 | 1 |
| Houston Oilers | 4 | 10 | 0 |

### Western Division

| Team | Win | Lost | Tie |
|------|-----|------|-----|
| San Diego Chargers | 8 | 5 | 1 |
| Kansas City Chiefs | 7 | 7 | 0 |
| Oakland Raiders | 5 | 7 | 2 |
| Denver Broncos | 2 | 11 | 1 |

**Champion: Buffalo Bills defeat the San Diego Chargers in Buffalo, 20-7.**

### Season Awards

*Most Valuable Player*        Gino Capilletti, Flanker/Kicker, Boston Patriots

---

1964 was the last season ABC would broadcast AFL games. The original 1960 agreement with the AFL gave ABC a valuable sports property to broadcast and gave the league valuable exposure and money to start up operations. The 1965 NBC television contract ensured the viability of the AFL and gave it additional dollars for its talent war with the NFL.

## 1965 – National Football League

## Eastern Conference

| Team | Win | Lost | Tie |
|------|-----|------|-----|
| Cleveland Browns | 11 | 3 | 0 |
| Dallas Cowboys | 7 | 7 | 0 |
| New York Giants | 7 | 7 | 0 |
| Washington Redskins | 6 | 8 | 0 |
| Philadelphia Eagles | 5 | 9 | 0 |
| St. Louis Cardinals | 5 | 9 | 0 |
| Pittsburgh Steelers | 2 | 12 | 0 |

## Western Conference

| Team | Win | Lost | Tie |
|------|-----|------|-----|
| Green Bay Packers | 10 | 3 | 1 |
| Baltimore Colts | 10 | 3 | 1 |
| Chicago Bears | 9 | 5 | 0 |
| San Francisco 49ers | 7 | 6 | 1 |
| Minnesota Vikings | 7 | 7 | 0 |
| Detroit Lions | 6 | 7 | 1 |
| Los Angeles Rams | 4 | 10 | 0 |

**Champion:  Green Bay Packers defeat the Cleveland Browns in Green Bay, 23-12.**

**Playoff Bowl:** Baltimore Colts defeat the Dallas Cowboys in Miami, 35-3.

## Season Awards
*Most Valuable Player*          Jim Brown, Running Back, Cleveland Browns
*Coach of the Year*             George Halas, Chicago Bears

The Green Bay Packers and Baltimore Colts tied for the best record in the Western Conference, even though the Packers defeated the Colts in both games they played during the regular season. The NFL, however, did not have tie-breaker rules in place at this time and so a playoff game was necessary. The Packers defeated the Colts in the playoff for the Western Conference title, 13-10 (in overtime).

# 1965 –American Football League

## Eastern Division

| Team | Win | Lost | Tie |
|------|-----|------|-----|
| Buffalo Bills | 10 | 3 | 1 |
| New York Jets | 5 | 8 | 1 |
| Boston Patriots | 4 | 8 | 2 |
| Houston Oilers | 4 | 10 | 0 |

## Western Division

| Team | Win | Lost | Tie |
|------|-----|------|-----|
| San Diego Chargers | 9 | 2 | 3 |
| Oakland Raiders | 8 | 5 | 1 |
| Kansas City Chiefs | 7 | 5 | 2 |
| Denver Broncos | 4 | 10 | 0 |

**Champion: Buffalo Bills defeat the San Diego Chargers in San Diego, 23-0.**

## Season Awards

Most Valuable Player                         Jack Kemp, Quarterback, San Diego Chargers

---

The AFL's New York Jets beat out the St. Louis Cardinals of the NFL for the services of Joe Namath, quarterback from Alabama. The Jets gave Namath a then record $427,000 multi-year contract. The escalating bidding war between the NFL and the AFL for players would lead to the 1966 announcement of a merger of the leagues.

# 1966 – National Football League

## Eastern Conference

| Team | Win | Lost | Tie |
|------|-----|------|-----|
| Dallas Cowboys | 10 | 3 | 1 |
| Philadelphia Eagles | 9 | 5 | 0 |
| Cleveland Browns | 9 | 5 | 0 |
| St. Louis Cardinals | 8 | 5 | 1 |
| Washington Redskins | 7 | 7 | 0 |
| Pittsburgh Steelers | 5 | 8 | 1 |
| Atlanta Falcons | 3 | 11 | 0 |
| New York Giants | 1 | 12 | 1 |

## Western Conference

| Team | Win | Lost | Tie |
|------|-----|------|-----|
| Green Bay Packers | 12 | 2 | 0 |
| Baltimore Colts | 9 | 5 | 0 |
| Los Angeles Rams | 8 | 6 | 0 |
| San Francisco 49ers | 6 | 6 | 2 |
| Chicago Bears | 5 | 7 | 2 |
| Detroit Lions | 4 | 9 | 1 |
| Minnesota Vikings | 4 | 9 | 1 |

**Champion: Green Bay Packers defeat the Dallas Cowboys in Dallas, 34-27.**

**Playoff Bowl:** Baltimore Colts defeat the Philadelphia Eagles in Miami, 20-14.

## Season Awards

*Most Valuable Player*          Bart Starr, Quarterback, Green Bay Packers
*Coach of the Year*             Tom Landry, Dallas Cowboys

---

Prior to the start of the 1966 season the NFL and AFL announced that they would merge. Initially, the league champions would meet in a post-season game called the NFL-AFL World Championship Game (later known as the "Super Bowl") beginning after the 1966 season. The leagues would fully merge in 1970 with the NFL being the surviving league and all AFL members becoming NFL franchises. Until then, the leagues would play separate schedules (like the American and National Leagues in baseball until the advent of interleague play). The NFL and AFL agreed that AFL records would count as part of the records of the NFL. The NFL added the Atlanta Falcons as an expansion team prior to the start of the 1966 season. This was the first NFL franchise in the South. The New Orleans Saints would join the league in 1967. After beating the Dallas Cowboys for the NFL title, the Green Bay Packers would be the NFL's first representative in the Super Bowl.

# 1966 –American Football League

## Eastern Division

| Team | Win | Lost | Tie |
|------|-----|------|-----|
| Buffalo Bills | 9 | 4 | 1 |
| Boston Patriots | 8 | 4 | 2 |
| New York Jets | 6 | 6 | 2 |
| Houston Oilers | 3 | 11 | 0 |
| Miami Dolphins | 3 | 11 | 0 |

## Western Division

| Team | Win | Lost | Tie |
|------|-----|------|-----|
| Kansas City Chiefs | 11 | 2 | 1 |
| Oakland Raiders | 8 | 5 | 1 |
| San Diego Chargers | 7 | 6 | 1 |
| Denver Broncos | 4 | 10 | 0 |

**Champion: Kansas City Chiefs defeat the Buffalo Bills in Buffalo, 31-7.**

## Season Awards

*Most Valuable Player* Jim Nance, Fullback, Boston Patriots

---

The Kansas Chiefs defeated the Buffalo Bills in the AFL championship game to become the AFL's first representative in the Super Bowl. The AFL added its first expansion team in 1966, the Miami Dolphins.

# Playoffs

## 1967 – Super Bowl I
## Los Angeles

**Green Bay Packers** (NFL) defeat the Kansas City Chiefs (AFL), 35-10.

––––––––––

Due to the fact that each league had its own exclusive television contract, the first Super Bowl was broadcast on both CBS and NBC.

# 1967 – National Football League

## EASTERN CONFERENCE

### Capitol Division

| Team | Win | Lost | Tie |
|---|---|---|---|
| Dallas Cowboys | 9 | 5 | 0 |
| Philadelphia Eagles | 6 | 7 | 1 |
| Washington Redskins | 5 | 6 | 3 |
| New Orleans Saints | 3 | 11 | 0 |

### Century Division

| Team | Win | Lost | Tie |
|---|---|---|---|
| Cleveland Browns | 9 | 5 | 0 |
| New York Giants | 7 | 7 | 0 |
| St. Louis Cardinals | 6 | 7 | 1 |
| Pittsburgh Steelers | 4 | 9 | 1 |

## WESTERN CONFERENCE

### Central Division

| Team | Win | Lost | Tie |
|---|---|---|---|
| Green Bay Packers | 9 | 4 | 1 |
| Chicago Bears | 7 | 6 | 1 |
| Detroit Lions | 5 | 7 | 2 |
| Minnesota Vikings | 3 | 8 | 3 |

### Coastal Division

| Team | Win | Lost | Tie |
|---|---|---|---|
| Los Angeles Rams | 11 | 1 | 2 |
| Baltimore Colts | 11 | 1 | 2 |
| San Francisco 49ers | 7 | 7 | 0 |
| Atlanta Falcons | 1 | 12 | 1 |

---

The NFL expanded in New Orleans prior to the 1967 season. Some speculate that placing a team in New Orleans was part of the political price the NFL paid to get United States Senator Russell Long (D-LA) to help pass legislation alleviating any antitrust concerns with the NFL-AFL merger. With the addition of the New Orleans Saints, the NFL divided the Eastern and Western Conferences into divisions. The Eastern Conference was broken into the Capitol and Century Divisions, the Western Conference into the Central and Coastal Divisions. A glance at the location of the teams in the divisions tells you that geography was not a top consideration in dividing the teams. The division winners would play each other for the conference title and the conference title winners would play for the right to go to the Super Bowl vs. the AFL champion.

# 1967 –American Football League

## Eastern Division

| Team | Win | Lost | Tie |
|------|-----|------|-----|
| Houston Oilers | 9 | 4 | 1 |
| New York Jets | 8 | 5 | 1 |
| Buffalo Bills | 4 | 10 | 0 |
| Miami Dolphins | 4 | 10 | 0 |
| Boston Patriots | 3 | 10 | 1 |

## Western Division

| Team | Win | Lost | Tie |
|------|-----|------|-----|
| Oakland Raiders | 13 | 1 | 0 |
| Kansas City Chiefs | 9 | 5 | 0 |
| San Diego Chargers | 8 | 5 | 1 |
| Denver Broncos | 3 | 11 | 0 |

## 1967-1968 Playoffs

### NFL Playoffs

*Eastern Conference* (in Dallas) - Dallas Cowboys 52, Cleveland Browns 14

*Western Conference* (in Milwaukee) - Green Bay Packers 28, Los Angeles Rams 7

NFL Championship (in Green Bay) - Green Bay Packers 21, Dallas Cowboys 17

*NFL Playoff Bowl* (in Miami) – Los Angeles Rams 30, Cleveland Browns 6

### AFL Playoffs

AFL Championship (in Oakland) – Oakland Raiders 40, Houston Oilers 7

---

The Baltimore Colts tied the Los Angeles Rams for the best record in the NFL. The Rams and Colts tied, 24-24, in October and the Rams defeated the Colts on the last Sunday of the regular season 34-10. Because of tie-breaker rules implemented in 1967 based on point differential in head-to-head games, the Rams won the division on the strength of a +24 point differential. The 1967 NFL Championship game played in Green Bay between the Packers and the Dallas Cowboys is commonly referred to as the "Ice Bowl" because of the brutal weather conditions (-13 degrees with a wind chill of -48 degrees). It is considered one of the classic games in NFL history.

# 1968 – Super Bowl II
## Miami

**Green Bay Packers** (NFL) defeat the Oakland Raiders (AFL), 33-14.

## Season Awards

*Most Valuable Player (NFL)*             Johnny Unitas, Quarterback,
                                         Baltimore Colts

*Coach of the Year (NFL)*                George Allen, Los Angeles Rams/Don
                                         Shula Baltimore Colts (tie)

*Offensive Rookie of the Year (NFL)*     Mel Farr, Running Back, Detroit Lions

*Defensive Rookie of the Year (NFL)*     Lem Barney, Cornerback, Detroit Lions

*Most Valuable Player (AFL)*             Daryle Lamonica, Quarterback,
                                         Oakland Raiders

# 1968 – National Football League

## EASTERN CONFERENCE

### Capitol Division

| Team | Win | Lost | Tie |
|------|-----|------|-----|
| Dallas Cowboys | 12 | 2 | 0 |
| New York Giants | 7 | 7 | 0 |
| Washington Redskins | 5 | 9 | 0 |
| Philadelphia Eagles | 2 | 12 | 0 |

### Century Division

| Team | Win | Lost | Tie |
|------|-----|------|-----|
| Cleveland Browns | 10 | 4 | 0 |
| St. Louis Cardinals | 9 | 4 | 1 |
| New Orleans Saints | 4 | 9 | 1 |
| Pittsburgh Steelers | 2 | 11 | 1 |

## WESTERN CONFERENCE

### Central Division

| Team | Win | Lost | Tie |
|------|-----|------|-----|
| Minnesota Vikings | 8 | 6 | 0 |
| Chicago Bears | 7 | 7 | 0 |
| Green Bay Packers | 6 | 7 | 1 |
| Detroit Lions | 4 | 8 | 2 |

### Coastal Division

| Team | Win | Lost | Tie |
|------|-----|------|-----|
| Baltimore Colts | 13 | 1 | 0 |
| Los Angeles Rams | 10 | 3 | 1 |
| San Francisco 49ers | 7 | 6 | 1 |
| Atlanta Falcons | 2 | 12 | 0 |

---

Prior to the start of the 1968 season the New York Giants and the New Orleans Saints switched divisions. The Giants moved to the Capitol Division and the Saints moved to the Century Division.

# 1968 –American Football League

## Eastern Division

| Team | Win | Lost | Tie |
|------|-----|------|-----|
| New York Jets | 11 | 3 | 0 |
| Houston Oilers | 7 | 7 | 0 |
| Miami Dolphins | 5 | 8 | 1 |
| Boston Patriots | 4 | 10 | 0 |
| Buffalo Bills | 1 | 12 | 1 |

## Western Division

| Team | Win | Lost | Tie |
|------|-----|------|-----|
| Oakland Raiders | 12 | 2 | 0 |
| Kansas City Chiefs | 12 | 2 | 0 |
| San Diego Chargers | 9 | 5 | 0 |
| Denver Broncos | 5 | 9 | 0 |
| Cincinnati Bengals | 3 | 11 | 0 |

---

The AFL expanded in 1968 with the addition of the Cincinnati Bengals. Paul Brown, long-time coach of the Cleveland Browns who was fired in January 1963, was head coach and part-owner.

## 1968-1969 Playoffs

## NFL Playoffs

*Eastern Conference* (in Cleveland) - Cleveland Browns 31, Dallas Cowboys 20

*Western Conference* (in Baltimore) – Baltimore Colts 24, Minnesota Vikings 14

NFL Championship (in Cleveland) – Baltimore Colts 34, Cleveland Browns 0

*NFL Playoff Bowl* (in Miami) – Dallas Cowboys 17, Minnesota Vikings 13

## AFL Playoffs

*Western Division playoff* (in Oakland) – Oakland Raiders 41, Kansas City Chiefs 6

AFL Championship (in New York) – New York Jets 27, Oakland Raiders 23

————————

The Oakland Raiders and Kansas City Chiefs tied for the best record in the AFL Western Division. The AFL did not have a tie-breaker system. The teams met in a playoff game for the right to face the New York Jets for the AFL title.

# 1969 – Super Bowl III

## Miami

**New York Jets** (AFL) defeat the Baltimore Colts (NFL), 16-7.

## Season Awards

*Most Valuable Player (NFL)*              Earl Morrall, Quarterback,
                                          Baltimore Colts

*Coach of the Year (NFL)*                 Don Shula, Baltimore Colts

*Offensive Rookie of the Year (NFL)*      Earl McCullouch, Wide Receiver,
                                          Detroit Lions

*Defensive Rookie of the Year (NFL)*      Claude Humphrey, Defensive End,
                                          Atlanta Falcons

*Most Valuable Player (AFL)*              Joe Namath, Quarterback,
                                          New York Jets

---

The New York Jets were double-digit underdogs to the NFL champion Baltimore Colts. The Jets upset of the Colts is considered by many to be one of the greatest upsets in sports history. The Jets victory helped establish the credibility of the AFL in the minds of both the NFL and fans.

# 1969 – National Football League

## EASTERN CONFERENCE

### Capitol Division

| Team | Win | Lost | Tie |
|------|-----|------|-----|
| Dallas Cowboys | 11 | 2 | 1 |
| Washington Redskins | 7 | 5 | 2 |
| New Orleans Saints | 5 | 9 | 0 |
| Philadelphia Eagles | 4 | 9 | 1 |

### Century Division

| Team | Win | Lost | Tie |
|------|-----|------|-----|
| Cleveland Browns | 10 | 3 | 1 |
| New York Giants | 6 | 8 | 0 |
| St. Louis Cardinals | 4 | 9 | 1 |
| Pittsburgh Steelers | 1 | 13 | 0 |

## WESTERN CONFERENCE

### Central Division

| Team | Win | Lost | Tie |
|------|-----|------|-----|
| Minnesota Vikings | 12 | 2 | 0 |
| Detroit Lions | 9 | 4 | 1 |
| Green Bay Packers | 8 | 6 | 0 |
| Chicago Bears | 1 | 13 | 0 |

### Coastal Division

| Team | Win | Lost | Tie |
|------|-----|------|-----|
| Los Angeles Rams | 11 | 3 | 0 |
| Baltimore Colts | 8 | 5 | 1 |
| Atlanta Falcons | 6 | 8 | 0 |
| San Francisco 49ers | 4 | 8 | 2 |

Prior to the start of the 1969 season the New York Giants and the New Orleans Saints switched divisions (again). The Giants moved to the Century Division and the Saints moved to the Capitol Division. In 1969 the Philadelphia Eagles became the first NFL team to play their home games on artificial turf. The Houston Oilers of the AFL played their home games on artificial turf inside the first domed stadium, the Astrodome.

# 1969 –American Football League

## Eastern Division

| Team | Win | Lost | Tie |
|------|-----|------|-----|
| New York Jets | 10 | 4 | 0 |
| Houston Oilers | 6 | 6 | 2 |
| Boston Patriots | 4 | 10 | 0 |
| Buffalo Bills | 4 | 10 | 0 |
| Miami Dolphins | 3 | 10 | 1 |

## Western Division

| Team | Win | Lost | Tie |
|------|-----|------|-----|
| Oakland Raiders | 12 | 1 | 1 |
| Kansas City Chiefs | 11 | 3 | 0 |
| San Diego Chargers | 8 | 6 | 0 |
| Denver Broncos | 5 | 8 | 1 |
| Cincinnati Bengals | 4 | 9 | 1 |

---

The AFL celebrated its 10th season with a special anniversary patch worn by the Kansas City Chiefs in the Super Bowl. The NFL celebrated its 50th season in 1969 and also developed a special logo patch that was worn by each NFL team during the season.

## 1969-1970 Playoffs

## NFL Playoffs

*Eastern Conference* (in Dallas) - Cleveland Browns 38, Dallas Cowboys 14

*Western Conference* (in Minneapolis) –Minnesota Vikings 23, Los Angeles Rams 20

NFL Championship (in Minneapolis) – Minnesota Vikings 27, Cleveland Browns 7

*NFL Playoff Bowl* (in Miami) – Los Angeles Rams 31, Dallas Cowboys 0

## AFL Playoffs

*Divisional playoff* (in New York) – Kansas City Chiefs 13, New York Jets 6

*Divisional playoff* (in Oakland) – Oakland Raiders 56, Houston Oilers 7

AFL Championship (in Oakland) – Kansas City Chiefs 17, Oakland Raiders 7

---

The 1969 season was the last season where the NFL and AFL operated as separate entities, each with their own championship game with their champions meeting in the Super Bowl. In 1970 the NFL dramatically realigned the conferences and divisions to incorporate the AFL into the NFL.

The 1970 Playoff Bowl was the last in the series. There was discussion between the NFL and AFL about keeping the Playoff Bowl post-merger with the runners up in the NFC and AFC title games playing in the bowl. It was decided that a game featuring "losers" would not have much further appeal given the rise in popularity of the Super Bowl and the more attractive Pro Bowl. For the 1969 season the AFL added two teams to its playoffs. The first place team in the Eastern Division would host the second place team in the Western Division. The first place team in the Western Division would host the second place team in the Eastern Division. The winners would meet for the (final) AFL title.

# 1970 – Super Bowl IV

## Miami

**Kansas City Chiefs** (AFL) defeat the Minnesota Vikings (NFL), 23-7.

## Season Awards

*Most Valuable Player (NFL)*            Roman Gabriel, Quarterback,
                                        Los Angeles Rams

*Coach of the Year (NFL)*               Bud Grant, Minnesota Vikings

*Offensive Rookie of the Year (NFL)*    Calvin Hill, Running Back,
                                        Dallas Cowboys

*Defensive Rookie of the Year (NFL)*    Joe Greene, Defensive End,
                                        Pittsburgh Steelers

*Most Valuable Player (AFL)*            Daryle Lamonica,
                                        Quarterback, Oakland Raiders

---

The Kansas City Chiefs, like the Jets in Super Bowl III, were decided underdogs to the NFL champion Minnesota Vikings. The Chiefs' upset of the Vikings put to rest any doubts that the AFL teams did not "belong" with the NFL teams and was the perfect segue to the fully merged league.

# 1970-1979

## 1970 – National Football Conference

### Eastern Division

| Team | Win | Lost | Tie |
|------|-----|------|-----|
| Dallas Cowboys | 10 | 4 | 0 |
| New York Giants | 9 | 5 | 0 |
| St. Louis Cardinals | 8 | 5 | 1 |
| Washington Redskins | 6 | 8 | 0 |
| Philadelphia Eagles | 3 | 10 | 1 |

### Central Division

| Team | Win | Lost | Tie |
|------|-----|------|-----|
| Minnesota Vikings | 12 | 2 | 0 |
| Detroit Lions | 10 | 4 | 0 |
| Chicago Bears | 6 | 8 | 0 |
| Green Bay Packers | 6 | 8 | 0 |

### Western Division

| Team | Win | Lost | Tie |
|------|-----|------|-----|
| San Francisco 49ers | 10 | 3 | 1 |
| Los Angeles Rams | 9 | 4 | 1 |
| Atlanta Falcons | 4 | 8 | 2 |
| New Orleans Saints | 2 | 11 | 1 |

**The 1970 season brought major** changes to the NFL as it merged completely with the AFL. The NFL divided into two conferences, the National Football Conference (made up primarily of the old NFL teams) and the American Football Conference (made up primarily of the old AFL teams). Three NFL teams needed to move to the AFC in order to balance the conferences. Those teams were the Baltimore Colts, Pittsburgh Steelers and the Cleveland Browns. Additionally, each conference was divided into three divisions: Eastern, Central, and Western. Due to an uneven number of teams, the Eastern Divisions of both the NFC and AFC had five teams vs. four teams in the Central and Western Divisions respectively. As part of the merger the NFL's rules applied, meaning innovations like the AFL's two-point conversion option were eliminated. However, the NFL adopted the AFL innovation of using the stadium clock as the official game clock. Further, the NFL adopted the AFL rule of placing the player's last name on the back of their jersey.

## 1970 – American Football Conference

### Eastern Division

| Team | Win | Lost | Tie |
|------|-----|------|-----|
| Baltimore Colts | 11 | 2 | 1 |
| Miami Dolphins | 10 | 4 | 0 |
| New York Jets | 4 | 10 | 1 |
| Buffalo Bills | 3 | 10 | 1 |
| Boston Patriots | 2 | 12 | 0 |

### Central Division

| Team | Win | Lost | Tie |
|------|-----|------|-----|
| Cincinnati Bengals | 8 | 6 | 0 |
| Cleveland Browns | 7 | 7 | 0 |
| Pittsburgh Steelers | 5 | 9 | 0 |
| Houston Oilers | 3 | 10 | 1 |

### Western Division

| Team | Win | Lost | Tie |
|------|-----|------|-----|
| Oakland Raiders | 8 | 4 | 2 |
| Kansas City Chiefs | 7 | 5 | 2 |
| San Diego Chargers | 5 | 6 | 3 |
| Denver Broncos | 5 | 8 | 1 |

---

The AFC games were broadcast on NBC (home of the old AFL) while CBS retained the NFC games. For intra-conference games, CBS would broadcast if the visiting team was from the NFC, and vice versa for NBC. 1970 was also the debut of ABC's *Monday Night Football*, making the NFL the first professional sports league to have regular prime-time broadcasts.

## 1970-1971 Playoffs

## NFC Playoffs

*Divisional playoff* (in Dallas) - Dallas Cowboys 5, Detroit Lions 0

*Divisional playoff* (in Minneapolis) – San Francisco 49ers 17, Minnesota Vikings 14

NFC Championship (in San Francisco) – Dallas Cowboys 17, San Francisco 49ers 10

## AFC Playoffs

*Divisional playoff* (in Oakland) – Oakland Raiders 21, Miami Dolphins 14

*Divisional playoff* (in Baltimore) – Baltimore Colts 17, Cincinnati Bengals 0

AFC Championship (in Baltimore) – Baltimore Colts 27, Oakland Raiders 17

---

Beginning with the 1970 season and the realignment of the NFL's conferences and divisions, the winners of each division and a fourth "wild card" team based on the record of best non-division winner would advance to the conference playoffs. Tiebreaker rules were changed based on the following (in order): 1) head-to-head competition; 2) record within the division; 3) records of common opponents; and 4) record within the conference. The winner of each conference (i.e., NFC and AFC) would advance to the Super Bowl. Playoff games would be hosted by the top-two division winners with the wild card playing the team with the best record and the third best team playing the second best team. The conference championship game would be played at the home stadium of the higher remaining seed. The Super Bowl would continue to be played at a pre-determined site and would, for the first time, become the NFL championship game.

# 1971 – Super Bowl V

# Miami

**Baltimore Colts** (AFC) defeat the Dallas Cowboys (NFC), 16-13.

## Season Awards

| | |
|---|---|
| *Most Valuable Player* | John Brodie, Quarterback, San Francisco 49ers |
| *Coach of the Year* | Dick Nolan, San Francisco 49ers |
| *Offensive Rookie of the Year* | Dennis Shaw, Quarterback, Buffalo Bills |
| *Defensive Rookie of the Year* | Bruce Taylor, Cornerback, San Francisco 49ers |

---

Super Bowl V is the only Super Bowl where the MVP award was given to a player of the losing team, Dallas linebacker Chuck Howley.

# 1971 – National Football Conference

## Eastern Division

| Team | Win | Lost | Tie |
|------|-----|------|-----|
| Dallas Cowboys | 11 | 3 | 0 |
| Washington Redskins | 9 | 4 | 1 |
| Philadelphia Eagles | 6 | 7 | 1 |
| St. Louis Cardinals | 4 | 9 | 1 |
| New York Giants | 4 | 10 | 0 |

## Central Division

| Team | Win | Lost | Tie |
|------|-----|------|-----|
| Minnesota Vikings | 11 | 3 | 0 |
| Detroit Lions | 7 | 6 | 1 |
| Chicago Bears | 6 | 8 | 0 |
| Green Bay Packers | 4 | 8 | 2 |

## Western Division

| Team | Win | Lost | Tie |
|------|-----|------|-----|
| San Francisco 49ers | 9 | 5 | 0 |
| Los Angeles Rams | 8 | 5 | 1 |
| Atlanta Falcons | 7 | 6 | 1 |
| New Orleans Saints | 4 | 8 | 2 |

# 1971 – American Football Conference

## Eastern Division

| Team | Win | Lost | Tie |
|------|-----|------|-----|
| Miami Dolphins | 10 | 3 | 1 |
| Baltimore Colts | 10 | 4 | 0 |
| New England Patriots | 6 | 8 | 0 |
| New York Jets | 6 | 8 | 0 |
| Buffalo Bills | 1 | 13 | 0 |

## Central Division

| Team | Win | Lost | Tie |
|------|-----|------|-----|
| Cleveland Browns | 9 | 5 | 0 |
| Pittsburgh Steelers | 6 | 8 | 0 |
| Houston Oilers | 4 | 9 | 1 |
| Cincinnati Bengals | 4 | 10 | 0 |

## Western Division

| Team | Win | Lost | Tie |
|------|-----|------|-----|
| Kansas City Chiefs | 10 | 3 | 1 |
| Oakland Raiders | 8 | 4 | 2 |
| San Diego Chargers | 6 | 8 | 0 |
| Denver Broncos | 4 | 9 | 1 |

---

In 1971, the Boston Patriots changed their name to the New England Patriots, hoping to appeal to a larger geographic area.

# 1971-1972 Playoffs

## NFC Playoffs

*Divisional playoff* (in San Francisco) – San Francisco 49ers 24, Washington Redskins 20

*Divisional playoff* (in Minneapolis) – Dallas Cowboys 20, Minnesota Vikings 12

NFC Championship (in Dallas) – Dallas Cowboys 14, San Francisco 49ers 3

## AFC Playoffs

*Divisional playoff* (in Kansas City) – Miami Dolphins 27, Kansas City Chiefs 24 (2OT)

*Divisional playoff* (in Cleveland) – Baltimore Colts 20, Cleveland Browns 3

AFC Championship (in Miami) – Miami Dolphins 21, Baltimore Colts 0

# 1972 – Super Bowl VI

# New Orleans

**Dallas Cowboys** (NFC) defeat the Miami Dolphins (AFC), 24-3.

## Season Awards

*Most Valuable Player*                  Alan Page, Defensive Tackle,
                                        Minnesota Vikings

*Coach of the Year*                     George Allen, Washington Redskins

*Offensive Rookie of the Year*          John Brockington, Running Back,
                                        Green Bay Packers

*Defensive Rookie of the Year*          Isiah Robertson, Linebacker,
                                        Los Angeles Rams

## 1972 – National Football Conference

### Eastern Division

| Team | Win | Lost | Tie |
|------|-----|------|-----|
| Washington Redskins | 11 | 3 | 0 |
| Dallas Cowboys | 10 | 4 | 0 |
| New York Giants | 8 | 6 | 0 |
| St. Louis Cardinals | 4 | 9 | 1 |
| Philadelphia Eagles | 2 | 11 | 1 |

### Central Division

| Team | Win | Lost | Tie |
|------|-----|------|-----|
| Green Bay Packers | 10 | 4 | 0 |
| Detroit Lions | 8 | 5 | 1 |
| Minnesota Vikings | 7 | 7 | 0 |
| Chicago Bears | 4 | 9 | 1 |

### Western Division

| Team | Win | Lost | Tie |
|------|-----|------|-----|
| San Francisco 49ers | 8 | 5 | 1 |
| Atlanta Falcons | 7 | 7 | 0 |
| Los Angeles Rams | 6 | 7 | 1 |
| New Orleans Saints | 2 | 11 | 1 |

In 1971, tie games, previously ignored in terms of winning percentage calculations, became equal to a half-game win and a half-game loss in the standings.

# 1972 – American Football Conference

## Eastern Division

| Team | Win | Lost | Tie |
|------|-----|------|-----|
| Miami Dolphins | 14 | 0 | 0 |
| New York Jets | 7 | 7 | 0 |
| Baltimore Colts | 5 | 9 | 0 |
| Buffalo Bills | 4 | 9 | 1 |
| New England Patriots | 3 | 11 | 0 |

## Central Division

| Team | Win | Lost | Tie |
|------|-----|------|-----|
| Pittsburgh Steelers | 11 | 3 | 0 |
| Cleveland Browns | 10 | 4 | 0 |
| Cincinnati Bengals | 8 | 6 | 0 |
| Houston Oilers | 1 | 13 | 0 |

## Western Division

| Team | Win | Lost | Tie |
|------|-----|------|-----|
| Oakland Raiders | 10 | 3 | 1 |
| Kansas City Chiefs | 8 | 6 | 0 |
| Denver Broncos | 5 | 9 | 0 |
| San Diego Chargers | 4 | 9 | 1 |

---

The Miami Dolphins were the first (and only team to date) to finish an NFL championship season undefeated through the playoffs. The Chicago Bears had perfect regular seasons in 1934 and 1942 but lost the championship game both years. 1972 marked the first ever playoff appearance for the Pittsburgh Steelers, one of the NFL's oldest franchises.

## 1972-1973 Playoffs

## NFC Playoffs

*Divisional playoff* (in San Francisco) – Dallas Cowboys 30, San Francisco 49ers 28

*Divisional playoff* (in Washington DC) – Washington Redskins 16, Green Bay Packers 3

NFC Championship (in Washington DC) – Washington Redskins 26, Dallas Cowboys 3

## AFC Playoffs

*Divisional playoff* (in Miami) – Miami Dolphins 20, Cleveland Browns 14

*Divisional playoff* (in Pittsburgh) – Pittsburgh Steelers 13, Oakland Raiders 7

AFC Championship (in Miami) – Miami Dolphins 21, Pittsburgh Steelers 17

---

The divisional playoff game between the Oakland Raiders and Pittsburgh Steelers ended in controversy when Franco Harris (running back – Pittsburgh), caught a deflected pass and scored a touchdown with seconds left on the clock, giving the Steelers a 13-7 win. The controversy was over whether the ball was illegally touched by a Pittsburgh player before Harris caught the ball. The catch is commonly known as the "Immaculate Reception." If you fly into the Pittsburgh airport you will find a statue of Franco Harris making the Immaculate Reception waiting for you at the top of the escalators, next to George Washington and a 15-foot tall Tyrannosaurus Rex skeleton.

# 1973 – Super Bowl VII

## New Orleans

**Miami Dolphins** (AFC) defeat the Washington Redskins (NFC), 14-7.

## Season Awards

| | |
|---|---|
| *Most Valuable Player* | Larry Brown, Running Back, Washington Redskins |
| *Coach of the Year* | Don Shula, Miami Dolphins |
| *Offensive Players of the Year* | Larry Brown, Running Back, Washington Redskins |
| *Defensive Player of the Year* | Joe Greene, Defensive Tackle, Pittsburgh Steelers |
| *Offensive Rookie of the Year* | Franco Harris, Running Back, Pittsburgh Steelers |
| *Defensive Rookie of the Year* | Willie Buchanon, Cornerback, Green Bay Packers |

---

Until the 1972 season, all NFL games (including championship games and Super Bowls) were blacked-out on television in the "home" team's home city. The NFL made an exception for the 1973 Super Bowl (given the political pressure coming out of Washington DC, home of the Redskins). Congress intervened before the 1973 season, passing a law which eliminated the blackout of games in the home market so long as the game was sold out by 72 hours before game time.

# 1973 – National Football Conference

## Eastern Division

| Team | Win | Lost | Tie |
|------|-----|------|-----|
| Dallas Cowboys | 10 | 4 | 0 |
| Washington Redskins | 10 | 4 | 0 |
| Philadelphia Eagles | 5 | 8 | 1 |
| St. Louis Cardinals | 4 | 9 | 1 |
| New York Giants` | 2 | 11 | 1 |

## Central Division

| Team | Win | Lost | Tie |
|------|-----|------|-----|
| Minnesota Vikings | 12 | 2 | 0 |
| Detroit Lions | 6 | 7 | 1 |
| Green Bay Packers | 5 | 7 | 2 |
| Chicago Bears | 3 | 11 | 0 |

## Western Division

| Team | Win | Lost | Tie |
|------|-----|------|-----|
| Los Angeles Rams | 12 | 2 | 0 |
| Atlanta Falcons | 9 | 5 | 0 |
| San Francisco 49ers | 5 | 9 | 0 |
| New Orleans Saints | 5 | 9 | 0 |

---

In 1973 the NFL introduced a new numbering system for players: 1–19: Quarterbacks and specialists; 20–49: Running backs and defensive backs; 50–59: Centers and linebackers; 60–79: Defensive linemen and offensive linemen other than centers; 80–89: Wide receivers and tight ends; Numbers 0, 00, and 90–99 were no longer allowed to be issued, even though these numbers were rarely issued anyway. Numbers 90–99 would be allowed again in 1984 for defensive linemen and linebackers in addition to the above mentioned numbers. The Dallas Cowboys won the Eastern Division title over the Washington Redskins due to a higher point differential in head-to-head games (+13).

# 1973 – American Football Conference

## Eastern Division

| Team | Win | Lost | Tie |
|------|-----|------|-----|
| Miami Dolphins | 12 | 2 | 0 |
| Buffalo Bills | 9 | 5 | 0 |
| New England Patriots | 5 | 9 | 0 |
| New York Jets | 4 | 10 | 0 |
| Baltimore Colts | 4 | 10 | 0 |

## Central Division

| Team | Win | Lost | Tie |
|------|-----|------|-----|
| Cincinnati Bengals | 10 | 4 | 0 |
| Pittsburgh Steelers | 10 | 4 | 0 |
| Cleveland Browns | 7 | 5 | 2 |
| Houston Oilers | 1 | 13 | 0 |

## Western Division

| Team | Win | Lost | Tie |
|------|-----|------|-----|
| Oakland Raiders | 9 | 4 | 1 |
| Denver Broncos | 7 | 5 | 2 |
| Kansas City Chiefs | 7 | 5 | 2 |
| San Diego Chargers | 2 | 11 | 1 |

---

The Cincinnati Bengals won the Central Division title over the Pittsburgh Steelers due to a better AFC conference record (8-4 vs. 7-5 for Steelers).

# 1973-1974 Playoffs

## NFC Playoffs

*Divisional playoff* (in Minneapolis) – Minnesota Vikings 27, Washington Redskins 20

*Divisional playoff* (in Dallas) – Dallas Cowboys 27, Los Angeles Rams 16

NFC Championship (in Dallas) – Minnesota Vikings 27, Dallas Cowboys 10

## AFC Playoffs

*Divisional playoff* (in Miami) – Miami Dolphins 34, Cincinnati Bengals 16

*Divisional playoff* (in Oakland) – Oakland Raiders 33, Pittsburgh Steelers 14

AFC Championship (in Miami) – Miami Dolphins 27, Oakland Raiders 10

# 1974 – Super Bowl VIII

## Houston

**Miami Dolphin**s (AFC) defeat the Minnesota Vikings (NFC), 24-7.

## Season Awards

| | |
|---|---|
| *Most Valuable Player* | O.J. Simpson, Running Back, Buffalo Bills |
| *Coach of the Year* | Chuck Knox, Los Angeles Rams |
| *Offensive Player of the Year* | O.J. Simpson, Running Back, Buffalo Bills |
| *Defensive Player of the Year* | Dick Anderson, Safety, Miami Dolphins |
| *Offensive Rookie of the Year* | Chuck Foreman, Running Back, Minnesota Vikings |
| *Defensive Rookie of the Year* | Wally Chambers, Defensive Tackle, Chicago Bears |

League MVP O.J. Simpson became the first NFL running back to rush for over 2,000 yards in a season when he ran for 2,003 yards during the 1973 season.

## 1974 – National Football Conference

## Eastern Division

| Team | Win | Lost | Tie |
|------|-----|------|-----|
| St. Louis Cardinals | 10 | 4 | 0 |
| Washington Redskins | 10 | 4 | 0 |
| Dallas Cowboys | 8 | 6 | 0 |
| Philadelphia Eagles | 7 | 7 | 0 |
| New York Giants | 2 | 12 | 0 |

## Central Division

| Team | Win | Lost | Tie |
|------|-----|------|-----|
| Minnesota Vikings | 10 | 4 | 0 |
| Detroit Lions | 7 | 7 | 0 |
| Green Bay Packers | 6 | 8 | 0 |
| Chicago Bears | 4 | 10 | 0 |

## Western Division

| Team | Win | Lost | Tie |
|------|-----|------|-----|
| Los Angeles Rams | 10 | 4 | 0 |
| San Francisco 49ers | 6 | 8 | 0 |
| New Orleans Saints | 5 | 9 | 0 |
| Atlanta Falcons | 3 | 11 | 0 |

---

The St. Louis Cardinals took the Eastern Division title over the Washington Redskins as a result of a 2-0 record vs. Washington in head-to-head games between the two teams. To decrease the number of tie games, the NFL adopted a new overtime rule. One sudden death overtime period (15 minutes) was added to all tied games; if no team scored in this period, the game would result in a tie. The first ever regular season overtime period was played on September 22, 1974 between the Pittsburgh Steelers and the Denver Broncos. Neither team scored during the overtime period and the game ended in a draw. For playoff games, the sudden death rules remained unchanged and the teams would play until there was a winner, i.e., the first team to score.

# 1974 – American Football Conference

## Eastern Division

| Team | Win | Lost | Tie |
|------|-----|------|-----|
| Miami Dolphins | 11 | 3 | 0 |
| Buffalo Bills | 9 | 5 | 0 |
| New England Patriots | 7 | 7 | 0 |
| New York Jets | 7 | 7 | 0 |
| Baltimore Colts | 2 | 12 | 0 |

## Central Division

| Team | Win | Lost | Tie |
|------|-----|------|-----|
| Pittsburgh Steelers | 10 | 3 | 1 |
| Cincinnati Bengals | 7 | 7 | 0 |
| Houston Oilers | 7 | 7 | 0 |
| Cleveland Browns | 4 | 10 | 0 |

## Western Division

| Team | Win | Lost | Tie |
|------|-----|------|-----|
| Oakland Raiders | 12 | 2 | 0 |
| Denver Broncos | 7 | 6 | 1 |
| Kansas City Chiefs | 5 | 9 | 0 |
| San Diego Chargers | 5 | 9 | 0 |

---

The NFL moved the goal posts from the goal line to the back line of the end zone (as they were in 1932). The league did this to increase player safety (reducing collisions with the goal post base) and to cut down on the number of field goals by making them 10 yards longer and, thus, more difficult.

# 1974-1975 Playoffs

## NFC Playoffs

*Divisional playoff* (in Los Angeles) – Los Angeles Rams 19, Washington Redskins 10

*Divisional playoff* (in Minneapolis) – Minnesota Vikings 30, St. Louis Cardinals 14

NFC Championship (in Minneapolis) – Minnesota Vikings 14, Los Angeles Rams 10

## AFC Playoffs

*Divisional playoff* (in Pittsburgh) – Pittsburgh Steelers 32, Buffalo Bills 14

*Divisional playoff* (in Oakland) – Oakland Raiders 28, Miami Dolphins 26

AFC Championship (in Oakland) – Pittsburgh Steelers 24, Oakland Raiders 13

# 1975 – Super Bowl IX
# New Orleans

**Pittsburgh Steelers** (AFC) defeat the Minnesota Vikings (NFC), 16-6.

## Season Awards

| | |
|---|---|
| *Most Valuable Player* | Ken Stabler, Quarterback, Oakland Raiders |
| *Coach of the Year* | Don Coryell, St. Louis Cardinals |
| *Offensive Player of the Year* | Ken Stabler, Quarterback, Oakland Raiders |
| *Defensive Player of the Year* | Joe Greene, Defensive End, Pittsburgh Steelers |
| *Offensive Rookie of the Year* | Don Woods, Running Back, San Diego Chargers |
| *Defensive Rookie of the Year* | Jack Lambert, Linebacker, Pittsburgh Steelers |

# 1975 – National Football Conference

## Eastern Division

| Team | Win | Lost | Tie |
|------|-----|------|-----|
| St. Louis Cardinals | 11 | 3 | 0 |
| Dallas Cowboys | 10 | 4 | 0 |
| Washington Redskins | 8 | 6 | 0 |
| New York Giants | 5 | 9 | 0 |
| Philadelphia Eagles | 4 | 10 | 0 |

## Central Division

| Team | Win | Lost | Tie |
|------|-----|------|-----|
| Minnesota Vikings | 12 | 2 | 0 |
| Detroit Lions | 7 | 7 | 0 |
| Green Bay Packers | 4 | 10 | 0 |
| Chicago Bears | 4 | 10 | 0 |

## Western Division

| Team | Win | Lost | Tie |
|------|-----|------|-----|
| Los Angeles Rams | 12 | 2 | 0 |
| San Francisco 49ers | 5 | 9 | 0 |
| Atlanta Falcons | 4 | 10 | 0 |
| New Orleans Saints | 2 | 12 | 0 |

---

1975 was the first NFL season without any tie games. For the first time since the 1966 season, the Dallas Cowboys did not host a Thanksgiving Day football game. Instead, the league selected the Buffalo Bills at St. Louis Cardinals as the featured contest.

# 1975 – American Football Conference

## Eastern Division

| Team | Win | Lost | Tie |
|------|-----|------|-----|
| Baltimore Colts | 10 | 4 | 0 |
| Miami Dolphins | 10 | 4 | 0 |
| Buffalo Bills | 8 | 6 | 0 |
| New England Patriots | 3 | 11 | 0 |
| New York Jets | 3 | 11 | 0 |

## Central Division

| Team | Win | Lost | Tie |
|------|-----|------|-----|
| Pittsburgh Steelers | 12 | 2 | 0 |
| Cincinnati Bengals | 11 | 3 | 0 |
| Houston Oilers | 10 | 4 | 0 |
| Cleveland Browns | 3 | 11 | 0 |

## Western Division

| Team | Win | Lost | Tie |
|------|-----|------|-----|
| Oakland Raiders | 11 | 3 | 0 |
| Denver Broncos | 6 | 8 | 0 |
| Kansas City Chiefs | 5 | 9 | 0 |
| San Diego Chargers | 2 | 12 | 0 |

---

Baltimore finished ahead of Miami and won the AFC East based on a 2-0 sweep of their regular season games. In 1975, the NFL pioneered the use of wireless microphones for referees, allowing them to announce penalties and other important information to the stadium crowd and the television audience.

## 1975-1976 Playoffs

## NFC Playoffs

*Divisional playoff* (in Los Angeles) – Los Angeles Rams 35, St. Louis Cardinals 23

*Divisional playoff* (in Minneapolis) – Dallas Cowboys 17, Minnesota Vikings 14

NFC Championship (in Los Angeles) – Dallas Cowboys 37, Los Angeles Rams 7

## AFC Playoffs

*Divisional playoff* (in Pittsburgh) – Pittsburgh Steelers 28, Baltimore Colts 10

*Divisional playoff* (in Oakland) – Oakland Raiders 31, Cincinnati Bengals 28

AFC Championship (in Pittsburgh) – Pittsburgh Steelers 16, Oakland Raiders 10

––––––––––

For the 1975 season playoffs, the NFL changed the site of playoffs games to the surviving team with the best overall record. Prior to 1975, the site of playoff games rotated by division. The Super Bowl remained a pre-selected neutral site game.

# 1976 – Super Bowl X

## Miami

**Pittsburgh Steelers** (AFC) defeat the Dallas Cowboys (NFC), 16-10.

## Season Awards

| | |
|---|---|
| *Most Valuable Player* | Fran Tarkenton, Quarterback, Minnesota Vikings |
| *Coach of the Year* | Ted Marchibroda, Baltimore Colts |
| *Offensive Player of the Year* | Fran Tarkenton, Quarterback, Minnesota Vikings |
| *Defensive Player of the Year* | Mel Blount, Cornerback, Pittsburgh Steelers |
| *Offensive Rookie of the Year* | Mike Thomas, Running Back, Washington Redskins |
| *Defensive Rookie of the Year* | Robert Brazile, Linebacker, Houston Oilers |

# 1976 – National Football Conference

## Eastern Division

| Team | Win | Lost | Tie |
|---|---|---|---|
| Dallas Cowboys | 11 | 3 | 0 |
| Washington Redskins | 10 | 4 | 0 |
| St. Louis Cardinals | 10 | 4 | 0 |
| Philadelphia Eagles | 4 | 10 | 0 |
| New York Giants | 3 | 11 | 0 |

## Central Division

| Team | Win | Lost | Tie |
|---|---|---|---|
| Minnesota Vikings | 11 | 2 | 1 |
| Chicago Bears | 7 | 7 | 0 |
| Detroit Lions | 6 | 8 | 0 |
| Green Bay Packers | 5 | 9 | 0 |

## Western Division

| Team | Win | Lost | Tie |
|---|---|---|---|
| Los Angeles Rams | 10 | 3 | 1 |
| San Francisco 49ers | 8 | 6 | 0 |
| Atlanta Falcons | 4 | 10 | 0 |
| New Orleans Saints | 4 | 10 | 0 |
| Seattle Seahawks | 2 | 12 | 0 |

The NFL added two expansion teams in 1976, the Seattle Seahawks and the Tampa Bay Buccaneers. The Seahawks were placed in the NFC West and the Buccaneers in the AFC West. This expansion fulfilled part of the 1966 NFL-AFL merger agreement. In particular, the agreement that the league would expand by two additional teams by 1970 or "soon thereafter."

## 1976 – American Football Conference

## Eastern Division

| Team | Win | Lost | Tie |
|------|-----|------|-----|
| Baltimore Colts | 11 | 3 | 0 |
| New England Patriots | 11 | 3 | 0 |
| Miami Dolphins | 6 | 8 | 0 |
| New York Jets | 3 | 11 | 0 |
| Buffalo Bills | 2 | 12 | 0 |

## Central Division

| Team | Win | Lost | Tie |
|------|-----|------|-----|
| Pittsburgh Steelers | 10 | 4 | 0 |
| Cincinnati Bengals | 10 | 4 | 0 |
| Cleveland Browns | 9 | 5 | 0 |
| Houston Oilers | 5 | 9 | 0 |

## Western Division

| Team | Win | Lost | Tie |
|------|-----|------|-----|
| Oakland Raiders | 13 | 1 | 0 |
| Denver Broncos | 9 | 5 | 0 |
| San Diego Chargers | 6 | 8 | 0 |
| Kansas City Chiefs | 5 | 9 | 0 |
| Tampa Bay Buccaneers | 0 | 14 | 0 |

---

In addition to joining the league as an expansion team in 1976, the Tampa Bay Buccaneers set a modern day record as the first NFL franchise to lose all of its games in a season.

## 1976-1977 Playoffs

## NFC Playoffs

*Divisional playoff* (in Dallas) – Los Angeles Rams 14, Dallas Cowboys 12

*Divisional playoff* (in Minneapolis) – Minnesota Vikings 35, Washington Redskins 20[1]

NFC Championship (in Minneapolis) – Minnesota Vikings 24, Los Angeles Rams 13

## AFC Playoffs

*Divisional playoff* (in Baltimore) – Pittsburgh Steelers 40[2], Baltimore Colts 14[3]

*Divisional playoff* (in Oakland) –Oakland Raiders 24, New England Patriots 21

AFC Championship (in Oakland) – Oakland Raiders 24, Pittsburgh Steelers 7

---

1      The Washington Redskins finished ahead of the St. Louis Cardinals in the NFC East on the basis of a 2-0 sweep in head-to-head games in 1976.

2      The Pittsburgh Steelers finished ahead of the Cincinnati Bengals in the AFC Central on the basis of a 2-0 sweep in head-to-head games in 1976.

3      The Baltimore Colts finished ahead of the New England Patriots in the AFC East on the basis of a better record within the division, 7-1 to 6-2 respectively.

# 1977 – Super Bowl XI
# Los Angeles (Rose Bowl)

**Oakland Raiders** (AFC) defeat the Minnesota Vikings (NFC), 32-14.

## Season Awards

| | |
|---|---|
| *Most Valuable Player* | Bert Jones, Quarterback, Baltimore Colts |
| *Coach of the Year* | Forrest Gregg, Cleveland Browns |
| *Offensive Player of the Year* | Bert Jones, Quarterback, Baltimore Colts |
| *Defensive Player of the Year* | Jack Lambert, Linebacker, Pittsburgh Steelers |
| *Offensive Rookie of the Year* | Sammy White, Wide Receiver, Minnesota Vikings |
| *Defensive Rookie of the Year* | Mike Haynes, Cornerback, New England Patriots |

# 1977 – National Football Conference

## Eastern Division

| Team | Win | Lost | Tie |
|------|-----|------|-----|
| Dallas Cowboys | 12 | 2 | 0 |
| Washington Redskins | 9 | 5 | 0 |
| St. Louis Cardinals | 7 | 7 | 0 |
| Philadelphia Eagles | 5 | 9 | 0 |
| New York Giants | 5 | 9 | 0 |

## Central Division

| Team | Win | Lost | Tie |
|------|-----|------|-----|
| Minnesota Vikings | 9 | 5 | 0 |
| Chicago Bears | 9 | 5 | 0 |
| Detroit Lions | 6 | 8 | 0 |
| Green Bay Packers | 4 | 10 | 0 |
| Tampa Bay Buccaneers | 2 | 12 | 0 |

## Western Division

| Team | Win | Lost | Tie |
|------|-----|------|-----|
| Los Angeles Rams | 10 | 4 | 0 |
| Atlanta Falcons | 7 | 7 | 0 |
| San Francisco 49ers | 5 | 9 | 0 |
| New Orleans Saints | 3 | 11 | 0 |

The NFL moved the Tampa Bay Buccaneers from the AFC West to the NFC Central. The Dallas Cowboys did not play on Thanksgiving Day for the second consecutive year. The NFL featured the Miami Dolphins at St. Louis Cardinals instead. This would be the last year the Cowboys did not play on Thanksgiving Day (as of the 2014-15 season).

## 1977 – American Football Conference

## Eastern Division

| Team | Win | Lost | Tie |
|------|-----|------|-----|
| Baltimore Colts | 10 | 4 | 0 |
| Miami Dolphins | 10 | 4 | 0 |
| New England Patriots | 9 | 5 | 0 |
| Buffalo Bills | 3 | 11 | 0 |
| New York Jets | 3 | 11 | 0 |

## Central Division

| Team | Win | Lost | Tie |
|------|-----|------|-----|
| Pittsburgh Steelers | 9 | 5 | 0 |
| Cincinnati Bengals | 8 | 6 | 0 |
| Houston Oilers | 8 | 6 | 0 |
| Cleveland Browns | 6 | 8 | 0 |

## Western Division

| Team | Win | Lost | Tie |
|------|-----|------|-----|
| Denver Broncos | 12 | 2 | 0 |
| Oakland Raiders | 11 | 3 | 0 |
| San Diego Chargers | 7 | 7 | 0 |
| Seattle Seahawks | 5 | 9 | 0 |
| Kansas City Chiefs | 2 | 12 | 0 |

The NFL moved the Seattle Seahawks from the NFC West to the AFC West. To open up scoring the league changed it rules to allow the defensive player to only make contact with a receiver once anywhere on the field.

## 1977-1978 Playoffs

## NFC Playoffs

*Divisional playoff* (in Dallas) – Dallas Cowboys 37, Chicago Bears 7

*Divisional playoff* (in Los Angeles) – Minnesota Vikings 14[4], Los Angeles Rams 7

NFC Championship (in Dallas) – Dallas Cowboys 23, Minnesota Vikings 6

## AFC Playoffs

*Divisional playoff* (in Baltimore) – Oakland Raiders 37, Baltimore Colts 31[5] (2OT)

*Divisional playoff* (in Denver) – Denver Broncos 34, Pittsburgh Steelers 21

AFC Championship (in Denver) – Denver Broncos 20, Oakland Raiders 17

---

4       The Minnesota Vikings finished ahead of the Chicago Bears in the NFC Central based on fewer losses by common opponents. The Vikings lost to common opponents with a sum total of 11 losses, the Bears lost to common opponents with a sum total of 14 losses. Chicago, in turn, won the NFC Wild Card spot over the Washington Redskins due to better net points in conference games, 48 to 4.

5       The Baltimore Colts finished ahead of the Miami Dolphins in the AFC East based on a better conference record, 9-3 to 8-4 respectively.

# 1978 – Super Bowl XII

## New Orleans

**Dallas Cowboys** (NFC) defeat the Denver Broncos (AFC), 27-10.

## Season Awards

| | |
|---|---|
| *Most Valuable Player* | Walter Payton, Running Back, Chicago Bears |
| *Coach of the Year* | Red Miller, Denver Broncos |
| *Offensive Player of the Year* | Walter Payton, Running Back, Chicago Bears |
| *Defensive Player of the Year* | Harvey Martin, Defensive End, Dallas Cowboys |
| *Offensive Rookie of the Year* | Tony Dorsett, Running Back, Dallas Cowboys |
| *Defensive Rookie of the Year* | A.J. Duhe, Defensive End, Miami Dolphins |

## 1978  – National Football Conference

## Eastern Division

| Team | Win | Lost | Tie |
|---|---|---|---|
| Dallas Cowboys | 12 | 4 | 0 |
| Philadelphia Eagles | 9 | 7 | 0 |
| Washington Redskins | 8 | 8 | 0 |
| St. Louis Cardinals | 6 | 10 | 0 |
| New York Giants | 6 | 10 | 0 |

## Central Division

| Team | Win | Lost | Tie |
|---|---|---|---|
| Minnesota Vikings | 8 | 7 | 1 |
| Green Bay Packers | 8 | 7 | 1 |
| Detroit Lions | 7 | 9 | 0 |
| Chicago Bears | 7 | 9 | 0 |
| Tampa Bay Buccaneers | 5 | 11 | 0 |

## Western Division

| Team | Win | Lost | Tie |
|---|---|---|---|
| Los Angeles Rams | 12 | 4 | 0 |
| Atlanta Falcons | 9 | 7 | 0 |
| New Orleans Saints | 7 | 9 | 0 |
| San Francisco 49ers | 2 | 14 | 0 |

---

The NFL moved to a 16 game regular season schedule in 1978. The league also began a new scheduling format as well. A division in one conference would play a division in another conference, rotating every season and repeating the process every three years. Previously, teams played random opponents in the other conference. This format remains in effect today.

## 1978 – American Football Conference

### Eastern Division

| Team | Win | Lost | Tie |
|------|-----|------|-----|
| New England Patriots | 11 | 5 | 0 |
| Miami Dolphins | 11 | 5 | 0 |
| New York Jets | 8 | 8 | 0 |
| Buffalo Bills | 5 | 11 | 0 |
| Baltimore Colts | 5 | 11 | 0 |

### Central Division

| Team | Win | Lost | Tie |
|------|-----|------|-----|
| Pittsburgh Steelers | 14 | 2 | 0 |
| Houston Oilers | 10 | 6 | 0 |
| Cleveland Browns | 8 | 8 | 0 |
| Cincinnati Bengals | 4 | 12 | 0 |

### Western Division

| Team | Win | Lost | Tie |
|------|-----|------|-----|
| Denver Broncos | 10 | 6 | 0 |
| Oakland Raiders | 9 | 7 | 0 |
| San Diego Chargers | 9 | 7 | 0 |
| Seattle Seahawks | 9 | 7 | 0 |
| Kansas City Chiefs | 4 | 12 | 0 |

To open up scoring even further, the league changed its contact rule to only allow the defensive player to contact a receiver once within five yards of the line of scrimmage.

## 1978-1979 Playoffs

## NFC Playoffs

*Wild Card playoff* (in Atlanta) – Atlanta Falcons 14[6], Philadelphia Eagles 13

*Divisional playoff* (in Dallas) – Dallas Cowboys 27, Atlanta Falcons 20

*Divisional playoff* (in Los Angeles) – Los Angeles Rams 34[7], Minnesota Vikings 10[8]

NFC Championship (in Los Angeles) – Dallas Cowboys 28, Los Angeles Rams 0

## AFC Playoffs

*Wild Card playoff* (in Miami) – Houston Oilers 17, Miami Dolphins 9

*Divisional playoff* (in Boston) – Houston Oilers 31, New England Patriots 14[9]

*Divisional playoff* (in Pittsburgh) – Pittsburgh Steelers 33, Denver Broncos 10

AFC Championship (in Pittsburgh) – Pittsburgh Steelers 34, Houston Oilers 5

––––––––––

The NFL expanded the playoffs beginning with the 1978 season. The league added another Wild Card team from each conference, expanding the number of playoff teams from eight to ten. The Wild Card teams would play each other (at the field of the team with the better record) with the winner advancing to the divisional playoff round.

––––––––––

6        The Atlanta Falcons were the top NFC Wild card team over the Philadelphia Eagles based a better conference record, 8-4 vs. 6-6, respectively. This was the first season the Falcons made the playoffs.

7        The Los Angeles Rams beat out the Dallas Cowboys for the NFC top seed based on a better head-to-head record, 1-0.

8        The Minnesota Vikings finished ahead of the Green Bay Packers in the NFC Central based on better head-to-head record, 1–0–1.

9        The New England Patriots finished ahead of the Miami Dolphins in the AFC East based on better division record 6–2 vs. 5–3, respectively.

# 1979 – Super Bowl XIII

## Miami

**Pittsburgh Steelers** (AFC) defeat the Dallas Cowboys (NFC), 35-31.

## Season Awards

*Most Valuable Player*  Terry Bradshaw, Quarterback,
Pittsburgh Steelers

*Coach of the Year*  Jack Patera, Seattle Seahawks

*Offensive Player of the Year*  Earl Campbell, Running Back, Houston Oilers

*Defensive Player of the Year*  Randy Gradishar, Linebacker, Denver Broncos

*Offensive Rookie of the Year*  Earl Campbell, Running Back, Houston Oilers

*Defensive Rookie of the Year*  Al Baker, Defensive End, Detroit Lions

## 1979  – National Football Conference

### Eastern Division

| Team | Win | Lost | Tie |
|---|---|---|---|
| Dallas Cowboys | 11 | 5 | 0 |
| Philadelphia Eagles | 11 | 5 | 0 |
| Washington Redskins | 10 | 6 | 0 |
| New York Giants | 6 | 10 | 0 |
| St. Louis Cardinals | 5 | 11 | 0 |

### Central Division

| Team | Win | Lost | Tie |
|---|---|---|---|
| Tampa Bay Buccaneers | 10 | 6 | 0 |
| Chicago Bears | 10 | 6 | 0 |
| Minnesota Vikings | 7 | 9 | 0 |
| Green Bay Packers | 5 | 11 | 0 |
| Detroit Lions | 2 | 14 | 0 |

### Western Division

| Team | Win | Lost | Tie |
|---|---|---|---|
| Los Angeles Rams | 9 | 7 | 0 |
| New Orleans Saints | 8 | 8 | 0 |
| Atlanta Falcons | 6 | 10 | 0 |
| San Francisco 49ers | 2 | 14 | 0 |

The NFL banned tear-away jerseys prior to the start of the 1979 season.

# 1979 – American Football Conference

## Eastern Division

| Team | Win | Lost | Tie |
|------|-----|------|-----|
| Miami Dolphins | 10 | 6 | 0 |
| New England Patriots | 9 | 7 | 0 |
| New York Jets | 8 | 8 | 0 |
| Buffalo Bills | 7 | 9 | 0 |
| Baltimore Colts | 5 | 11 | 0 |

## Central Division

| Team | Win | Lost | Tie |
|------|-----|------|-----|
| Pittsburgh Steelers | 12 | 4 | 0 |
| Houston Oilers | 11 | 5 | 0 |
| Cleveland Browns | 9 | 7 | 0 |
| Cincinnati Bengals | 4 | 12 | 0 |

## Western Division

| Team | Win | Lost | Tie |
|------|-----|------|-----|
| San Diego Chargers | 12 | 4 | 0 |
| Denver Broncos | 10 | 6 | 0 |
| Oakland Raiders | 9 | 7 | 0 |
| Seattle Seahawks | 9 | 7 | 0 |
| Kansas City Chiefs | 7 | 9 | 0 |

## 1979-1980 Playoffs

## NFC Playoffs

*Wild Card playoff* (in Philadelphia) – Philadelphia Eagles 27, Chicago 17[10]

*Divisional playoff* (in Dallas) – Los Angeles Rams 21, Dallas Cowboys 19[11]

*Divisional playoff* (in Tampa Bay) – Tampa Bay Buccaneers 24[12], Philadelphia Eagles 17

NFC Championship (in Tampa Bay) – Los Angeles Rams 9, Tampa Bay Buccaneers 0

## AFC Playoffs

*Wild Card playoff* (in Houston) – Houston Oilers 13, Denver Broncos 7

*Divisional playoff* (in San Diego) – Houston Oilers 17, San Diego Chargers 14[13]

*Divisional playoff* (in Pittsburgh) – Pittsburgh Steelers 34, Miami Dolphins 14

AFC Championship (in Pittsburgh) – Pittsburgh Steelers 27, Houston Oilers 13

---

10      The Chicago Bears beat out the Washington Redskins for the second NFC Wild Card because of better net points in all games played, 57 to 53.

11      The Dallas Cowboys won the NFC East over the Philadelphia Eagles due to a better conference record, 10-2 vs. 9-3, respectively.

12      The Tampa Bay Buccaneers won the NFC Central over the Chicago Bears due to a better division record, 6-2 vs. 5-3, respectively.

13      The San Diego Chargers were the AFC top seed over the Pittsburgh Steelers due a head-to-head victory.

# 1980 – Super Bowl XIV
# Los Angeles (Rose Bowl)

**Pittsburgh Steelers** (AFC) defeat the Los Angeles Rams (NFC), 31-19.

## Season Awards

| | |
|---|---|
| *Most Valuable Player* | Earl Campbell, Running Back, Houston Oilers |
| *Coach of the Year* | Jack Pardee, Washington Redskins |
| *Offensive Player of the Year* | Earl Campbell, Running Back, Houston Oilers |
| *Defensive Player of the Year* | Lee Roy Selmon, Defensive End, Tampa Bay Buccaneers |
| *Offensive Rookie of the Year* | Ottis Anderson, Running Back, St. Louis Cardinals |
| *Defensive Rookie of the Year* | Jim Haslett, Linebacker, Buffalo Bills |

# 1980-1989

## 1980 – National Football Conference

## Eastern Division

| Team | Win | Lost | Tie |
|------|-----|------|-----|
| Philadelphia Eagles | 12 | 4 | 0 |
| Dallas Cowboys | 12 | 4 | 0 |
| Washington Redskins | 6 | 10 | 0 |
| St. Louis Cardinals | 5 | 11 | 0 |
| New York Giants | 4 | 12 | 0 |

## Central Division

| Team | Win | Lost | Tie |
|------|-----|------|-----|
| Minnesota Vikings | 9 | 7 | 0 |
| Detroit Lions | 9 | 7 | 0 |
| Chicago Bears | 7 | 9 | 0 |
| Tampa Bay Buccaneers | 5 | 10 | 1 |
| Green Bay Packers | 5 | 10 | 1 |

## Western Division

| Team | Win | Lost | Tie |
|------|-----|------|-----|
| Atlanta Falcons | 12 | 4 | 0 |
| Los Angeles Rams | 11 | 5 | 0 |
| San Francisco 49ers | 6 | 10 | 0 |
| New Orleans Saints | 1 | 15 | 0 |

---

**In 1980, the NFL enacted a new rule** that prohibited striking, swinging, or clubbing to the head, face, or neck. Prior to this change, such activity was perfectly legal during games.

## 1980 – American Football Conference

### Eastern Division

| Team | Win | Lost | Tie |
|------|-----|------|-----|
| Buffalo Bills | 11 | 5 | 0 |
| New England Patriots | 10 | 6 | 0 |
| Miami Dolphins | 8 | 8 | 0 |
| Baltimore Colts | 7 | 9 | 0 |
| New York Jets | 4 | 12 | 0 |

### Central Division

| Team | Win | Lost | Tie |
|------|-----|------|-----|
| Cleveland Browns | 11 | 5 | 0 |
| Houston Oilers | 11 | 5 | 0 |
| Pittsburgh Steelers | 9 | 7 | 0 |
| Cincinnati Bengals | 6 | 10 | 0 |

### Western Division

| Team | Win | Lost | Tie |
|------|-----|------|-----|
| San Diego Chargers | 11 | 5 | 0 |
| Oakland Raiders | 11 | 5 | 0 |
| Kansas City Chiefs | 8 | 8 | 0 |
| Denver Broncos | 8 | 8 | 0 |
| Seattle Seahawks | 4 | 12 | 0 |

---

After the NFL refused to approve the move of the Oakland Raiders franchise to Los Angeles, the Raiders (run by legendary owner Al Davis) and the Los Angeles Coliseum sued the NFL for alleged antitrust violations. There was no verdict in the case until 1982.

## 1980-1981 Playoffs

## NFC Playoffs

*Wild Card playoff* (in Dallas) – Dallas Cowboys 34, Los Angeles Rams 13

*Divisional playoff* (in Atlanta) – Dallas Cowboys 30, Atlanta Falcons 27[1]

*Divisional playoff* (in Philadelphia) – Philadelphia Eagles 31[2], Minnesota Vikings 16[3]

NFC Championship (in Philadelphia) – Philadelphia Eagles 20, Dallas Cowboys 7

## AFC Playoffs

*Wild Card playoff* (in Oakland) – Oakland Raiders 27[4], Houston Oilers 7

*Divisional playoff* (in Cleveland) – Oakland Raiders 14, Cleveland Browns 12[5]

*Divisional playoff* (in San Diego) – San Diego Chargers 20[6], Buffalo Bills 14

AFC Championship (in San Diego) – Oakland Raiders 34, San Diego Chargers 27

---

1       The Atlanta Falcons were the top NFC seed over the Philadelphia Eagles based on a head-to-head victory over the Eagles.

2       The Philadelphia Eagles won the NFC East over the Dallas Cowboys based on better net points in division games, + 84 vs. +50.

3       The Minnesota Vikings won the NFC Central over the Detroit Lions based on a better conference record, 8-4 vs. 9-5.

4       Oakland was the top AFC Wild Card seed based on a better conference record than the Houston Oilers, 9-3 vs. 7-5.

5       The Cleveland Browns finished won the AFC Central over the Houston Oilers based on a better conference record, 8-4 vs. 7-5.

6       The San Diego Chargers bested the Oakland Raiders for the AFC West title based on net points in division games, +60 to +37, respectively.  The Chargers were the top AFC seed based on a better conference record than the Cleveland Browns or the Buffalo Bills, 9-3, to 8-4 each for the Browns and Bills.  The Browns won the second seed over the Bills based on a better record against common opponents, 5-2 vs. 5-3.

# 1981 – Super Bowl XV (15)

## New Orleans

**Oakland Raiders** (AFC) defeat the Philadelphia Eagles (NFC), 27-10.

## Season Awards

| | |
|---|---|
| *Most Valuable Player* | Brian Sipe, Quarterback, Cleveland Browns |
| *Coach of the Year* | Chuck Knox, Buffalo Bills |
| *Offensive Player of the Year* | Earl Campbell, Running Back, Houston Oilers |
| *Defensive Player of the Year* | Lester Hayes, Cornerback, Oakland Raiders |
| *Offensive Rookie of the Year* | Billy Sims, Running Back, Detroit Lions |
| *Defensive Rookie of the Year* | Buddy Curry & Al Richardson, Linebackers, Atlanta Falcons |

# 1981  – National Football Conference

## Eastern Division

| Team | Win | Lost | Tie |
|---|---|---|---|
| Dallas Cowboys | 12 | 4 | 0 |
| Philadelphia Eagles | 10 | 6 | 0 |
| New York Giants | 9 | 7 | 0 |
| Washington Redskins | 8 | 8 | 0 |
| St. Louis Cardinals | 7 | 9 | 0 |

## Central Division

| Team | Win | Lost | Tie |
|---|---|---|---|
| Tampa Bay Buccaneers | 9 | 7 | 0 |
| Detroit Lions | 8 | 8 | 0 |
| Green Bay Packers | 8 | 8 | 0 |
| Minnesota Vikings | 7 | 9 | 0 |
| Chicago Bears | 6 | 10 | 0 |

## Western Division

| Team | Win | Lost | Tie |
|---|---|---|---|
| San Francisco 49ers | 13 | 3 | 0 |
| Atlanta Falcons | 7 | 9 | 0 |
| Los Angeles Rams | 6 | 10 | 0 |
| New Orleans Saints | 4 | 12 | 0 |

---

Beginning with the 1981 season, the NFL made it illegal for a player to use any type of adhesive on his body, equipment or uniform. This effectively banned "stickum" a substance made famous by Oakland Raider wide receiver Fred Biletnikoff to make it easier to catch and hold onto passes.

# 1981 – American Football Conference

## Eastern Division

| Team | Win | Lost | Tie |
|------|-----|------|-----|
| Miami Dolphins | 11 | 4 | 1 |
| New York Jets | 10 | 5 | 1 |
| Buffalo Bills | 10 | 6 | 0 |
| Baltimore Colts | 2 | 14 | 0 |
| New England Patriots | 2 | 14 | 0 |

## Central Division

| Team | Win | Lost | Tie |
|------|-----|------|-----|
| Cincinnati Bengals | 12 | 4 | 0 |
| Pittsburgh Steelers | 8 | 8 | 0 |
| Houston Oilers | 7 | 9 | 0 |
| Cleveland Browns | 5 | 11 | 0 |

## Western Division

| Team | Win | Lost | Tie |
|------|-----|------|-----|
| San Diego Chargers | 10 | 6 | 0 |
| Denver Broncos | 10 | 6 | 0 |
| Kansas City Chiefs | 9 | 7 | 0 |
| Oakland Raiders | 7 | 9 | 0 |
| Seattle Seahawks | 6 | 10 | 0 |

## 1981-1982 Playoffs

## NFC Playoffs

*Wild Card playoff* (in Philadelphia) – New York Giants 27, Philadelphia Eagles 21

*Divisional playoff* (in Dallas) – Dallas Cowboys 38, Tampa Bay Buccaneers 0

*Divisional playoff* (in San Francisco) – San Francisco 49ers 38, New York Giants 24

NFC Championship (in San Francisco) – San Francisco 49ers 28, Dallas Cowboys 27

## AFC Playoffs

*Wild Card playoff* (in New York) – Buffalo Bills 31[7], New York Jets 27

*Divisional playoff* (in Miami) – San Diego Chargers 41[8], Miami Dolphins 38 (OT)

*Divisional playoff* (in Cincinnati) – Cincinnati Bengals 28, Buffalo Bills 21

AFC Championship (in Cincinnati) – Cincinnati Bengals 27, San Diego Chargers 7

---

7       The Buffalo Bills were the second AFC Wild Card over the Denver Broncos based on a head-to-head victory.

8       The San Diego Chargers won the AFC West over the Denver Broncos based on a better division record, 6-2 vs. 5-3.

# 1982 – Super Bowl XVI (16)

## Detroit

**San Francisco 49ers** (NFC) defeat the Cincinnati Bengals (AFC), 26-21.

## Season Awards

| | |
|---|---|
| *Most Valuable Player* | Ken Anderson, Quarterback, Cincinnati Bengals |
| *Coach of the Year* | Bill Walsh, San Francisco 49ers |
| *Offensive Player of the Year* | Ken Anderson, Quarterback, Cincinnati Bengals |
| *Defensive Player of the Year* | Lawrence Taylor, Linebacker, New York Giants |
| *Offensive Rookie of the Year* | George Rogers, Running Back, New Orleans Saints |
| *Defensive Rookie of the Year* | Lawrence Taylor, Linebacker, New York Giants |

---

The 1981 Super Bowl was the first Super Bowl held in a "cold" weather city, i.e., Detroit. It was played inside a domed stadium, Pontiac Stadium.

## 1982  – National Football Conference

### Eastern Division

| Team | Win | Lost | Tie |
|------|-----|------|-----|
| Washington Redskins | 8 | 1 | 0 |
| Dallas Cowboys | 6 | 3 | 0 |
| St. Louis Cardinals | 5 | 4 | 0 |
| New York Giants | 4 | 5 | 0 |
| Philadelphia Eagles | 3 | 6 | 0 |

### Central Division

| Team | Win | Lost | Tie |
|------|-----|------|-----|
| Green Bay Packers | 5 | 3 | 1 |
| Minnesota Vikings | 5 | 4 | 0 |
| Tampa Bay Buccaneers | 5 | 4 | 0 |
| Detroit Lions | 4 | 5 | 0 |
| Chicago Bears | 3 | 6 | 0 |

### Western Division

| Team | Win | Lost | Tie |
|------|-----|------|-----|
| Atlanta Falcons | 5 | 4 | 0 |
| New Orleans Saints | 4 | 5 | 0 |
| San Francisco 49ers | 3 | 6 | 0 |
| Los Angeles Rams | 2 | 7 | 0 |

---

A players strike at the beginning of the 1982 season shortened the regular season to nine games. Also, the 1982 season was the first season the league began keeping track of quarterback "sacks" by defensive players as an official statistic.

## 1982 – American Football Conference

## Eastern Division

| Team | Win | Lost | Tie |
|------|-----|------|-----|
| Miami Dolphins | 7 | 2 | 0 |
| New York Jets | 6 | 3 | 0 |
| New England Patriots | 5 | 4 | 0 |
| Buffalo Bills | 4 | 5 | 0 |
| Baltimore Colts | 0 | 8 | 1 |

## Central Division

| Team | Win | Lost | Tie |
|------|-----|------|-----|
| Cincinnati Bengals | 7 | 2 | 0 |
| Pittsburgh Steelers | 6 | 3 | 0 |
| Cleveland Browns | 4 | 5 | 0 |
| Houston Oilers | 1 | 8 | 0 |

## Western Division

| Team | Win | Lost | Tie |
|------|-----|------|-----|
| Los Angeles Raiders | 8 | 1 | 0 |
| San Diego Chargers | 6 | 3 | 0 |
| Seattle Seahawks | 4 | 5 | 0 |
| Kansas City Chiefs | 3 | 6 | 0 |
| Denver Broncos | 2 | 7 | 0 |

---

The Raiders won their anti-trust lawsuit against the NFL and were allowed to move the franchise from Oakland to Los Angeles. The Raiders became the first NFL team to relocate to a new city since the Chicago Cardinals moved to St. Louis in 1960 (the AFL's Los Angeles Chargers moved to San Diego in 1961). The legal decision put into question whether a NFL franchise needed the consent of the league to move to a different city.

## 1982-1983 Playoffs

### NFC – Top Eight Teams[9]

|                        | W | L | T |
|------------------------|---|---|---|
| Washington Redskins    | 8 | 1 | 0 |
| Dallas Cowboys         | 6 | 3 | 0 |
| Green Bay Packers      | 5 | 3 | 1 |
| Minnesota Vikings      | 5 | 4 | 0 |
| Atlanta Falcons        | 5 | 4 | 0 |
| St. Louis Cardinals    | 5 | 4 | 0 |
| Tampa Bay Buccaneers   | 5 | 4 | 0 |
| Detroit Lions          | 4 | 5 | 0 |

### NFC - First Round

| In Green Bay:  | Green Bay Packers 41, St. Louis Cardinals 16 |
| In Dallas:     | Dallas Cowboys 30, Tampa Bay Buccaneers 17 |
| In Minneapolis:| Minnesota Vikings 30, Atlanta Falcons 24 |
| In Washington: | Washington Redskins 31, Detroit Lions 7 |

### NFC – Second Round

| In Dallas:     | Dallas Cowboys 37, Green Bay Packers 26 |
| In Washington: | Washington Redskins 21, Minnesota Vikings 7 |

### NFC Championship

| In Washington: | Washington Redskins 31, Dallas Cowboys 17 |

---

9       The Minnesota Vikings, Atlanta Falcons, St. Louis Cardinals, and Tampa Bay Buccaneers playoff seeds were determined by best won-lost record in conference games. The Detroit Lions finished ahead of the New Orleans Saints and the New York Giants based on a better conference record (4–4, vs. 3–5 vs. 3–5, respectively). The San Francisco 49ers finished ahead of the Chicago Bears, and the Bears finished ahead of the Philadelphia Eagles based on conference record, 2–3 vs. 2–5 vs. 1–5, respectively. The Dallas Cowboys lost their third straight NFC championship game. They played in 10 of the first 13 NFC championship games.

Due to the strike-shortened season, the NFL adopted a special 16-team playoff tournament. For the most part, division standings were ignored. The eight best teams from each conference were seeded 1 to 8 based on their regular season records. For the first time, teams qualified for the playoffs with losing records.

## AFC – Top Eight Teams[10]

|  | W | L | T |
|---|---|---|---|
| Los Angeles Raiders | 8 | 1 | 0 |
| Miami Dolphins | 7 | 2 | 0 |
| Cincinnati Bengals | 7 | 2 | 0 |
| Pittsburgh Steelers | 6 | 3 | 0 |
| San Diego Chargers | 6 | 3 | 0 |
| New York Jets | 6 | 3 | 0 |
| New England Patriots | 5 | 4 | 0 |
| Cleveland Browns | 4 | 5 | 0 |

## AFC – First Round

| In Cincinnati: | New York Jets 44, Cincinnati Bengals 17 |
| In Los Angeles: | Los Angeles Raiders 27, Cleveland Browns 10 |
| In Pittsburgh: | San Diego Chargers 31, Pittsburgh 28 |
| In Miami: | Miami Dolphins 28, New England Patriots 13 |

## AFC – Second Round

| In Los Angeles: | New York Jets 17, Los Angeles Raiders 14 |
| In Miami: | Miami Dolphins 34, San Diego 14 |

## AFC Championship

| In Miami: | Miami Dolphins 14, New York Jets 0 |

---

10     The Miami Dolphins finished ahead of the Cincinnati Bengals based on a better conference record, 6–1 vs. 6–2. The Pittsburgh Steelers finished ahead of the San Diego Chargers based on a better record against common opponents, 3–1 vs. 2–1, after the New York Jets were bumped to the sixth seed from the three-way tie based on conference record, 5–3 to 2–3. The Cleveland Browns finished ahead of the Buffalo Bills and the Seattle Seahawks based on better conference record, 4–3 vs. 3–3 vs. 3–5, respectively.

# 1983 – Super Bowl XVII (17)

# Miami

**Washington Redskins** (NFC) defeat the Miami Dolphins (AFC), 27-17.

## Season Awards

*Most Valuable Player*            Mark Moseley, Placekicker,
                                  Washington Redskins

*Coach of the Year*               Joe Gibbs, Washington Redskins

*Offensive Player of the Year*    Dan Fouts, Quarterback, San Diego Chargers

*Defensive Player of the Year*    Lawrence Taylor, Linebacker, New York Giants

*Offensive Rookie of the Year*    Marcus Allen, Running Back,
                                  Los Angeles Raiders

*Defensive Rookie of the Year*    Chip Banks, Linebacker, Cleveland Browns

---

Mark Mosely remains the only kicker to win the league MVP award. It was during a strike-shortened season and Mosely made a NFL record 23 straight field goals including several game winners.

## 1983 – National Football Conference

## Eastern Division

| Team | Win | Lost | Tie |
|------|-----|------|-----|
| Washington Redskins | 14 | 2 | 0 |
| Dallas Cowboys | 12 | 4 | 0 |
| St. Louis Cardinals | 8 | 7 | 1 |
| Philadelphia Eagles | 5 | 11 | 0 |
| New York Giants | 3 | 12 | 1 |

## Central Division

| Team | Win | Lost | Tie |
|------|-----|------|-----|
| Detroit Lions | 9 | 7 | 0 |
| Green Bay Packers | 8 | 8 | 0 |
| Chicago Bears | 8 | 8 | 0 |
| Minnesota Vikings | 8 | 8 | 0 |
| Tampa Bay Buccaneers | 2 | 14 | 0 |

## Western Division

| Team | Win | Lost | Tie |
|------|-----|------|-----|
| San Francisco 49ers | 10 | 6 | 0 |
| Los Angeles Rams | 9 | 7 | 0 |
| New Orleans Saints | 8 | 8 | 0 |
| Atlanta Falcons | 7 | 9 | 0 |

# 1983 – American Football Conference

## Eastern Division

| Team | Win | Lost | Tie |
|------|-----|------|-----|
| Miami Dolphins | 12 | 4 | 0 |
| New England Patriots | 8 | 8 | 0 |
| Buffalo Bills | 8 | 8 | 0 |
| Baltimore Colts | 7 | 9 | 0 |
| New York Jets | 7 | 9 | 0 |

## Central Division

| Team | Win | Lost | Tie |
|------|-----|------|-----|
| Pittsburgh Steelers | 10 | 6 | 0 |
| Cleveland Brown | 9 | 7 | 0 |
| Cincinnati Bengals | 7 | 9 | 0 |
| Houston Oilers | 2 | 14 | 0 |

## Western Division

| Team | Win | Lost | Tie |
|------|-----|------|-----|
| Los Angeles Raiders | 12 | 4 | 0 |
| Seattle Seahawks | 9 | 7 | 0 |
| Denver Broncos | 9 | 7 | 0 |
| Kansas City Chiefs | 6 | 10 | 0 |
| San Diego Chargers | 6 | 10 | 0 |

# 1983-1984 Playoffs

## NFC Playoffs

*Wild Card playoff* (in Dallas) – Los Angeles Rams 24, Dallas Cowboys 17

*Divisional playoff* (in Washington) – Washington Redskins 51, Los Angeles Rams 7

*Divisional playoff* (in San Francisco) – San Francisco 49ers 24, Detroit Lions 23

NFC Championship (in Washington) – Washington Redskins 24, San Francisco 49ers 21

## AFC Playoffs

*Wild Card playoff* (in Seattle) – Seattle Seahawks 31[11], Denver Broncos 7

*Divisional playoff* (in Miami) – Seattle Seahawks 27, Miami Dolphins 20

*Divisional playoff* (in Los Angeles) – Los Angeles Raiders 38[12], Pittsburgh Steelers 10

AFC Championship (in Los Angeles) – Los Angeles Raiders 30, Seattle Seahawks 14

---

11    The Seattle Seahawks were the AFC Wild Card first seed over the Denver Broncos based on a better division record, 5-3 vs. 3-5, after the Cleveland Browns were eliminated from the three-way tie based on the head-to-head records, 2-1 vs. 2-1 vs. 0-2.

12    The Los Angeles Raiders were the AFC top seed based on their head-to-head victory over the Miami Dolphins.

# 1984 – Super Bowl XVIII (18)

## Tampa

**Los Angeles Raiders** (AFC) defeat the Washington Redskins (NFC), 38-9.

## Season Awards

| | |
|---|---|
| *Most Valuable Player* | Joe Theismann, Quarterback, Washington Redskins |
| *Coach of the Year* | Joe Gibbs, Washington Redskins |
| *Offensive Player of the Year* | Joe Theismann, Quarterback, Washington Redskins |
| *Defensive Player of the Year* | Doug Betters, Defensive End, Miami Dolphins |
| *Offensive Rookie of the Year* | Eric Dickerson, Running Back, Los Angeles Rams |
| *Defensive Rookie of the Year* | Vernon Maxwell, Linebacker, Baltimore Colts |

------------

The NFL Films highlight package for Super Bowl XVIII, entitled "Black Sunday" for the victorious Raiders, was the last performance by fabled narrator John Facenda. Facenda, known as "The Voice," died eight months later.

# 1984 – National Football Conference

## Eastern Division

| Team | Win | Lost | Tie |
|------|-----|------|-----|
| Washington Redskins | 11 | 5 | 0 |
| New York Giants | 9 | 7 | 0 |
| Dallas Cowboys | 9 | 7 | 0 |
| St. Louis Cardinals | 9 | 7 | 0 |
| Philadelphia Eagles | 6 | 9 | 1 |

## Central Division

| Team | Win | Lost | Tie |
|------|-----|------|-----|
| Chicago Bears | 10 | 6 | 0 |
| Green Bay Packers | 8 | 8 | 0 |
| Tampa Bay Buccaneers | 6 | 10 | 0 |
| Detroit Lions | 4 | 11 | 1 |
| Minnesota Vikings | 3 | 13 | 0 |

## Western Division

| Team | Win | Lost | Tie |
|------|-----|------|-----|
| San Francisco 49ers | 15 | 1 | 0 |
| Los Angeles Rams | 10 | 6 | 0 |
| New Orleans Saints | 7 | 9 | 0 |
| Atlanta Falcons | 4 | 12 | 0 |

---

The San Francisco 49ers became the first NFL team to win 15 games during the regular season. In 1984, the NFL changed its rules to prohibit any prolonged, excessive, or pre-meditated celebration by individual players or a group of players leading some to comment that "NFL" stood for "No Fun League."

# 1984 – American Football Conference

## Eastern Division

| Team | Win | Lost | Tie |
|------|-----|------|-----|
| Miami Dolphins | 14 | 2 | 0 |
| New England Patriots | 9 | 7 | 0 |
| New York Jets | 7 | 9 | 0 |
| Indianapolis Colts | 4 | 12 | 0 |
| Buffalo Bills | 2 | 14 | 0 |

## Central Division

| Team | Win | Lost | Tie |
|------|-----|------|-----|
| Pittsburgh Steelers | 9 | 7 | 0 |
| Cincinnati Bengals | 8 | 8 | 0 |
| Cleveland Browns | 5 | 11 | 0 |
| Houston Oilers | 3 | 13 | 0 |

## Western Division

| Team | Win | Lost | Tie |
|------|-----|------|-----|
| Denver Broncos | 13 | 3 | 0 |
| Seattle Seahawks | 12 | 4 | 0 |
| Los Angeles Raiders | 11 | 5 | 0 |
| Kansas City Chiefs | 8 | 8 | 0 |
| San Diego Chargers | 7 | 9 | 0 |

The Colts relocated from Baltimore to Indianapolis. The move was made in the middle of the night without notice or NFL pre-approval, a direct result of the Los Angeles Raiders antitrust lawsuit. The move devastated the Colts fans in Baltimore, among the most dedicated and loyal fans in all the NFL.

## 1984-1985 Playoffs

## NFC Playoffs

*Wild Card playoff* (in Los Angeles) – New York Giants 16[13], Los Angeles Rams 13

*Divisional playoff* (in Washington) – Chicago Bears 23, Washington Redskins 19

*Divisional playoff* (in San Francisco) – San Francisco 49ers 21, New York Giants 10

NFC Championship (in San Francisco) – San Francisco 49ers 23, Chicago Bears 0

## AFC Playoffs

*Wild Card playoff* (in Seattle) – Seattle Seahawks 13, Los Angeles Raiders 7

*Divisional playoff* (in Miami) – Miami Dolphins 31, Seattle Seahawks 10

*Divisional playoff* (in Denver) – Pittsburgh Steelers 24, Denver Broncos 17

AFC Championship (in Miami) – Miami Dolphins 45, Pittsburgh Steelers 28

---

13     The New York Giants beat out the St. Louis Cardinals and the Dallas Cowboys for the NFC East title based on best head-to-head record, 3-1 vs. 2-2 vs. 1-3. The Cardinals finished ahead of the Cowboys for the Wild Card based on a better division record (5-3 vs. 3-5).

# 1985 – Super Bowl XIX (19)
## Palo Alto, CA

**San Francisco 49ers** (NFC) defeat the Miami Dolphins (AFC), 38-16.

## Season Awards

| | |
|---|---|
| *Most Valuable Player* | Dan Marino, Quarterback, Miami Dolphins |
| *Coach of the Year* | Chuck Knox, Seattle Seahawks |
| *Offensive Player of the Year* | Dan Marino, Quarterback, Miami Dolphins |
| *Defensive Player of the Year* | Kenny Easley, Safety, Seattle Seahawks |
| *Offensive Rookie of the Year* | Louis Lipps, Wide Receiver, Pittsburgh Steelers |
| *Defensive Rookie of the Year* | Bill Maas, Defensive Tackle, Kansas City Chiefs |

# 1985 – National Football Conference

## Eastern Division

| Team | Win | Lost | Tie |
|------|-----|------|-----|
| Dallas Cowboys | 10 | 6 | 0 |
| New York Giants | 10 | 6 | 0 |
| Washington Redskins | 10 | 6 | 0 |
| Philadelphia Eagles | 7 | 9 | 0 |
| St. Louis Cardinals | 5 | 11 | 0 |

## Central Division

| Team | Win | Lost | Tie |
|------|-----|------|-----|
| Chicago Bears | 15 | 1 | 0 |
| Green Bay Packers | 8 | 8 | 0 |
| Minnesota Vikings | 7 | 9 | 0 |
| Detroit Lions | 7 | 9 | 0 |
| Tampa Bay Buccaneers | 2 | 14 | 0 |

## Western Division

| Team | Win | Lost | Tie |
|------|-----|------|-----|
| Los Angeles Rams | 11 | 5 | 0 |
| San Francisco 49ers | 10 | 6 | 0 |
| New Orleans Saints | 5 | 11 | 0 |
| Atlanta Falcons | 4 | 12 | 0 |

---

In 1985 the Chicago Bears were on the cusp of an undefeated season, including a dominating Super Bowl win. They would have been the second team to accomplish that feat. The team that prevented them from doing so? The only team to go undefeated in the regular season and win the Super Bowl, the Miami Dolphins, who beat the Bears 38-24 in Miami on *Monday Night Football*. The Bears were 12-0 heading into the game, in what proved to be their only loss in 1985.

# 1985 – American Football Conference

## Eastern Division

| Team | Win | Lost | Tie |
| --- | --- | --- | --- |
| Miami Dolphins | 12 | 4 | 0 |
| New York Jets | 11 | 5 | 0 |
| New England Patriots | 11 | 5 | 0 |
| Indianapolis Colts | 5 | 11 | 0 |
| Buffalo Bills | 2 | 14 | 0 |

## Central Division

| Team | Win | Lost | Tie |
| --- | --- | --- | --- |
| Cleveland Browns | 8 | 8 | 0 |
| Cincinnati Bengals | 7 | 9 | 0 |
| Pittsburgh Steelers | 7 | 9 | 0 |
| Houston Oilers | 5 | 11 | 0 |

## Western Division

| Team | Win | Lost | Tie |
| --- | --- | --- | --- |
| Los Angeles Raiders | 12 | 4 | 0 |
| Denver Broncos | 11 | 5 | 0 |
| Seattle Seahawks | 8 | 8 | 0 |
| San Diego Chargers | 8 | 8 | 0 |
| Kansas City Chiefs | 6 | 10 | 0 |

## 1985-1986 Playoffs

## NFC Playoffs

*Wild Card playoff* (in San Francisco) – New York Giants 17, San Francisco 49ers 3

*Divisional playoff* (in Los Angeles) – Los Angeles Rams 20, Dallas Cowboys 0[14]

*Divisional playoff* (in Chicago) – Chicago Bears 21, New York Giants 0

NFC Championship (in Chicago) – Chicago Bears 24, Los Angeles Rams 0

## AFC Playoffs

*Wild Card playoff* (in New York) – New England Patriots 26, New York Jets 14[15]

*Divisional playoff* (in Miami) – Miami Dolphins 24, Cleveland Browns 21

*Divisional playoff* (in Los Angeles) – New England Patriots 27, Los Angeles Raiders 20[16]

AFC Championship (in Miami) – New England Patriots 31, Miami Dolphins 14

---

14      The Dallas Cowboys beat out the New York Giants and Washington Redskins for the NFC East title based on a better head-to-head record, 4-0 vs. 1-3 vs. 1-3. The New York Giants were the NFC first Wild Card over the San Francisco 49ers and the Washington Redskins based on a better conference record, 8-4 vs. 7-5 vs. 6-6. The 49ers were the NFC second Wild Card over the Redskins based on its head-to-head victory over the Redskins.

15      The New York Jets were the AFC first Wild Card over the New England Patriots and Denver Broncos based on a better conference record, 9-3 vs. 8-4 vs. 8-4. The Patriots were the AFC second Wild Card based over the Broncos based on a better record against common opponents, 4-2 vs. 3-3.

16      The Los Angeles Raiders were the AFC first seed over the Miami Dolphins based on a better record against common opponents, 5-1 vs. 4-2.

# 1986 – Super Bowl XX (20)

## New Orleans

**Chicago Bears** (NFC) defeat the New England Patriots (AFC), 46-10.

## Season Awards

| | |
|---|---|
| *Most Valuable Player* | Marcus Allen, Running Back, Los Angeles Raiders |
| *Coach of the Year* | Mike Ditka, Chicago Bears |
| *Offensive Player of the Year* | Marcus Allen, Running Back, Los Angeles Raiders |
| *Defensive Player of the Year* | Mike Singletary, Linebacker, Chicago Bears |
| *Offensive Rookie of the Year* | Eddie Brown, Wide Receiver, Cincinnati Bengals |
| *Defensive Rookie of the Year* | Duane Bickett, Linebacker, Indianapolis Colts |

---

This was the last Super Bowl to feature "Up with People" as the halftime entertainment.

## 1986  – National Football Conference

## Eastern Division

| Team | Win | Lost | Tie |
|------|-----|------|-----|
| New York Giants | 14 | 2 | 0 |
| Washington Redskins | 12 | 4 | 0 |
| Dallas Cowboys | 7 | 9 | 0 |
| Philadelphia Eagles | 5 | 10 | 1 |
| St. Louis Cardinals | 4 | 11 | 1 |

## Central Division

| Team | Win | Lost | Tie |
|------|-----|------|-----|
| Chicago Bears | 14 | 2 | 0 |
| Minnesota Vikings | 9 | 7 | 0 |
| Detroit Lions | 5 | 11 | 0 |
| Green Bay Packers | 4 | 12 | 0 |
| Tampa Bay Buccaneers | 2 | 14 | 0 |

## Western Division

| Team | Win | Lost | Tie |
|------|-----|------|-----|
| San Francisco 49ers | 10 | 5 | 1 |
| Los Angeles Rams | 10 | 6 | 0 |
| Atlanta Falcons | 7 | 8 | 1 |
| New Orleans Saints | 7 | 9 | 0 |

---

A limited instant replay system was implemented for the 1986 season. An official in the booth decided which plays to review. There was no time limit on how long the replay review could take. The system was repealed in 1992 but reinstituted in 1999 under different rules.

# 1986 – American Football Conference

## Eastern Division

| Team | Win | Lost | Tie |
|------|-----|------|-----|
| New England Patriots | 11 | 5 | 0 |
| New York Jets | 10 | 6 | 0 |
| Miami Dolphins | 8 | 8 | 0 |
| Buffalo Bills | 4 | 12 | 0 |
| Indianapolis Colts | 3 | 13 | 0 |

## Central Division

| Team | Win | Lost | Tie |
|------|-----|------|-----|
| Cleveland Browns | 12 | 4 | 0 |
| Cincinnati Bengals | 10 | 6 | 0 |
| Pittsburgh Steelers | 6 | 10 | 0 |
| Houston Oilers | 5 | 11 | 0 |

## Western Division

| Team | Win | Lost | Tie |
|------|-----|------|-----|
| Denver Broncos | 11 | 5 | 0 |
| Kansas City Chiefs | 10 | 6 | 0 |
| Seattle Seahawks | 10 | 6 | 0 |
| Los Angeles Raiders | 8 | 8 | 0 |
| San Diego Chargers | 4 | 12 | 0 |

## 1986-1987 Playoffs

## NFC Playoffs

*Wild Card playoff* (in Washington) – Washington Redskins 19, Los Angeles Rams 7

*Divisional playoff* (in Chicago) – Washington Redskins 27, Chicago Bears 13

*Divisional playoff* (in New York) – New York Giants 49[17], San Francisco 49ers 3

NFC Championship (in New York) – New York Giants 17, Washington Redskins 0

## AFC Playoffs

*Wild Card playoff* (in New York) – New York Jets 35[18], Kansas City Chiefs 15

*Divisional playoff* (in Cleveland) – Cleveland Browns 23, New York Jets 20 (2OT)

*Divisional playoff* (in Denver) – Denver Broncos 22[19], New England Patriots 17

AFC Championship (in Denver) – Denver Broncos 23, Cleveland Browns 20 (OT)

---

17    The New York Giants captured the NFC first seed based on a better conference record than the Chicago Bears, 11-1 vs. 10-2.

18    The New York Jets were the AFC Wild Card first seed over the Kansas City Chiefs, the Seattle Seahawks, and the Cincinnati Bengals based on a better conference record, 9-5 vs. 8-4 vs. 7-5 vs. 7-5. The Kansas City Chiefs were the AFC Wild Card second seed based on a better conference record than the Seahawks or the Bengals, 8-4 vs. 7-5 vs. 7-5.

19    The Denver Broncos were the AFC second seed based on their head-to-head victory over the New England Patriots.

# 1987 – Super Bowl XXI (21)

## Los Angeles

**New York Giants** (NFC) defeat the Denver Broncos (AFC), 39-20.

## Season Awards

| | |
|---|---|
| *Most Valuable Player* | Lawrence Taylor, Linebacker, New York Giants |
| *Coach of the Year* | Bill Parcells, New York Giants |
| *Offensive Player of the Year* | Eric Dickerson, Running Back, Los Angeles Rams |
| *Defensive Player of the Year* | Lawrence Taylor, Linebacker, New York Giants |
| *Offensive Rookie of the Year* | Reuben Mayes, Running Back, New Orleans Saints |
| *Defensive Rookie of the Year* | Leslie O'Neal, Defensive End, San Diego Chargers |

## 1987 – National Football Conference

### Eastern Division

| Team | Win | Lost | Tie |
|------|-----|------|-----|
| Washington Redskins | 11 | 4 | 0 |
| St. Louis Cardinals | 7 | 8 | 0 |
| Philadelphia Eagles | 7 | 8 | 0 |
| Dallas Cowboys | 7 | 8 | 0 |
| New York Giants | 6 | 9 | 0 |

### Central Division

| Team | Win | Lost | Tie |
|------|-----|------|-----|
| Chicago Bears | 11 | 4 | 0 |
| Minnesota Vikings | 8 | 7 | 0 |
| Green Bay Packers | 5 | 9 | 1 |
| Tampa Bay Buccaneers | 4 | 11 | 0 |
| Detroit Lions | 4 | 11 | 0 |

### Western Division

| Team | Win | Lost | Tie |
|------|-----|------|-----|
| San Francisco 49ers | 13 | 2 | 0 |
| New Orleans Saints | 12 | 3 | 0 |
| Los Angeles Rams | 6 | 9 | 0 |
| Atlanta Falcons | 3 | 12 | 0 |

---

There was a 24-day players' strike after week two of the 1987 season. The games scheduled for week three were canceled (and thus only a 15 game season was played that year). Replacement players were used for weeks four through six, though a notable percentage of regular NFL players crossed the picket line during the strike. Also, in 1987, the NFL began playing games on Sunday night. The games were broadcast by ESPN, a turning point in that network's history and the beginning of the phenomenal growth of ESPN.

# 1987 – American Football Conference

## Eastern Division

| Team | Win | Lost | Tie |
|------|-----|------|-----|
| Indianapolis Colts | 9 | 6 | 0 |
| New England Patriots | 8 | 7 | 0 |
| Miami Dolphins | 8 | 7 | 0 |
| Buffalo Bills | 7 | 8 | 0 |
| New York Jets | 6 | 9 | 0 |

## Central Division

| Team | Win | Lost | Tie |
|------|-----|------|-----|
| Cleveland Browns | 10 | 5 | 0 |
| Houston Oilers | 9 | 6 | 0 |
| Pittsburgh Steelers | 8 | 7 | 0 |
| Cincinnati Bengals | 4 | 11 | 0 |

## Western Division

| Team | Win | Lost | Tie |
|------|-----|------|-----|
| Denver Broncos | 10 | 4 | 1 |
| Seattle Seahawks | 9 | 6 | 0 |
| San Diego Chargers | 8 | 7 | 0 |
| Los Angeles Raiders | 5 | 10 | 0 |
| Kansas City Chiefs | 4 | 11 | 0 |

## 1987-1988 Playoffs

## NFC Playoffs

*Wild Card playoff* (in New Orleans) – Minnesota Vikings 44, New Orleans Saints 10

*Divisional playoff* (in San Francisco) – Minnesota Vikings 36, San Francisco 49ers 24

*Divisional playoff* (in Chicago) – Washington Redskins 21, Chicago Bears 17[20]

NFC Championship (in Washington) – Washington Redskins 17, Minnesota Vikings 10

## AFC Playoffs

*Wild Card playoff* (in Houston) – Houston Oilers 23[21], Seattle Seahawks 10 (OT)

*Divisional playoff* (in Cleveland) – Cleveland Browns 38, Indianapolis Colts 21

*Divisional playoff* (in Denver) – Denver Broncos 34, Houston Oilers 10

AFC Championship (in Denver) – Denver Broncos 38, Cleveland Browns 33

---

20      The Chicago Bears were the NFC second seed over the Washington Redskins based on a better conference record, 9-2 vs. 9-3.

21      The Houston Oilers won the AFC fourth seed over the Seattle Seahawks based on a better conference record, 7-4 vs. 5-6.

# 1988 – Super Bowl XXII (22)

# San Diego

**Washington Redskins** (NFC) defeat the Denver Broncos (AFC), 42-10.

## Season Awards

| | |
|---|---|
| *Most Valuable Player* | John Elway, Quarterback, Denver Broncos |
| *Coach of the Year* | Jim Mora, New Orleans Saints |
| *Offensive Player of the Year* | Jerry Rice, Wide Receiver, San Francisco 49ers |
| *Defensive Player of the Year* | Reggie White, Defensive End, Philadelphia Eagles |
| *Offensive Rookie of the Year* | Troy Stradford, Running Back, Miami Dolphins |
| *Defensive Rookie of the Year* | Shane Conlan, Linebackers, Buffalo Bills |

# 1988 – National Football Conference

## Eastern Division

| Team | Win | Lost | Tie |
|---|---|---|---|
| Philadelphia Eagles | 10 | 6 | 0 |
| New York Giants | 10 | 6 | 0 |
| Washington Redskins | 7 | 9 | 0 |
| Phoenix Cardinals | 7 | 9 | 0 |
| Dallas Cowboys | 3 | 13 | 0 |

## Central Division

| Team | Win | Lost | Tie |
|---|---|---|---|
| Chicago Bears | 12 | 4 | 0 |
| Minnesota Vikings | 11 | 5 | 0 |
| Tampa Bay Buccaneers | 5 | 11 | 0 |
| Detroit Lions | 4 | 12 | 0 |
| Green Bay Packers | 4 | 12 | 0 |

## Western Division

| Team | Win | Lost | Tie |
|---|---|---|---|
| San Francisco 49ers | 10 | 6 | 0 |
| Los Angeles Rams | 10 | 6 | 0 |
| New Orleans Saints | 10 | 6 | 0 |
| Atlanta Falcons | 5 | 11 | 0 |

---

Before the start of the 1988 season the St. Louis Cardinals relocated to Phoenix, Arizona and became the Phoenix Cardinals. Five NFC teams finished with 10-6 records, giving the NFL tie-breaker rules a real workout.

# 1988 – American Football Conference

## Eastern Division

| Team | Win | Lost | Tie |
|------|-----|------|-----|
| Buffalo Bills | 12 | 4 | 0 |
| Indianapolis Colts | 9 | 7 | 0 |
| New England Patriots | 9 | 7 | 0 |
| New York Jets | 8 | 7 | 1 |
| Miami Dolphins | 6 | 10 | 0 |

## Central Division

| Team | Win | Lost | Tie |
|------|-----|------|-----|
| Cincinnati Bengals | 12 | 4 | 0 |
| Cleveland Browns | 10 | 6 | 0 |
| Houston Oilers | 10 | 6 | 0 |
| Pittsburgh Steelers | 5 | 11 | 0 |

## Western Division

| Team | Win | Lost | Tie |
|------|-----|------|-----|
| Seattle Seahawks | 9 | 7 | 0 |
| Denver Broncos | 8 | 8 | 0 |
| Los Angeles Raiders | 7 | 9 | 0 |
| San Diego Chargers | 6 | 10 | 0 |
| Kansas City Chiefs | 4 | 11 | 1 |

## 1988-1989 Playoffs

## NFC Playoffs

*Wild Card playoff* (in Minneapolis) – Minnesota Vikings 28, Los Angeles Rams 17[22]

*Divisional playoff* (in San Francisco) – San Francisco 49ers 34[23], Minnesota Vikings 9

*Divisional playoff* (in Chicago) – Chicago Bears 20, Philadelphia Eagles 12[24]

NFC Championship (in Chicago) – San Francisco 49ers 28, Chicago Bears 3

## AFC Playoffs

*Wild Card playoff* (in Cleveland) – Houston Oilers 24, Cleveland Browns 23[25]

*Divisional playoff* (in Buffalo) – Buffalo Bills 17, Houston Oilers 10

*Divisional playoff* (in Cincinnati) – Cincinnati Bengals 21[26], Seattle Seahawks 13

AFC Championship (in Cincinnati) – Cincinnati Bengals 21, Buffalo Bills 10

---

22      The Los Angeles Rams finished second in the NFC West over the New Orleans Saints based on a better division record, 4-2 vs. 3-3 and earned the second NFC Wild Card over the New York Giants and the New Orleans Saints based on a better conference record, 8-4 vs. 9-5 vs. 6-6.

23      The San Francisco 49ers were the NFC second seed over the Philadelphia Eagles based on a better record against common opponents, 6-3 vs. 5-4. The 49ers finished first in the NFC West over the Los Angeles Rams and the New Orleans Saints based on a better head-to-head record against those teams, 3-1 vs. 2-2 vs. 1-3.

24      The Philadelphia Eagles won the NFC East Division over the New York Giants based on a head-to-head sweep.

25      The Cleveland Browns Finished ahead of the Houston Oilers in the AFC Central Division based on a better division record, 4-2 vs. 3-3.

26      The Cincinnati Bengals beat out the Buffalo Bills for the AFC top seed based on a head-to-head victory.

# 1989 – Super Bowl XXIII (23)

## Miami

**San Francisco 49ers** (NFC) defeat the Cincinnati Bengals (AFC), 20-16.

## Season Awards

*Most Valuable Player*            Boomer Esiason, Quarterback,
                                  Cincinnati Bengals

*Coach of the Year*               Mike Ditka, Chicago Bears

*Offensive Player of the Year*    Roger Craig, Running Back,
                                  San Francisco 49ers

*Defensive Player of the Year*    Mike Singletary, Linebacker, Chicago Bears

*Offensive Rookie of the Year*    John Stephens, Running Back,
                                  New England Patriots

*Defensive Rookie of the Year*    Erik McMillan Safety, New York Jets

# 1989 – National Football Conference

## Eastern Division

| Team | Win | Lost | Tie |
|------|-----|------|-----|
| New York Giants | 12 | 4 | 0 |
| Philadelphia Eagles | 11 | 5 | 0 |
| Washington Redskins | 10 | 6 | 0 |
| Phoenix Cardinals | 5 | 11 | 0 |
| Dallas Cowboys | 1 | 15 | 0 |

## Central Division

| Team | Win | Lost | Tie |
|------|-----|------|-----|
| Minnesota Vikings | 10 | 6 | 0 |
| Green Bay Packers | 10 | 6 | 0 |
| Detroit Lions | 7 | 9 | 0 |
| Chicago Bears | 6 | 10 | 0 |
| Tampa Bay Buccaneers | 5 | 11 | 0 |

## Western Division

| Team | Win | Lost | Tie |
|------|-----|------|-----|
| San Francisco 49ers | 14 | 2 | 0 |
| Los Angeles Rams | 11 | 5 | 0 |
| New Orleans Saints | 9 | 7 | 0 |
| Atlanta Falcons | 3 | 13 | 0 |

# 1989 – American Football Conference

## Eastern Division

| Team | Win | Lost | Tie |
|------|-----|------|-----|
| Buffalo Bills | 9 | 7 | 0 |
| Miami Dolphins | 8 | 8 | 0 |
| Indianapolis Colts | 8 | 8 | 0 |
| New England Patriots | 5 | 11 | 0 |
| New York Jets | 4 | 12 | 0 |

## Central Division

| Team | Win | Lost | Tie |
|------|-----|------|-----|
| Cleveland Browns | 9 | 6 | 1 |
| Houston Oilers | 9 | 7 | 0 |
| Pittsburgh Steelers | 9 | 7 | 0 |
| Cincinnati Bengals | 8 | 8 | 0 |

## Western Division

| Team | Win | Lost | Tie |
|------|-----|------|-----|
| Denver Broncos | 11 | 5 | 0 |
| Kansas City Chiefs | 8 | 7 | 1 |
| Los Angeles Raiders | 8 | 8 | 0 |
| Seattle Seahawks | 7 | 9 | 0 |
| San Diego Chargers | 6 | 10 | 0 |

## 1989-1990 Playoffs

## NFC Playoffs

*Wild Card playoff* (in Philadelphia) – Los Angeles Rams 21, Philadelphia Eagles 7[27]

*Divisional playoff* (in San Francisco) – San Francisco 49ers 41, Minnesota Vikings 13[28]

*Divisional playoff* (in New York) – Los Angeles Rams 19, New York Giants 13 (OT)

NFC Championship (in San Francisco) – San Francisco 49ers 30, Los Angeles Rams 3

## AFC Playoffs

*Wild Card playoff* (in Houston) – Pittsburgh Steelers 26, Houston Oilers 23[29] (OT)

*Divisional playoff* (in Denver) – Denver Broncos 24, Pittsburgh Steelers 23

*Divisional playoff* (in Cleveland) – Cleveland Browns 34, Buffalo Bills 30

AFC Championship (in Denver) – Denver Broncos 37, Cleveland Browns 21

---

27    The Philadelphia Eagles were the NFC Wild Card first seed over the Los Angeles Rams based on a better record against common opponents, 6-3 vs. 5-4.

28    The Minnesota Vikings beat out the Green Bay Packers for the NFC Central Division title based on a better record in the division, 6-2 vs. 5-3.

29    The Houston Oilers finished ahead of the Pittsburgh Steelers in the AFC Central Division based on head-to-head sweep of games played between the two teams.

# 1990 – Super Bowl XXIV (24)

## New Orleans

**San Francisco 49ers** (NFC) defeat the Denver Broncos (AFC), 55-10.

## Season Awards

| | |
|---|---|
| *Most Valuable Player* | Joe Montana, Quarterback, San Francisco 49ers |
| *Coach of the Year* | Lindy Infante, Green Bay Packers |
| *Offensive Player of the Year* | Joe Montana, Quarterback, San Francisco 49ers |
| *Defensive Player of the Year* | Keith Millard, Defensive Tackle, Minnesota Vikings |
| *Offensive Rookie of the Year* | Barry Sanders, Running Back, Detroit |
| *Defensive Rookie of the Year* | Derrick Thomas, Linebacker, Kansas City Chiefs |

# 1990-1999

## 1990 – National Football Conference

### Eastern Division

| Team | Win | Lost | Tie |
|------|-----|------|-----|
| New York Giants | 13 | 3 | 0 |
| Philadelphia Eagles | 10 | 6 | 0 |
| Washington Redskins | 10 | 6 | 0 |
| Dallas Cowboys | 7 | 9 | 0 |
| Phoenix Cardinals | 5 | 11 | 0 |

### Central Division

| Team | Win | Lost | Tie |
|------|-----|------|-----|
| Chicago Bears | 11 | 5 | 0 |
| Tampa Bay Buccaneers | 6 | 10 | 0 |
| Detroit Lions | 6 | 10 | 0 |
| Green Bay Packers | 6 | 10 | 0 |
| Minnesota Vikings | 6 | 10 | 0 |

### Western Division

| Team | Win | Lost | Tie |
|------|-----|------|-----|
| San Francisco 49ers | 14 | 2 | 0 |
| New Orleans Saints | 8 | 8 | 0 |
| Los Angeles Rams | 5 | 11 | 0 |
| Atlanta Falcons | 5 | 11 | 0 |

---

**At the beginning of the 1990 season,** the NFL changed the regular season schedule so that all teams would play 16 games over 17 weeks. This meant each team had "bye" week at some point during the season. The league also expanded the playoffs by adding another Wild Card team from each conference. The lowest seeded Wild Card would play the lowest seeded division winner (at the home stadium of the division winner). The two remaining Wild Card teams would play each other (at the home stadium of the higher seed). The Wild Cards are referred to herein as first Wild Card, second Wild Card, and third Wild Card.

## 1990 – American Football Conference

### Eastern Division

| Team | Win | Lost | Tie |
|---|---|---|---|
| Buffalo Bills | 13 | 3 | 0 |
| Miami Dolphins | 12 | 4 | 0 |
| Indianapolis Colts | 7 | 9 | 0 |
| New York Jets | 6 | 10 | 0 |
| New England Patriots | 1 | 15 | 0 |

### Central Division

| Team | Win | Lost | Tie |
|---|---|---|---|
| Cincinnati Bengals | 9 | 7 | 0 |
| Houston Oilers | 9 | 7 | 0 |
| Pittsburgh Steelers | 9 | 7 | 0 |
| Cleveland Browns | 3 | 13 | 0 |

### Western Division

| Team | Win | Lost | Tie |
|---|---|---|---|
| Los Angeles Raiders | 12 | 4 | 0 |
| Kansas City Chiefs | 11 | 5 | 0 |
| Seattle Seahawks | 9 | 7 | 0 |
| San Diego Chargers | 6 | 10 | 0 |
| Denver Broncos | 5 | 11 | 0 |

---

Paul Tagliabue completed his first full year as Commissioner after replacing the retiring Pete Rozelle halfway through the 1989 season.

## 1990 - 1991 Playoffs

## NFC Playoffs

*Wild Card playoff* (in Chicago) – Chicago Bears 16, New Orleans Saints 6

*Wild Card playoff* (in Philadelphia) – Washington Redskins 20, Philadelphia Eagles 6[1]

*Divisional playoff* (in San Francisco) – San Francisco 49ers 28, Washington Redskins 10

*Divisional playoff* (in New York) – New York Giants 31, Chicago Bears 3

NFC Championship (in San Francisco) – New York Giants 15, San Francisco 49ers 13

## AFC Playoffs

*Wild Card playoff* (in Cincinnati) – Cincinnati Bengals 41[2], Houston Oilers 14

*Wild Card playoff* (in Miami) – Miami Dolphins 17, Kansas City Chiefs 16

*Divisional playoff* (in Los Angeles) – Los Angeles Raiders 20, Cincinnati Bengals 10

*Divisional playoff* (in Buffalo) – Buffalo Bills 44, Miami Dolphins 34

AFC Championship (in Buffalo) – Buffalo Bills 51, Los Angeles Raiders 3

--------

1        The Philadelphia Eagles beat the Washington Redskins for the NFC East title based on a better division record, 5-3 vs. 4-4.

2        The Cincinnati Bengals beat out the Pittsburgh Steelers and Houston Oilers for the AFC Central title based on the best head-to-head record, 3-1 vs. 1-3 vs. 2-2. The Oilers beat out the Steelers and the Seattle Seahawks for the third AFC Wild Card based on a better conference record, 8-4 vs. 6-6 vs. 7-5.

# 1991 – Super Bowl XXV (25)

## Tampa

**New York Giants** (NFC) defeat the Buffalo Bills (AFC), 20-19.

## Season Awards

| | |
|---|---|
| *Most Valuable Player* | Joe Montana, Quarterback, San Francisco 49ers |
| *Coach of the Year* | Jimmy Johnson, Dallas Cowboys |
| *Offensive Player of the Year* | Warren Moon, Quarterback, Houston Oilers |
| *Defensive Player of the Year* | Bruce Smith, Defensive End, Buffalo Bills |
| *Offensive Rookie of the Year* | Emmitt Smith, Running Back, Dallas Cowboys |
| *Defensive Rookie of the Year* | Mark Carrier, Safety, Chicago Bears |

## 1991  – National Football Conference

### Eastern Division

| Team | Win | Lost | Tie |
|---|---|---|---|
| Washington Redskins | 14 | 2 | 0 |
| Dallas Cowboys | 11 | 5 | 0 |
| Philadelphia Eagles | 10 | 6 | 0 |
| New York Giants | 8 | 8 | 0 |
| Phoenix Cardinals | 4 | 12 | 0 |

### Central Division

| Team | Win | Lost | Tie |
|---|---|---|---|
| Detroit Lions | 12 | 4 | 0 |
| Chicago Bears | 11 | 5 | 0 |
| Minnesota Vikings | 8 | 8 | 0 |
| Green Bay Packers | 4 | 12 | 0 |
| Tampa Bay Buccaneers | 3 | 13 | 0 |

### Western Division

| Team | Win | Lost | Tie |
|---|---|---|---|
| New Orleans Saints | 11 | 5 | 0 |
| Atlanta Falcons | 10 | 6 | 0 |
| San Francisco 49ers | 10 | 6 | 0 |
| Los Angeles Rams | 3 | 13 | 0 |

# 1991 – American Football Conference

## Eastern Division

| Team | Win | Lost | Tie |
|------|-----|------|-----|
| Buffalo Bills | 13 | 3 | 0 |
| New York Jets | 8 | 8 | 0 |
| Miami Dolphins | 8 | 8 | 0 |
| New England Patriots | 6 | 10 | 0 |
| Indianapolis Colts | 1 | 15 | 0 |

## Central Division

| Team | Win | Lost | Tie |
|------|-----|------|-----|
| Houston Oilers | 11 | 5 | 0 |
| Pittsburgh Steelers | 7 | 9 | 0 |
| Cleveland Browns | 6 | 10 | 0 |
| Cincinnati Bengals | 3 | 13 | 0 |

## Western Division

| Team | Win | Lost | Tie |
|------|-----|------|-----|
| Denver Broncos | 12 | 4 | 0 |
| Kansas City Chiefs | 10 | 6 | 0 |
| Los Angeles Raiders | 9 | 7 | 0 |
| Seattle Seahawks | 7 | 9 | 0 |
| San Diego Chargers | 4 | 12 | 0 |

## 1991 - 1992 Playoffs

## NFC Playoffs

*Wild Card playoff* (in Chicago) – Dallas Cowboys 17, Chicago Bears 13[3]

*Wild Card playoff* (in New Orleans) – Atlanta Falcons 27[4], New Orleans Saints 20

*Divisional playoff* (in Washington) – Washington Redskins 24, Atlanta Falcons 7

*Divisional playoff* (in Detroit) – Detroit Lions 38, Dallas Cowboys 6

NFC Championship (in Washington) – Washington Redskins 41, Detroit Lions 10

## AFC Playoffs

*Wild Card playoff* (in Houston) – Houston Oilers 17, New York Jets 10[5]

*Wild Card playoff* (in Kansas City) – Kansas City Chiefs 10, Los Angeles Raiders 6

*Divisional playoff* (in Denver) – Denver Broncos 26, Houston Oilers 24

*Divisional playoff* (in Buffalo) – Buffalo Bills 27, Kansas City Chiefs 14

AFC Championship (in Buffalo) – Buffalo Bills 10, Denver Broncos 7

---

3        The Chicago Bears beat out the Dallas Cowboys for the first Wild Card seed based on a better conference record, 9-3 vs. 8-4.

4        The Atlanta Falcons finished ahead of the San Francisco 49ers in the NFC West based on a head-to-head sweep of games played between the two teams.  The Falcons were the third Wild Card seed ahead of the Philadelphia Eagles based on a better conference record, 7-5 vs. 6-6.

5        The New York Jets finished ahead of the Miami Dolphins for first place in the AFC East based on a head-to-head sweep of games played between the two teams.

## 1992 – Super Bowl XXVI (26)

## Minneapolis

**Washington Redskins** (NFC) defeat the Buffalo Bills (AFC), 37-24.

## Season Awards

| | |
|---|---|
| *Most Valuable Player* | Thurman Thomas, Running Back, Buffalo Bills |
| *Coach of the Year* | Wayne Fontes, Detroit Lions |
| *Offensive Player of the Year* | Thurman Thomas, Running Back, Buffalo Bills |
| *Defensive Player of the Year* | Pat Swilling, Linebacker, New Orleans Saints |
| *Offensive Rookie of the Year* | Leonard Russell, Running Back, New England Patriots |
| *Defensive Rookie of the Year* | Mike Croel, Linebacker, Denver Broncos |

---

The halftime show for Super Bowl XXVI was "Winter Magic," a salute to winter and the Winter Olympics. The Fox Network ran a live version of its hit show *In Living Color* in opposition and drew a huge audience away from the Super Bowl broadcast. This led the NFL to rethink its halftime entertainment.

## 1992 – National Football Conference

## Eastern Division

| Team | Win | Lost | Tie |
|------|-----|------|-----|
| Dallas Cowboys | 13 | 3 | 0 |
| Philadelphia Eagles | 11 | 5 | 0 |
| Washington Redskins | 9 | 7 | 0 |
| New York Giants | 6 | 10 | 0 |
| Phoenix Cardinals | 4 | 12 | 0 |

## Central Division

| Team | Win | Lost | Tie |
|------|-----|------|-----|
| Minnesota Vikings | 11 | 5 | 0 |
| Green Bay Packers | 9 | 7 | 0 |
| Tampa Bay Buccaneers | 5 | 11 | 0 |
| Chicago Bears | 5 | 11 | 0 |
| Detroit Lions | 5 | 11 | 0 |

## Western Division

| Team | Win | Lost | Tie |
|------|-----|------|-----|
| San Francisco 49ers | 14 | 2 | 0 |
| New Orleans Saints | 12 | 4 | 0 |
| Atlanta Falcons | 6 | 10 | 0 |
| Los Angeles Rams | 6 | 10 | 0 |

---

The instant replay system in effect since 1986 was repealed. Instant replay would not return until 1999.

# 1992 – American Football Conference

## Eastern Division

| Team | Win | Lost | Tie |
|------|-----|------|-----|
| Miami Dolphins | 11 | 5 | 0 |
| Buffalo Bills | 11 | 5 | 0 |
| Indianapolis Colts | 9 | 7 | 0 |
| New York Jets | 4 | 12 | 0 |
| New England Patriots | 2 | 14 | 0 |

## Central Division

| Team | Win | Lost | Tie |
|------|-----|------|-----|
| Pittsburgh Steelers | 11 | 5 | 0 |
| Houston Oilers | 10 | 6 | 0 |
| Cleveland Browns | 7 | 9 | 0 |
| Cincinnati Bengals | 5 | 11 | 0 |

## Western Division

| Team | Win | Lost | Tie |
|------|-----|------|-----|
| San Diego Chargers | 11 | 5 | 0 |
| Kansas City Chiefs | 10 | 6 | 0 |
| Denver Broncos | 8 | 8 | 0 |
| Los Angeles Raiders | 7 | 9 | 0 |
| Seattle Seahawks | 2 | 14 | 0 |

## 1992 - 1993 Playoffs

## NFC Playoffs

*Wild Card playoff* (in Minneapolis) – Washington Redskins 24[6], Minnesota Vikings 7

*Wild Card playoff* (in New Orleans) – Philadelphia Eagles 26, New Orleans Saints 20

*Divisional playoff* (in San Francisco) – San Francisco 49ers 20, Washington Redskins 13

*Divisional playoff* (in Dallas) – Dallas Cowboys 34, Philadelphia Eagles 10

NFC Championship (in San Francisco) – Dallas Cowboys 30, San Francisco 49ers 20

## AFC Playoffs

*Wild Card playoff* (in Buffalo) – Buffalo Bills 41, Houston Oilers 38[7] (OT)

*Wild Card playoff* (in San Diego) – San Diego Chargers 17, Kansas City Chiefs 0

*Divisional playoff* (in Miami) – Miami Dolphins 31[8], San Diego Chargers 0

*Divisional playoff* (in Pittsburgh) – Buffalo Bills 24, Pittsburgh 3[9]

AFC Championship (in Miami) – Buffalo Bills 29, Miami Dolphins 10

---

6        The Washington Redskins won the NFC Wild Card third seed over the Green Bay Packers based on a better conference record, 7-5 vs. 6-6.

7        The Houston Oilers were the AFC Wild Card second seed based on its head-to-head victory over the Kansas City Chiefs.

8        The Miami Dolphins won the AFC East over the Buffalo Bills based on a better conference record, 9-3 vs. 7-5.

9        The Pittsburgh Steelers were the AFC first seed ahead of the Miami Dolphins based on a better conference record, 10-2 vs. 9-3. The Dolphins beat out the San Diego Chargers for the AFC second seed due to a better conference record, 9-3 vs. 9-5.

# 1993 – Super Bowl XXVII (27)

# Los Angeles (Rose Bowl)

**Dallas Cowboys** (NFC) defeat the Buffalo Bills (AFC), 52-17.

## Season Awards

| | |
|---|---|
| *Most Valuable Player* | Steve Young, Quarterback, San Francisco 49ers |
| *Coach of the Year* | Bill Cowher, Pittsburgh Steelers |
| *Offensive Player of the Year* | Steve Young, Quarterback, San Francisco 49ers |
| *Defensive Player of the Year* | Cortez Kennedy, Defensive Tackle, Seattle Seahawks |
| *Offensive Rookie of the Year* | Carl Pickens, Wide Receiver, Cincinnati Bengals |
| *Defensive Rookie of the Year* | Dale Carter, Cornerback, Kansas City Chiefs |

---

Megastar Michael Jackson performed at halftime, a direct response to the Fox Network's *In Living Color* experiment the year before. In the past, the NFL had such halftime performers as Elvis Presto, 91 year-old comic George Burns, the Rockettes, and a salute to the cartoon strip *Peanuts*. By bringing in Jackson, the NFL upped the ante and turned its halftime show into a "must see" musical showcase with acts like Paul McCartney, U2, The Rolling Stones, and Tom Petty and the Heartbreakers.

## 1993 – National Football Conference

### Eastern Division

| Team | Win | Lost | Tie |
|---|---|---|---|
| Dallas Cowboys | 12 | 4 | 0 |
| New York Giants | 11 | 5 | 0 |
| Philadelphia Eagles | 8 | 8 | 0 |
| Phoenix Cardinals | 7 | 9 | 0 |
| Washington Redskins | 4 | 12 | 0 |

### Central Division

| Team | Win | Lost | Tie |
|---|---|---|---|
| Detroit Lions | 10 | 6 | 0 |
| Minnesota Vikings | 9 | 7 | 0 |
| Green Bay Packers | 9 | 7 | 0 |
| Chicago Bears | 7 | 9 | 0 |
| Tampa Bay Buccaneers | 5 | 11 | 0 |

### Western Division

| Team | Win | Lost | Tie |
|---|---|---|---|
| San Francisco 49ers | 10 | 6 | 0 |
| New Orleans Saints | 8 | 8 | 0 |
| Atlanta Falcons | 6 | 10 | 0 |
| Los Angeles Rams | 5 | 11 | 0 |

In 1993, the NFL played 16 games over an 18 week regular season, with each team getting two bye weeks. The hope was to generate more revenue for the league. Teams found the experiment too disruptive and the league went back to the 17 week season in 1994. In December 1993, CBS lost its television rights to NFL games to the upstart Fox Network, a change that brought on the era of huge television broadcast money for the NFL and gave instant credibility and sustainability to Fox.

# 1993 – American Football Conference

## Eastern Division

| Team | Win | Lost | Tie |
|---|---|---|---|
| Buffalo Bills | 12 | 4 | 0 |
| Miami Dolphins | 9 | 7 | 0 |
| New York Jets | 8 | 8 | 0 |
| New England Patriots | 5 | 11 | 0 |
| Indianapolis Colts | 4 | 12 | 0 |

## Central Division

| Team | Win | Lost | Tie |
|---|---|---|---|
| Houston Oilers | 12 | 4 | 0 |
| Pittsburgh Steelers | 9 | 7 | 0 |
| Cleveland Browns | 7 | 9 | 0 |
| Cincinnati Bengals | 3 | 13 | 0 |

## Western Division

| Team | Win | Lost | Tie |
|---|---|---|---|
| Kansas City Chiefs | 11 | 5 | 0 |
| Los Angeles Raiders | 10 | 6 | 0 |
| Denver Broncos | 9 | 7 | 0 |
| San Diego Chargers | 8 | 8 | 0 |
| Seattle Seahawks | 6 | 10 | 0 |

## 1993 - 1994 Playoffs

## NFC Playoffs

*Wild Card playoff* (in Detroit) – Green Bay Packers 28, Detroit Lions 24

*Wild Card playoff* (in New York) – New York Giants 17, Minnesota Vikings 10[10]

*Divisional playoff* (in San Francisco) – San Francisco 49ers 44[11], New York Giants 3

*Divisional playoff* (in Dallas) – Dallas Cowboys 27, Green Bay Packers 17

NFC Championship (in Dallas) – Dallas Cowboys 38, San Francisco 49ers 21

## AFC Playoffs

*Wild Card playoff* (in Kansas City) – Kansas City Chiefs 27, Pittsburgh Steelers 24[12] (OT)

*Wild Card playoff* (in Los Angeles) – Los Angeles Raiders 42, Denver Broncos 24[13]

*Divisional playoff* (in Buffalo) – Buffalo Bills 29[14], Los Angeles Raiders 23

*Divisional playoff* (in Houston) – Kansas City Chiefs 28, Houston Oilers 20

AFC Championship (in Buffalo) – Buffalo Bills 30, Kansas City Chiefs 13

---

10    The Minnesota Vikings finished ahead of the Green bay Packers in the NFC Central, winning the NFC fifth seed based on a season sweep of the head-to-head meetings.

11    The San Francisco 49ers edged the Detroit Lions for the NFC second seed based on their head-to-head victory over the Lions.

12    The Pittsburgh Steelers were the AFC Wild Card third seed based on their head-to-head victory over the Miami Dolphins.

13    The Denver Broncos were the AFC Wild Card second seed ahead of the Pittsburgh Steelers and the Miami Dolphins based on a better conference record, 8-4 vs. 7-5 vs. 6-6.

14    The Buffalo Bills were the AFC first seed based on their head-to-head victory over the Houston Oilers.

# 1994 – Super Bowl XXVIII (28)

## Atlanta

**Dallas Cowboys** (NFC) defeat the Buffalo Bills (AFC), 30-13.

## Season Awards

| | |
|---|---|
| *Most Valuable Player* | Emmitt Smith, Running Back, Dallas Cowboys |
| *Coach of the Year* | Dan Reeves, Denver Broncos |
| *Offensive Player of the Year* | Jerry Rice, Wide Receiver, San Francisco 49ers |
| *Defensive Player of the Year* | Ron Woodson, Cornerback, Pittsburgh Steelers |
| *Offensive Rookie of the Year* | Jerome Bettis, Running Back, Los Angeles Rams |
| *Defensive Rookie of the Year* | Dana Stubblefield, Defensive Tackle, San Francisco 49ers |

The Buffalo Bills lost their fourth straight Super Bowl. The game was also the first time the same two teams met in consecutive Super Bowls.

## 1994 – National Football Conference

### Eastern Division

| Team | Win | Lost | Tie |
|------|-----|------|-----|
| Dallas Cowboys | 12 | 4 | 0 |
| New York Giants | 9 | 7 | 0 |
| Arizona Cardinals | 8 | 8 | 0 |
| Philadelphia Eagles | 7 | 9 | 0 |
| Washington Redskins | 3 | 13 | 0 |

### Central Division

| Team | Win | Lost | Tie |
|------|-----|------|-----|
| Minnesota Vikings | 10 | 6 | 0 |
| Green Bay Packers | 9 | 7 | 0 |
| Detroit Lions | 9 | 7 | 0 |
| Chicago Bears | 9 | 7 | 0 |
| Tampa Bay Buccaneers | 6 | 10 | 0 |

### Western Division

| Team | Win | Lost | Tie |
|------|-----|------|-----|
| San Francisco 49ers | 13 | 3 | 0 |
| New Orleans Saints | 7 | 9 | 0 |
| Atlanta Falcons | 7 | 9 | 0 |
| Los Angeles Rams | 4 | 12 | 0 |

---

The NFL adopted the two-point conversion (a former AFL innovation) prior to the start of the 1994 season. The NFL also adopted a salary cap for each team. The initial cap was set at $34.6 million per team. The 2015 salary cap is $148,578,313. The cap would be instrumental in improving parity between the teams, meaning fewer dynasties and giving each team a better chance to reach the playoffs and the Super Bowl. For an explanation of how the salary cap works, see the Appendix. The Phoenix Cardinals changed their name to the Arizona Cardinals. This name change made them the second franchise to adopt the name of a state vs. a city, the other being the Minnesota Vikings.

# 1994 – American Football Conference

## Eastern Division

| Team | Win | Lost | Tie |
|------|-----|------|-----|
| Miami Dolphins | 10 | 6 | 0 |
| New England Patriots | 10 | 6 | 0 |
| Indianapolis Colts | 8 | 8 | 0 |
| Buffalo Bills | 7 | 9 | 0 |
| New York Jets | 6 | 10 | 0 |

## Central Division

| Team | Win | Lost | Tie |
|------|-----|------|-----|
| Pittsburgh Steelers | 12 | 4 | 0 |
| Cleveland Browns | 11 | 5 | 0 |
| Cincinnati Bengals | 3 | 13 | 0 |
| Houston Oilers | 2 | 14 | 0 |

## Western Division

| Team | Win | Lost | Tie |
|------|-----|------|-----|
| San Diego Chargers | 11 | 5 | 0 |
| Kansas City Chiefs | 9 | 7 | 0 |
| Los Angeles Raiders | 9 | 7 | 0 |
| Denver Broncos | 7 | 9 | 0 |
| Seattle Seahawks | 6 | 10 | 0 |

## 1994 - 1995 Playoffs

## NFC Playoffs

*Wild Card playoff* (in Green Bay) – Green Bay Packers 16[15], Detroit Lions 12[16]

*Wild Card playoff* (in Minneapolis) – Chicago Bears 35, Minnesota Vikings 18

*Divisional playoff* (in San Francisco) – San Francisco 49ers 44, Chicago Bears 15

*Divisional playoff* (in Dallas) – Dallas Cowboys 35, Green Bay Packers 9

NFC Championship (in San Francisco) – San Francisco 49ers 38, Dallas Cowboys 28

## AFC Playoffs

*Wild Card playoff* (in Miami) – Miami Dolphins 27[17], Kansas City Chiefs 17[18]

*Wild Card playoff* (in Cleveland) – Cleveland Browns 20, New England Patriots 13

*Divisional playoff* (in San Diego) – San Diego Chargers 22, Miami Dolphins 21

*Divisional playoff* (in Pittsburgh) – Pittsburgh Steelers 29, Cleveland Browns 9

AFC Championship (in Pittsburgh) – San Diego Chargers 17, Pittsburgh Steelers 13

---

15      The Green Bay Packers were the NFC Wild Card first seed over the Detroit Lions and the Chicago Bears based on a better head-to-head record against those teams and over the New York Giants based on a better conference record, 8-4 vs. 6-6.

16      The Detroit Lions won the NFC Wild Card second seed over the Bears based on a better division record, 4-4 vs. 3-5, and over the Giants based on a head-to-head win.

17      The Miami Dolphins beat out the New England Patriots for the AFC East title based on a sweep of both games between the teams.

18      The Kansas City Chiefs beat out the Los Angeles Raiders for the final AFC Wild Card based on a sweep of both games between the teams.

# 1995 – Super Bowl XXIX (29)

## Miami

**San Francisco 49ers** (NFC) defeat the San Diego Chargers (AFC), 49-26.

## Season Awards

| | |
|---|---|
| *Most Valuable Player* | Steve Young, Quarterback, San Francisco 49ers |
| *Coach of the Year* | Bill Parcells, New England Patriots |
| *Offensive Player of the Year* | Barry Sanders, Running Back, Detroit Lions |
| *Defensive Player of the Year* | Deion Sanders, Cornerback, San Francisco 49ers |
| *Offensive Rookie of the Year* | Marshall Faulk, Running Back, Indianapolis Colts |
| *Defensive Rookie of the Year* | Tim Bowens, Defensive Tackles, Miami Dolphins |

## 1995 – National Football Conference

### Eastern Division

| Team | Win | Lost | Tie |
|------|-----|------|-----|
| Dallas Cowboys | 12 | 4 | 0 |
| Philadelphia Eagles | 10 | 6 | 0 |
| Washington Redskins | 6 | 10 | 0 |
| New York Giants | 5 | 11 | 0 |
| Arizona Cardinals | 4 | 12 | 0 |

### Central Division

| Team | Win | Lost | Tie |
|------|-----|------|-----|
| Green Bay Packers | 11 | 5 | 0 |
| Detroit Lions | 10 | 6 | 0 |
| Chicago Bears | 9 | 7 | 0 |
| Minnesota Vikings | 8 | 8 | 0 |
| Tampa Bay Buccaneers | 7 | 9 | 0 |

### Western Division

| Team | Win | Lost | Tie |
|------|-----|------|-----|
| San Francisco 49ers | 11 | 5 | 0 |
| Atlanta Falcons | 9 | 7 | 0 |
| St. Louis Rams | 7 | 9 | 0 |
| Carolina Panthers | 7 | 9 | 0 |
| New Orleans Saints | 7 | 9 | 0 |

---

The NFL expanded by two teams in 1995 adding the Carolina Panthers (NFC Western Division) and the Jacksonville Jaguars (AFC Central Division). The Panthers became the first team named after a region (North Carolina and South Carolina) vs. a state or city. Additionally, the Los Angeles Rams moved to St. Louis and the Los Angeles Raiders moved back to Oakland, leaving Los Angeles without an NFL team for the first time since 1946 (and, as of 2015, still without a NFL team). The league also permitted quarterbacks to receive radio communications from the bench. The radio receivers were in the quarterback's helmet. This change repealed a ban in place since 1956.

# 1995 – American Football Conference

## Eastern Division

| Team | Win | Lost | Tie |
|------|-----|------|-----|
| Buffalo Bills | 10 | 6 | 0 |
| Indianapolis Colts | 9 | 7 | 0 |
| Miami Dolphins | 9 | 7 | 0 |
| New England Patriots | 6 | 10 | 0 |
| New York Jets | 3 | 13 | 0 |

## Central Division

| Team | Win | Lost | Tie |
|------|-----|------|-----|
| Pittsburgh Steelers | 11 | 5 | 0 |
| Cincinnati Bengals | 7 | 9 | 0 |
| Houston Oilers | 7 | 9 | 0 |
| Cleveland Browns | 5 | 11 | 0 |
| Jacksonville Jaguars | 4 | 12 | 0 |

## Western Division

| Team | Win | Lost | Tie |
|------|-----|------|-----|
| Kansas City Chiefs | 13 | 3 | 0 |
| San Diego Chargers | 9 | 7 | 0 |
| Seattle Seahawks | 8 | 8 | 0 |
| Denver Broncos | 8 | 8 | 0 |
| Oakland Raiders | 8 | 8 | 0 |

## 1995 - 1996 Playoffs

## NFC Playoffs

*Wild Card playoff* (in Green Bay) – Green Bay Packers 37, Atlanta Falcons 20[19]

*Wild Card playoff* (in Philadelphia) – Philadelphia Eagles 58[20], Detroit Lions 37

*Divisional playoff* (in San Francisco) – Green Bay Packers 27, San Francisco 49ers 17[21]

*Divisional playoff* (in Dallas) – Dallas Cowboys 30, Philadelphia Eagles 11

NFC Championship (in Dallas) – Dallas Cowboys 38, Green Bay Packers 27

## AFC Playoffs

*Wild Card playoff* (in Buffalo) – Buffalo Bills 37, Miami Dolphins 22

*Wild Card playoff* (in San Diego) – Indianapolis Colts 35[22], San Diego Chargers 20[23]

*Divisional playoff* (in Kansas City) – Indianapolis Colts 10, Kansas City Chiefs 7

*Divisional playoff* (in Pittsburgh) – Pittsburgh Steelers 40, Buffalo Bills 21

AFC Championship (in Pittsburgh) – Pittsburgh Steelers 20, Indianapolis Colts 16

---

19      The Atlanta Falcons took the NFC Wild Card third seed ahead of the Chicago Bears based on a better record against common opponents, 4-2 vs. 3-3.

20      The Philadelphia Eagles took the NFC Wild Card first seed over the Detroit Lions based on a better conference record, 9-3 vs. 7-5.

21      The San Francisco 49ers won the NFC second seed over the Green Bay Packers based a better conference record, 8-4 vs. 7-5.

22      The Indianapolis Colts beat out the Miami Dolphins for the AFC East title based on a sweep of head-to-head games.

23      The San Diego Chargers were the AFC Wild Card first seed over the Colts based on a head-to-head victory.

# 1996 – Super Bowl XXX (30)
## Tempe, AZ

**Dallas Cowboys** (NFC) defeat the Pittsburgh Steelers (AFC), 27-17.

## Season Awards

| | |
|---|---|
| *Most Valuable Player* | Brett Favre, Quarterback, Green Bay Packers |
| *Coach of the Year* | Ray Rhodes, Philadelphia Eagles |
| *Offensive Player of the Year* | Brett Favre, Quarterback, Green Bay Packers |
| *Defensive Player of the Year* | Bryce Paup, Linebacker, Buffalo Bills |
| *Offensive Rookie of the Year* | Curtis Martin, Running Back, New England Patriots |
| *Defensive Rookie of the Year* | Hugh Douglas, Defensive End, New York Jets |

# 1996 – National Football Conference

## Eastern Division

| Team | Win | Lost | Tie |
|------|-----|------|-----|
| Dallas Cowboys | 10 | 6 | 0 |
| Philadelphia Eagles | 10 | 6 | 0 |
| Washington Redskins | 9 | 7 | 0 |
| Arizona Cardinals | 7 | 9 | 0 |
| New York Giants | 6 | 10 | 0 |

## Central Division

| Team | Win | Lost | Tie |
|------|-----|------|-----|
| Green Bay Packers | 13 | 3 | 0 |
| Minnesota Vikings | 9 | 7 | 0 |
| Chicago Bears | 7 | 9 | 0 |
| Tampa Bay Buccaneers | 6 | 10 | 0 |
| Detroit Lions | 5 | 11 | 0 |

## Western Division

| Team | Win | Lost | Tie |
|------|-----|------|-----|
| Carolina Panthers | 12 | 4 | 0 |
| San Francisco 49ers | 12 | 4 | 0 |
| St. Louis Rams | 6 | 10 | 0 |
| Atlanta Falcons | 3 | 13 | 0 |
| New Orleans Saints | 3 | 13 | 0 |

# 1996 – American Football Conference

## Eastern Division

| Team | Win | Lost | Tie |
|------|-----|------|-----|
| New England Patriots | 11 | 5 | 0 |
| Buffalo Bills | 10 | 6 | 0 |
| Indianapolis Colts | 9 | 7 | 0 |
| Miami Dolphins | 8 | 8 | 0 |
| New York Jets | 1 | 15 | 0 |

## Central Division

| Team | Win | Lost | Tie |
|------|-----|------|-----|
| Pittsburgh Steelers | 10 | 6 | 0 |
| Jacksonville Jaguars | 9 | 7 | 0 |
| Cincinnati Bengals | 8 | 8 | 0 |
| Houston Oilers | 8 | 8 | 0 |
| Baltimore Ravens | 4 | 12 | 0 |

## Western Division

| Team | Win | Lost | Tie |
|------|-----|------|-----|
| Denver Broncos | 13 | 3 | 0 |
| Kansas City Chiefs | 9 | 7 | 0 |
| San Diego Chargers | 8 | 8 | 0 |
| Oakland Raiders | 7 | 9 | 0 |
| Seattle Seahawks | 7 | 9 | 0 |

---

In a controversial move over the city's unwillingness to build a new stadium, the Cleveland Browns relocated to Baltimore before the start of the 1996 season. Because of the uproar in Cleveland over the decision (and the ensuing political and public relations mess), the league made an agreement with the cities of Cleveland and Baltimore. The name, colors, and records of the Browns would remain in Cleveland and that city would receive a new franchise within a few years. Baltimore would, in essence, get an "expansion team", though it was the fully-formed Browns organization. The team was renamed the Ravens and started with fresh records and history.

## 1996 - 1997 Playoffs

## NFC Playoffs

*Wild Card playoff* (in Dallas) – Dallas Cowboys 40[24], Minnesota Vikings 15[25]

*Wild Card playoff* (in San Francisco) – San Francisco 49ers 14, Philadelphia Eagles 0

*Divisional playoff* (in San Francisco) – Green Bay Packers 35, San Francisco 49ers 14

*Divisional playoff* (in Charlotte) – Carolina Panthers 26[26], Dallas Cowboys 17

NFC Championship (in Green Bay) – Green Bay Packers 30, Carolina Panthers 13

## AFC Playoffs

*Wild Card playoff* (in Buffalo) – Jacksonville Jaguars 30[27], Buffalo Bills 27

*Wild Card playoff* (in Pittsburgh) – Pittsburgh Steelers 42, Indianapolis Colts 14

*Divisional playoff* (in Denver) – Jacksonville Jaguars 30, Denver Broncos 27

*Divisional playoff* (in Boston) – New England Patriots 28, Pittsburgh Steelers 3

AFC Championship (in Boston) – New England Patriots 20, Jacksonville Jaguars 6

---

The Carolina Panthers and the Jacksonville Jaguars both advanced to their respective conference title games each in only their second year of existence.

---

24      The Dallas Cowboys won the NFC East over the Philadelphia Eagles based on a better record against common opponents, 8-5 vs. 7-6.

25      The Minnesota Vikings won the NFC Wild Card third seed over the Washington Redskins based on a better conference record, 8-4 vs. 6-6.

26      The Carolina Panthers won the NFC West over the San Francisco 49ers based on a head-to-head sweep.

27      The Jacksonville Jaguars were the AFC Wild Card second seed over the Indianapolis Colts and the Kansas City Chiefs based on a better conference record, 7-5 vs. 6-6 vs. 5-7. The Colts beat out the Chiefs for the AFC Wild Card third seed based on a head-to-head victory over the Chiefs.

# 1997 – Super Bowl XXXI (31)

## New Orleans

**Green Bay Packers** (NFC) defeat the New England Patriots (AFC), 35-21.

## Season Awards

| | |
|---|---|
| *Most Valuable Player* | Brett Favre, Quarterback, Green Bay Packers |
| *Coach of the Year* | Dom Capers, Carolina Panthers |
| *Offensive Player of the Year* | Terrell Davis, Running Back, Denver Broncos |
| *Defensive Player of the Year* | Bruce Smith, Defensive End, Buffalo Bills |
| *Offensive Rookie of the Year* | Eddie George, Running Back, Houston Oilers |
| *Defensive Rookie of the Year* | Simeon Rice, Defensive End, Arizona Cardinals |

## 1997 – National Football Conference

### Eastern Division

| Team | Win | Lost | Tie |
|------|-----|------|-----|
| New York Giants | 10 | 5 | 1 |
| Washington Redskins | 8 | 7 | 1 |
| Philadelphia Eagles | 6 | 9 | 1 |
| Dallas Cowboys | 6 | 10 | 0 |
| Arizona Cardinals | 4 | 12 | 0 |

### Central Division

| Team | Win | Lost | Tie |
|------|-----|------|-----|
| Green Bay Packers | 13 | 3 | 0 |
| Tampa Bay Buccaneers | 10 | 6 | 0 |
| Detroit Lions | 9 | 7 | 0 |
| Minnesota Vikings | 9 | 7 | 0 |
| Chicago Bears | 4 | 12 | 0 |

### Western Division

| Team | Win | Lost | Tie |
|------|-----|------|-----|
| San Francisco 49ers | 13 | 3 | 0 |
| Carolina Panthers | 7 | 9 | 0 |
| Atlanta Falcons | 7 | 9 | 0 |
| New Orleans Saints | 6 | 10 | 0 |
| St. Louis Rams | 5 | 11 | 0 |

## 1997 – American Football Conference

### Eastern Division

| Team | Win | Lost | Tie |
|------|-----|------|-----|
| New England Patriots | 10 | 6 | 0 |
| Miami Dolphins | 9 | 7 | 0 |
| New York Jets | 9 | 7 | 0 |
| Buffalo Bills | 6 | 10 | 0 |
| Indianapolis Colts | 3 | 13 | 0 |

### Central Division

| Team | Win | Lost | Tie |
|------|-----|------|-----|
| Pittsburgh Steelers | 11 | 5 | 0 |
| Jacksonville Jaguars | 11 | 5 | 0 |
| Tennessee Oilers | 8 | 8 | 0 |
| Cincinnati Bengals | 7 | 9 | 0 |
| Baltimore Ravens | 6 | 9 | 1 |

### Western Division

| Team | Win | Lost | Tie |
|------|-----|------|-----|
| Kansas City Chiefs | 13 | 3 | 0 |
| Denver Broncos | 12 | 4 | 0 |
| Seattle Seahawks | 8 | 8 | 0 |
| Oakland Raiders | 4 | 12 | 0 |
| San Diego Chargers | 4 | 12 | 0 |

---

In the aftermath of another stadium fight, the Houston Oilers relocated to Memphis, Tennessee before the start of the 1997 season and became the Tennessee Oilers (the third franchise to be named after a state). Memphis would be a temporary home while a new stadium was being built for the team in Nashville, Tennessee.

## 1997 - 1998 Playoffs

## NFC Playoffs

*Wild Card playoff* (in Tampa) – Tampa Bay Buccaneers 20, Detroit Lions 10[28]

*Wild Card playoff* (in New York) – Minnesota Vikings 23, New York Giants 22

*Divisional playoff* (in San Francisco) – San Francisco 49ers 28[29], Minnesota Vikings 22

*Divisional playoff* (in Green Bay) – Green Bay Packers 21, Tampa Bay Buccaneers 7

NFC Championship (in San Francisco) – Green Bay Packers 23, San Francisco 49ers 10

## AFC Playoffs

*Wild Card playoff* (in Denver) – Denver Broncos 42, Jacksonville Jaguars 17

*Wild Card playoff* (in Boston) – New England Patriots 17, Miami Dolphins 3[30]

*Divisional playoff* (in Denver) – Denver Broncos 14, Kansas City Chiefs 10

*Divisional playoff* (in Pittsburgh) – Pittsburgh Steelers 7[31], New England Patriots 6

AFC Championship (in Pittsburgh) – Denver Broncos 24, Pittsburgh Steelers 21

---

28      The Detroit Lions finished ahead of the Minnesota Vikings in the NFC Central based on a head-to-head sweep of their games.

29      The San Francisco 49ers took the NFC top seed over the Green Bay Packers due to a better conference record, 11-1 vs. 10-2.

30      The Miami Dolphins beat out the New York Jets for the final AFC Wild Card slot based on a head-to-head sweep of their games.

31      The Pittsburgh Steelers finished ahead of the Jacksonville Jaguars in the AFC Central due to better net division points, 78 vs. 23.

# 1998 – Super Bowl XXXII (32)
## San Diego

**Denver Broncos** (AFC) defeat the Green Bay Packers (NFC), 31-24.

## Season Awards

| | |
|---|---|
| *Most Valuable Player* | Brett Favre, Quarterback, Green Bay Packers/ Barry Sanders, Running Back, Detroit Lions (tie) |
| *Coach of the Year* | Jim Fassel, New York Giants |
| *Offensive Player of the Year* | Barry Sanders, Running Back, Detroit Lions |
| *Defensive Player of the Year* | Dana Stubblefield, Defensive Tackle, San Francisco 49ers |
| *Offensive Rookie of the Year* | Warrick Dunn, Running Back, Tampa Bay Buccaneers |
| *Defensive Rookie of the Year* | Peter Boulware, Linebacker, Baltimore Ravens |

---

The Denver Broncos became the first AFC team to win the Super Bowl in 14 seasons, since the Los Angeles Raiders beat the Washington Redskins in the 1984 - Super Bowl XVIII (18).

## 1998 – National Football Conference

### Eastern Division

| Team | Win | Lost | Tie |
|------|-----|------|-----|
| Dallas Cowboys | 10 | 6 | 0 |
| Arizona Cardinals | 9 | 7 | 0 |
| New York Giants | 8 | 8 | 0 |
| Washington Redskins | 6 | 10 | 0 |
| Philadelphia Eagles | 3 | 13 | 0 |

### Central Division

| Team | Win | Lost | Tie |
|------|-----|------|-----|
| Minnesota Vikings | 15 | 1 | 0 |
| Green Bay Packers | 11 | 5 | 0 |
| Tampa Bay Buccaneers | 8 | 8 | 0 |
| Detroit Lions | 5 | 11 | 0 |
| Chicago Bears | 4 | 12 | 0 |

### Western Division

| Team | Win | Lost | Tie |
|------|-----|------|-----|
| Atlanta Falcons | 14 | 2 | 0 |
| San Francisco 49ers | 12 | 4 | 0 |
| New Orleans Saints | 6 | 10 | 0 |
| Carolina Panthers | 4 | 12 | 0 |
| St. Louis Rams | 4 | 12 | 0 |

CBS got back in the business of broadcasting NFL games, taking over the AFC broadcasts from NBC.

# 1998 – American Football Conference

## Eastern Division

| Team | Win | Lost | Tie |
|------|-----|------|-----|
| New York Jets | 12 | 4 | 0 |
| Miami Dolphins | 10 | 6 | 0 |
| Buffalo Bills | 10 | 6 | 0 |
| New England Patriots | 9 | 7 | 0 |
| Indianapolis Colts | 3 | 13 | 0 |

## Central Division

| Team | Win | Lost | Tie |
|------|-----|------|-----|
| Jacksonville Jaguars | 11 | 5 | 0 |
| Tennessee Oilers | 8 | 8 | 0 |
| Pittsburgh Steelers | 7 | 9 | 0 |
| Baltimore Ravens | 6 | 10 | 0 |
| Cincinnati Bengals | 3 | 13 | 0 |

## Western Division

| Team | Win | Lost | Tie |
|------|-----|------|-----|
| Denver Broncos | 14 | 2 | 0 |
| Oakland Raiders | 8 | 8 | 0 |
| Seattle Seahawks | 8 | 8 | 0 |
| Kansas City Chiefs | 7 | 9 | 0 |
| San Diego Chargers | 5 | 11 | 0 |

---

In 1998, the Tennessee Oilers moved from Memphis to Nashville before the season started. Their new stadium was not ready, so the Oilers played their home games at Vanderbilt Stadium.

# 1998 - 1999 Playoffs

## NFC Playoffs

*Wild Card playoff* (in San Francisco) – San Francisco 49ers 30, Green Bay Packers 27

*Wild Card playoff* (in Dallas) – Arizona Cardinals 20, Dallas Cowboys 7

*Divisional playoff* (in Atlanta) – Atlanta Falcons 20, San Francisco 49ers 18

*Divisional playoff* (in Minneapolis) – Minnesota Vikings 41, Arizona Cardinals 21

NFC Championship (in Minneapolis) – Atlanta Falcons 30, Minnesota Vikings 27 (OT)

## AFC Playoffs

*Wild Card playoff* (in Jacksonville) – Jacksonville Jaguars 25, New England Patriots 10

*Wild Card playoff* (in Miami) – Miami Dolphins 24[32], Buffalo Bills 17

*Divisional playoff* (in Denver) – Denver Broncos 14, Kansas City Chiefs 10

*Divisional playoff* (in New York) – New York Jets 34, Jacksonville Jaguars 24

AFC Championship (in Denver) – Denver Broncos 23, New York Jets 10

---

The 1998 season was the first time four teams from one division, the AFC East, made the playoffs.

---

32    The Miami Dolphins finished ahead of the Buffalo Bills in the AFC East and for the first Wild Card (fourth seed) based on better net division points, 6 vs. 0.

# 1999 – Super Bowl XXXIII (33)
## Miami

**Denver Broncos** (AFC) defeat the Atlanta Falcons (NFC), 34-19.

## Season Awards

| | |
|---|---|
| *Most Valuable Player* | Terrell Davis, Running Back, Denver Broncos |
| *Coach of the Year* | Dan Reeves, Atlanta Falcons |
| *Offensive Player of the Year* | Terrell Davis, Running Back, Denver Broncos |
| *Defensive Player of the Year* | Reggie White, Defensive End, Green Bay Packers |
| *Offensive Rookie of the Year* | Randy Moss, Wide Receiver, Minnesota Vikings |
| *Defensive Rookie of the Year* | Charles Woodson, Cornerback, Oakland Raiders |
| *Comeback Player of the Year[33]* | Doug Flutie, Quarterback, Buffalo Bills |

---

33    The Associated Press renewed its "Comeback Player of the Year" award after the 1998 season.

## 1999 – National Football Conference

### Eastern Division

| Team | Win | Lost | Tie |
|------|-----|------|-----|
| Washington Redskins | 10 | 6 | 0 |
| Dallas Cowboys | 8 | 8 | 0 |
| New York Giants | 7 | 9 | 0 |
| Arizona Cardinals | 6 | 10 | 0 |
| Philadelphia Eagles | 5 | 11 | 0 |

### Central Division

| Team | Win | Lost | Tie |
|------|-----|------|-----|
| Tampa Bay Buccaneers | 11 | 5 | 0 |
| Minnesota Vikings | 10 | 6 | 0 |
| Detroit Lions | 8 | 8 | 0 |
| Green Bay Packers | 8 | 8 | 0 |
| Chicago Bears | 6 | 10 | 0 |

### Western Division

| Team | Win | Lost | Tie |
|------|-----|------|-----|
| St. Louis Rams | 13 | 3 | 0 |
| Carolina Panthers | 8 | 8 | 0 |
| Atlanta Falcons | 5 | 11 | 0 |
| San Francisco 49ers | 4 | 12 | 0 |
| New Orleans Saints | 3 | 13 | 0 |

---

The NFL reinstituted instant replay beginning with the 1999 season. This version of instant replay differed substantially from the prior system in effect from 1986 -1991. The key differences/improvements over past versions included:

- Cutting the number of challenges from three to two per half (to reduce delays).
- Coaches would be charged a timeout only for unsuccessful challenges.
- A replay assistant in the booth initiated all reviews inside the final two minutes of each half, taking the decision to challenge or not challenge a call out of the hands of the head coaches.

## 1999 – American Football Conference

## Eastern Division

| Team | Win | Lost | Tie |
|------|-----|------|-----|
| Indianapolis Colts | 13 | 3 | 0 |
| Buffalo Bills | 11 | 5 | 0 |
| Miami Dolphins | 9 | 7 | 0 |
| New York Jets | 8 | 8 | 0 |
| New England Patriots | 8 | 8 | 0 |

## Central Division

| Team | Win | Lost | Tie |
|------|-----|------|-----|
| Jacksonville Jaguars | 14 | 2 | 0 |
| Tennessee Titans | 13 | 3 | 0 |
| Baltimore Ravens | 8 | 8 | 0 |
| Pittsburgh Steelers | 4 | 12 | 0 |
| Cincinnati Bengals | 4 | 12 | 0 |
| Cleveland Browns | 2 | 14 | 0 |

## Western Division

| Team | Win | Lost | Tie |
|------|-----|------|-----|
| Seattle Seahawks | 9 | 7 | 0 |
| Kansas City Chiefs | 9 | 7 | 0 |
| San Diego Chargers | 8 | 8 | 0 |
| Oakland Raiders | 8 | 8 | 0 |
| Denver Broncos | 6 | 10 | 0 |

The Tennessee Oilers changed their name to the Tennessee Titans before the start of the season. The NFL retired the name "Oilers." The Titans kept a color scheme similar to the Oilers' colors.

NFL football returned to Cleveland when the expansion team the league awarded the city began play in the 1999 season. As previously agreed as part of the relocation of the original Cleveland franchise to Baltimore, the new Cleveland team kept the "Browns" name and colors, as well as all records of the previous Cleveland Browns teams. The addition of Cleveland and its placement in the AFC Central Division led to an uneven number of teams in the AFC and six teams in one division for the first time.

## 1999 - 2000 Playoffs

## NFC Playoffs

*Wild Card playoff* (in Washington) – Washington Redskins 27, Detroit Lions 13[34]

*Wild Card playoff* (in Minneapolis) – Minnesota Vikings 27, Dallas Cowboys 10[35]

*Divisional playoff* (in Tampa Bay) – Tampa Bay Buccaneers 14, Washington Redskins 13

*Divisional playoff* (in St. Louis) – St. Louis Rams 49, Minnesota Vikings 37

NFC Championship (in St. Louis) – St. Louis Rams 11, Tampa Bay Buccaneers 6

## AFC Playoffs

*Wild Card playoff* (in Nashville) – Tennessee Titans 22, Buffalo Bills 16

*Wild Card playoff* (in Seattle) – Miami Dolphins 20[36], Seattle Seahawks 17[37]

*Divisional playoff* (in Indianapolis) – Tennessee Titans 19, Indianapolis Colts 16

*Divisional playoff* (in Jacksonville) – Jacksonville Jaguars 62, Miami Dolphins 7 AFC
AFC Championship (in Jacksonville) – Tennessee Titans 33, Jacksonville Jaguars 14

---

34      The Detroit Lions were the NFC Wild Card third seed over the Green Bay Packers based on better conference record, 7–5 vs. 6–6, and over the Carolina Panthers based on a better conference record, 7–5 vs.6–6.

35      The Dallas Cowboys beat out the Detroit Lions for the NFC Wild Card second seed based on a better record against common opponents, 3-2 vs. 3-3, and the Carolina Panthers based on a better conference record, 7-5 vs. 6-6.

36      The Miami Dolphins beat out the Kansas City Chiefs for the AFC Wild Card third seed based on a better record against common opponents, 6-1 vs. 5-3.

37      The Seattle Seahawks topped the Kansas City Chiefs for the AFC West title based on a head-to-head sweep of their games.

## 2000– Super Bowl XXXIV (34)

## Atlanta

**St. Louis Rams** (NFC) defeat the Tennessee Titans (AFC), 23-16.

## Season Awards

| | |
|---|---|
| *Most Valuable Player* | Kurt Warner, Quarterback, St. Louis Rams |
| *Coach of the Year* | Dick Vermeil, St. Louis Rams |
| *Offensive Player of the Year* | Marshall Faulk, Running Back, St. Louis Rams |
| *Defensive Player of the Year* | Warren Sapp, Defensive Tackle, Tampa Bay Buccaneers |
| *Offensive Rookie of the Year* | Edgerrin James, Running Back, Indianapolis Colts |
| *Defensive Rookie of the Year* | Jevon Kearse, Defensive End, Tennessee Titans |
| *Comeback Player of the Year* | Bryant Young, Defensive Tackle, San Francisco 49ers |

---

The St. Louis Rams had nine losing seasons in a row before winning the Super Bowl in 2000, and laying a blueprint for other teams to follow in building a "worst to first" contender through free-agency, favorable scheduling, and a bit of luck (i.e., former grocery bagger Kurt Warner stepping up and leading the Rams to the promised land when starting quarterback Trent Green went down with a season ending injury in the third pre-season game of the season).

# 2000-2009

## 2000 – National Football Conference

## Eastern Division

| Team | Win | Lost | Tie |
| --- | --- | --- | --- |
| New York Giants | 12 | 4 | 0 |
| Philadelphia Eagles | 11 | 5 | 0 |
| Washington Redskins | 8 | 8 | 0 |
| Dallas Cowboys | 5 | 11 | 0 |
| Arizona Cardinals | 3 | 13 | 0 |

## Central Division

| Team | Win | Lost | Tie |
| --- | --- | --- | --- |
| Minnesota Vikings | 11 | 5 | 0 |
| Tampa Bay Buccaneers | 10 | 6 | 0 |
| Green Bay Packers | 9 | 7 | 0 |
| Detroit Lions | 9 | 7 | 0 |
| Chicago Bears | 5 | 11 | 0 |

## Western Division

| Team | Win | Lost | Tie |
| --- | --- | --- | --- |
| New Orleans Saints | 10 | 6 | 0 |
| St. Louis Rams | 10 | 6 | 0 |
| Carolina Panthers | 7 | 9 | 0 |
| San Francisco 49ers | 6 | 10 | 0 |
| Atlanta Falcons | 4 | 12 | 0 |

---

**Beginning with the 2000 season,** the NFL allowed any player wearing an eligible number, 1-49 and 80-89, to play quarterback without having to report to the referee before the play. This increased the number of trick plays teams could employ on offense, in particular the "Wildcat" formation where the quarterback lines up in a different position and another player (usually a running back or wide receiver) plays quarterback, trying to exploit mismatches caused by the formation. The 2008 Miami Dolphins made significant use of the play during that season.

## 2000 – American Football Conference

### Eastern Division

| Team | Win | Lost | Tie |
|------|-----|------|-----|
| Miami Dolphins | 11 | 5 | 0 |
| Indianapolis Colts | 10 | 6 | 0 |
| New York Jets | 9 | 7 | 0 |
| Buffalo Bills | 8 | 8 | 0 |
| New England Patriots | 5 | 11 | 0 |

### Central Division

| Team | Win | Lost | Tie |
|------|-----|------|-----|
| Tennessee Titans | 13 | 3 | 0 |
| Baltimore Ravens | 12 | 4 | 0 |
| Pittsburgh Steelers | 9 | 7 | 0 |
| Jacksonville Jaguars | 7 | 9 | 0 |
| Cincinnati Bengals | 4 | 12 | 0 |
| Cleveland Browns | 3 | 13 | 0 |

### Western Division

| Team | Win | Lost | Tie |
|------|-----|------|-----|
| Oakland Raiders | 12 | 4 | 0 |
| Denver Broncos | 11 | 5 | 0 |
| Kansas City Chiefs | 7 | 9 | 0 |
| Seattle Seahawks | 6 | 10 | 0 |
| San Diego Chargers | 1 | 15 | 0 |

## 2000-2001 Playoffs

## NFC Playoffs

*Wild Card playoff* (in New Orleans) – New Orleans Saints 31, St. Louis Rams 28

*Wild Card playoff* (in Philadelphia) – Philadelphia Eagles 21, Tampa Bay Buccaneers 3[1]

*Divisional playoff* (in Minneapolis) – Minnesota Vikings 34, New Orleans Saints 16[2]

*Divisional playoff* (in New York) – New York Giants 20, Philadelphia Eagles 10

NFC Championship (in New York) – New York Giants 41, Minnesota Vikings 0

## AFC Playoffs

*Wild Card playoff* (in Baltimore) – Baltimore Ravens 21, Denver Broncos 3

*Wild Card playoff* (in Miami) – Miami Dolphins 23, Indianapolis Colts 17 (OT)

*Divisional playoff* (in Nashville) – Baltimore Ravens 24, Tennessee Titans 10

*Divisional playoff* (in Oakland) – Oakland Raiders 27, Miami Dolphins 0

AFC Championship (in Oakland) – Baltimore Ravens 16, Oakland Raiders 3

---

1       The Tampa Bay Buccaneers were the NFC Wild Card second seed based on their head-to-head victory over the St. Louis Rams.

2       The New Orleans Saints beat out the St. Louis Ram for the NFC West title based on a better division record, 7-1 vs. 5-3.

# 2001– Super Bowl XXXV (35)

## Tampa

**Baltimore Ravens** (AFC) defeat the New York Giants (NFC), 34-7.

## Season Awards

*Most Valuable Player*              Marshall Faulk, Running Back, St. Louis Rams

*Coach of the Year*                  Jim Haslett, New Orleans Saints

*Offensive Player of the Year*       Marshall Faulk, Running Back, St. Louis Rams

*Defensive Player of the Year*       Ray Lewis, Linebacker, Baltimore Ravens

*Offensive Rookie of the Year*       Mike Anderson, Running Back,
                                     Denver Broncos

*Defensive Rookie of the Year*       Brian Urlacher, Linebacker, Chicago Bears

*Comeback Player of the Year*        Joe Johnson, Defensive End,
                                     New Orleans Saints

## 2001 – National Football Conference

## Eastern Division

| Team | Win | Lost | Tie |
| --- | --- | --- | --- |
| Philadelphia Eagles | 11 | 5 | 0 |
| Washington Redskins | 8 | 8 | 0 |
| New York Giants | 7 | 9 | 0 |
| Arizona Cardinals | 7 | 9 | 0 |
| Dallas Cowboys | 5 | 11 | 0 |

## Central Division

| Team | Win | Lost | Tie |
| --- | --- | --- | --- |
| Chicago Bears | 13 | 3 | 0 |
| Green Bay Packers | 12 | 4 | 0 |
| Tampa Bay Buccaneers | 9 | 7 | 0 |
| Minnesota Vikings | 5 | 11 | 0 |
| Detroit Lions | 2 | 14 | 0 |

## Western Division

| Team | Win | Lost | Tie |
| --- | --- | --- | --- |
| St. Louis Rams | 14 | 2 | 0 |
| San Francisco 49ers | 12 | 4 | 0 |
| New Orleans Saints | 7 | 9 | 0 |
| Atlanta Falcons | 7 | 9 | 0 |
| Carolina Panthers | 1 | 15 | 0 |

---

Due to the September 11, 2001 attacks on the United States, and not willing to repeat the error made after the assassination of President Kennedy, the NFL's games scheduled for September 16-17 were rescheduled to January 6-7. The Super Bowl was pushed out one week to allow the league to maintain its full regular season schedule and playoffs.

# 2001 – American Football Conference

## Eastern Division

| Team | Win | Lost | Tie |
|---|---|---|---|
| New England Patriots | 11 | 5 | 0 |
| Miami Dolphins | 11 | 5 | 0 |
| New York Jets | 10 | 6 | 0 |
| Indianapolis Colts | 6 | 10 | 0 |
| Buffalo Bills | 3 | 13 | 0 |

## Central Division

| Team | Win | Lost | Tie |
|---|---|---|---|
| Pittsburgh Steelers | 13 | 3 | 0 |
| Baltimore Ravens | 10 | 6 | 0 |
| Cleveland Browns | 7 | 9 | 0 |
| Tennessee Titans | 7 | 9 | 0 |
| Jacksonville Jaguars | 6 | 10 | 0 |
| Cincinnati Bengals | 6 | 10 | 0 |

## Western Division

| Team | Win | Lost | Tie |
|---|---|---|---|
| Oakland Raiders | 10 | 6 | 0 |
| Seattle Seahawks | 9 | 7 | 0 |
| Denver Broncos | 8 | 8 | 0 |
| Kansas City Chiefs | 6 | 10 | 0 |
| San Diego Chargers | 5 | 11 | 0 |

## 2001-2002 Playoffs

## NFC Playoffs

*Wild Card playoff* (in Tampa) – Philadelphia Eagles 31, Tampa Bay Buccaneers 9

*Wild Card playoff* (in Green Bay) – Green Bay Packers 25[3], San Francisco 49ers 15

*Divisional playoff* (in Chicago) – Philadelphia Eagles 33, Chicago Bears 19

*Divisional playoff* (in St. Louis) – St. Louis Rams 45, Green Bay Packers 17

NFC Championship (in St. Louis) – St. Louis Rams 29, Philadelphia Eagles 24

## AFC Playoffs

*Wild Card playoff* (in Oakland) – Oakland Raiders 38, New York Jets 24

*Wild Card playoff* (in Miami) – Baltimore Ravens 20[4], Miami Dolphins 3

*Divisional playoff* (in Boston) – New England Patriots 16[5], Oakland Raiders 13 (OT)

*Divisional playoff* (in Pittsburgh) – Pittsburgh Steelers 27, Baltimore Ravens 10

AFC Championship (in Pittsburgh) – New England Patriots 24, Pittsburgh Steelers 17

---

3          The Green Bay Packers were the NFC Wild Card first seed over the San Francisco 49ers based on a better conference record, 9-3 vs. 8-4.

4          The Baltimore Ravens were the AFC Wild Card second seed over the New York Jets based on a better record against common opponents, 3-2 vs. 2-2.

5          The New England Patriots beat the Miami Dolphins for the AFC East title based on a better division record, 6-2 v. 5-3.

# 2002– Super Bowl XXXVI (36)

## New Orleans

**New England Patriots** (AFC) defeat the St. Louis Rams (NFC), 20-17.

## Season Awards

| | |
|---|---|
| *Most Valuable Player* | Kurt Warner, Quarterback, St. Louis Rams |
| *Coach of the Year* | Dick Jauron, Chicago Bears |
| *Offensive Player of the Year* | Marshall Faulk, Running Back, St. Louis Rams |
| *Defensive Player of the Year* | Michael Strahan, Defensive End, New York Giants |
| *Offensive Rookie of the Year* | Anthony Thomas, Running Back, Chicago Bears |
| *Defensive Rookie of the Year* | Kendrell Bell, Linebacker, Pittsburgh Steelers |
| *Comeback Player of the Year* | Garrison Hearst, Running Back, San Francisco 49ers |

## 2002 – National Football Conference

### East Division

| Team | Win | Lost | Tie |
|---|---|---|---|
| Philadelphia Eagles | 12 | 4 | 0 |
| New York Giants | 10 | 6 | 0 |
| Washington Redskins | 7 | 9 | 0 |
| Dallas Cowboys | 5 | 11 | 0 |

### North Division

| Team | Win | Lost | Tie |
|---|---|---|---|
| Green Bay Packers | 12 | 4 | 0 |
| Minnesota Vikings | 6 | 10 | 0 |
| Chicago Bears | 4 | 12 | 0 |
| Detroit Lions | 3 | 13 | 0 |

### South Division

| Team | Win | Lost | Tie |
|---|---|---|---|
| Tampa Bay Buccaneers | 12 | 4 | 0 |
| Atlanta Falcons | 9 | 6 | 1 |
| New Orleans Saints | 9 | 7 | 0 |
| Carolina Panthers | 7 | 9 | 0 |

### West Division

| Team | Win | Lost | Tie |
|---|---|---|---|
| San Francisco 49ers | 10 | 6 | 0 |
| St. Louis Rams | 7 | 9 | 0 |
| Seattle Seahawks | 7 | 9 | 0 |
| Arizona Cardinals | 5 | 11 | 0 |

There were major alignment changes in the NFL to begin the 2002 season. The Houston Texans were added as the 32nd franchise and the league realigned each conference into four divisions of four teams each. The Seattle Seahawks moved from the AFC West to the NFC West. The Seahawks played their inaugural season in the NFC before moving to the AFC and now moved back to the NFC. The AFC Central and NFC Central divisions were renamed the "North", leaving four geographically based divisions in each conference: East, North, South, and West, with teams placed in their natural geographic region. The playoffs were modified to four division winners and two wild cards from each league (though the number of teams in the playoffs remained the same). Based on record, the division winners were seeded 1-4 and the Wild Card winners were seeded 5-6. The top two seeds received a bye and the remaining four teams play 1 vs. 4 and 2 vs. 3 with the higher seeds hosting the playoff game.

**Changes in the NFC**: In addition to the Seattle Seahawks move from the AFC West to the NFC West. The Arizona Cardinals moved from the NFC East to the NFC West. The Atlanta Falcons, Carolina Panthers, New Orleans Saints, and Tampa Bay Buccaneers moved to the newly formed NFC South.

**Changes in the AFC**: The Indianapolis Colts, Jacksonville Jaguars, Tennessee Titans moved to the newly formed AFC South. The Houston Texans expansion team was placed in the AFC South as well.

# 2002 – American Football Conference

## East Division

| Team | Win | Lost | Tie |
|------|-----|------|-----|
| New York Jets | 9 | 7 | 0 |
| New England Patriots | 9 | 7 | 0 |
| Miami Dolphins | 9 | 7 | 0 |
| Buffalo Bills | 8 | 8 | 0 |

## North Division

| Team | Win | Lost | Tie |
|------|-----|------|-----|
| Pittsburgh Steelers | 10 | 5 | 1 |
| Cleveland Browns | 9 | 7 | 0 |
| Baltimore Ravens | 7 | 9 | 0 |
| Cincinnati Bengals | 2 | 14 | 0 |

## South Division

| Team | Win | Lost | Tie |
|------|-----|------|-----|
| Tennessee Titans | 11 | 5 | 0 |
| Indianapolis Colts | 10 | 6 | 0 |
| Jacksonville Jaguars | 6 | 10 | 0 |
| Houston Texas | 4 | 12 | 0 |

## West Division

| Team | Win | Lost | Tie |
|------|-----|------|-----|
| Oakland Raiders | 11 | 5 | 0 |
| Denver Broncos | 9 | 7 | 0 |
| San Diego Chargers | 8 | 8 | 0 |
| Kansas City Chiefs | 8 | 8 | 0 |

---

The Houston Texans' new stadium, Reliant Stadium, was the first NFL stadium with a retractable roof. The NFL developed special rules for stadiums with retractable roofs: a) the home team must decide to have the roof open or closed at least 90 minutes before kick-off; b) if the roof is closed at kick-off, it cannot be opened during the game; and c) if open at kick-off, the roof can only be closed in the event of severe weather conditions.

# 2002-2003 Playoffs

## NFC Playoffs

*Wild Card playoff* (in San Francisco) – San Francisco 49ers 39, New York Giants 38

*Wild Card playoff* (in Green Bay) – Atlanta Falcons 27, Green Bay Packers 7

*Divisional playoff* (in Tampa) – Tampa Bay Buccaneers 31, San Francisco 49ers 6

*Divisional playoff* (in Philadelphia) – Philadelphia Eagles 20[6], Atlanta Falcons 6

NFC Championship (in Philadelphia) – Tampa Bay Buccaneers 27, Philadelphia Eagles 10

## AFC Playoffs

*Wild Card playoff* (in Pittsburgh) – Pittsburgh Steelers 36, Cleveland Browns 33[7]

*Wild Card playoff* (in New York) – New York Jets 41[8], Indianapolis Colts 0

*Divisional playoff* (in Nashville) – Tennessee Titans 34, Pittsburgh Steelers 31 (OT)

*Divisional playoff* (in Oakland) – Oakland Raiders 30[9], New York Jets 10

AFC Championship (in Oakland) – Oakland Raiders 41, Tennessee Titans 24

---

6      The Philadelphia Eagles secured the NFC number one seed over the Green Bay Packers and the Tampa Bay Buccaneers based on a better conference record, 11-1 vs. 9-3 vs. 9-3. The Buccaneers won the NFC second seed over the Packers based on a head-to-head victory.

7      The Cleveland Browns won the last AFC Wild Card slot over the Denver Broncos and the New England Patriots based on a better conference record, 7-5 vs. 5-7 vs. 6-6.

8      The New York Jets beat out the New England Patriots for the AFC East title based on a better record in games against common opponents, 8-4 vs. 7-5, and over the Miami Dolphins based on a better division record, 4-2 vs. 2-4. The Patriots finished ahead of the Dolphins based on a better division record, 4-2 vs. 2-4.

9      The Oakland Raiders won the AFC number one seed over the Tennessee Titans based on a head-to-head victory.

# 2003– Super Bowl XXXVII (37)
## San Diego

**Tampa Bay Buccaneers** (NFC) defeat the Oakland Raiders (AFC), 48-21.

## Season Awards

| | |
|---|---|
| *Most Valuable Player* | Rich Gannon, Quarterback, Oakland Raiders |
| *Coach of the Year* | Andy Reid, Philadelphia Eagles |
| *Offensive Player of the Year* | Priest Holmes, Running Back, Kansas City Chiefs |
| *Defensive Player of the Year* | Derrick Brooks, Linebacker, Tampa Bay Buccaneers |
| *Offensive Rookie of the Year* | Clinton Portis, Running Back, Denver Broncos |
| *Defensive Rookie of the Year* | Julius Peppers, Defensive End, Carolina Panthers |
| *Comeback Player of the Year* | Tommy Maddox, Quarterback, Pittsburgh Steelers |

# 2003 – National Football Conference

## East Division

| Team | Win | Lost | Tie |
|------|-----|------|-----|
| Philadelphia Eagles | 12 | 4 | 0 |
| Dallas Cowboys | 10 | 6 | 0 |
| Washington Redskins | 5 | 11 | 0 |
| New York Giants | 4 | 12 | 0 |

## North Division

| Team | Win | Lost | Tie |
|------|-----|------|-----|
| Green Bay Packers | 10 | 6 | 0 |
| Minnesota Vikings | 9 | 7 | 0 |
| Chicago Bears | 7 | 9 | 0 |
| Detroit Lions | 5 | 11 | 0 |

## South Division

| Team | Win | Lost | Tie |
|------|-----|------|-----|
| Carolina Panthers | 11 | 5 | 0 |
| New Orleans Saints | 8 | 8 | 0 |
| Tampa Bay Buccaneers | 7 | 9 | 0 |
| Atlanta Falcons | 5 | 11 | 0 |

## West Division

| Team | Win | Lost | Tie |
|------|-----|------|-----|
| St. Louis Rams | 12 | 4 | 0 |
| Seattle Seahawks | 10 | 6 | 0 |
| San Francisco | 7 | 9 | 0 |
| Arizona Cardinals | 4 | 12 | 0 |

# 2003 – American Football Conference

## East Division

| Team | Win | Lost | Tie |
|---|---|---|---|
| New England Patriots | 14 | 2 | 0 |
| Miami Dolphins | 10 | 6 | 0 |
| Buffalo Bills | 6 | 10 | 0 |
| New York Jets | 6 | 10 | 0 |

## North Division

| Team | Win | Lost | Tie |
|---|---|---|---|
| Baltimore Ravens | 10 | 6 | 0 |
| Cincinnati Bengals | 8 | 8 | 0 |
| Pittsburgh Steelers | 6 | 10 | 0 |
| Cleveland Browns | 5 | 11 | 0 |

## South Division

| Team | Win | Lost | Tie |
|---|---|---|---|
| Indianapolis Colts | 12 | 4 | 0 |
| Tennessee Titans | 12 | 4 | 0 |
| Jacksonville Jaguars | 5 | 11 | 0 |
| Houston Texas | 5 | 11 | 0 |

## West Division

| Team | Win | Lost | Tie |
|---|---|---|---|
| Kansas City Chiefs | 13 | 3 | 0 |
| Denver Broncos | 10 | 6 | 0 |
| Oakland Raiders | 4 | 12 | 0 |
| San Diego Chargers | 4 | 12 | 0 |

## 2003-2004 Playoffs

## NFC Playoffs

*Wild Card playoff* (in Charlotte) – Carolina Panthers 29, Dallas Cowboys 10

*Wild Card playoff* (in Green Bay) – Green Bay Packers 33, Seattle Seahawks 27 (OT)

*Divisional playoff* (in St. Louis) – Carolina Panthers 29, St. Louis Rams 23 (2OT)

*Divisional playoff* (in Philadelphia) – Philadelphia Eagles 20, Green Bay Packers 17 (OT)

NFC Championship (in Philadelphia) – Carolina Panthers 14, Philadelphia Eagles 3

## AFC Playoffs

*Wild Card playoff* (in Indianapolis) – Indianapolis Colts 41[10], Denver Broncos 10[11]

*Wild Card playoff* (in Baltimore) – Tennessee Titans 20, Baltimore Ravens 17

*Divisional playoff* (in Kansas City) – Indianapolis Colts 38, Kansas City Chiefs 31

*Divisional playoff* (in Boston) – New England Patriots 17, Tennessee Titans 14

AFC Championship (in Boston) – New England Patriots 24, Indianapolis Colts 14

---

10      The Indianapolis Colts beat out the Tennessee Titans for the AFC South title based on a sweep of their head-to-head games.

11      The Denver Broncos beat the Miami Dolphins for the AFC sixth seed (second Wild Card) based on a better conference record, 9-3 vs. 7-5.

# 2004– Super Bowl XXXVIII (38)

## Houston

**New England Patriots** (AFC) defeat the Carolina Panthers (NFC), 32-29.

## Season Awards

| | |
|---|---|
| *Most Valuable Player* | Peyton Manning, Quarterback, Indianapolis Colts and Steve McNair, Quarterback, Tennessee Titans (tie) |
| *Coach of the Year* | Bill Belichick, New England Patriots |
| *Offensive Player of the Year* | Jamal Lewis, Running Back, Baltimore Ravens |
| *Defensive Player of the Year* | Ray Lewis, Linebacker, Baltimore Ravens |
| *Offensive Rookie of the Year* | Anquan Boldin, Wide Receiver, Arizona Cardinals |
| *Defensive Rookie of the Year* | Terrell Suggs, Linebacker, Baltimore Ravens |
| *Comeback Player of the Year* | Jon Kitna, Quarterback, Cincinnati Bengals |

## 2004  – National Football Conference

### East Division

| Team | Win | Lost | Tie |
|------|-----|------|-----|
| Philadelphia Eagles | 13 | 3 | 0 |
| New York Giants | 6 | 10 | 0 |
| Dallas Cowboys | 6 | 10 | 0 |
| Washington Redskins | 6 | 10 | 0 |

### North Division

| Team | Win | Lost | Tie |
|------|-----|------|-----|
| Green Bay Packers | 10 | 6 | 0 |
| Minnesota Vikings | 8 | 8 | 0 |
| Detroit Lions | 6 | 10 | 0 |
| Chicago Bears | 5 | 11 | 0 |

### South Division

| Team | Win | Lost | Tie |
|------|-----|------|-----|
| Atlanta Falcons | 11 | 5 | 0 |
| New Orleans Saints | 8 | 8 | 0 |
| Carolina Panthers | 7 | 9 | 0 |
| Tampa Bay Buccaneers | 5 | 11 | 0 |

### West Division

| Team | Win | Lost | Tie |
|------|-----|------|-----|
| Seattle Seahawks | 9 | 7 | 0 |
| St. Louis Rams | 8 | 8 | 0 |
| Arizona Cardinals | 6 | 10 | 0 |
| San Francisco 49ers | 2 | 14 | 0 |

---

The NFL changed its rules to allow wide receivers to wear jersey numbers 10-19 in addition to 80-89. Additionally, the NFL banned the iconic "single-bar" facemask beginning with the 2004 season (with several players - primarily kickers - "grandfathered" to continue to use the single bar for several additional seasons).

## 2004 – American Football Conference

### East Division

| Team | Win | Lost | Tie |
| --- | --- | --- | --- |
| New England Patriots | 14 | 2 | 0 |
| New York Jets | 10 | 6 | 0 |
| Buffalo Bills | 9 | 7 | 0 |
| Miami Dolphins | 4 | 12 | 0 |

### North Division

| Team | Win | Lost | Tie |
| --- | --- | --- | --- |
| Pittsburgh Steelers | 15 | 1 | 0 |
| Baltimore Ravens | 9 | 7 | 0 |
| Cincinnati Bengals | 8 | 8 | 0 |
| Cleveland Browns | 4 | 12 | 0 |

### South Division

| Team | Win | Lost | Tie |
| --- | --- | --- | --- |
| Indianapolis Colts | 12 | 4 | 0 |
| Jacksonville Jaguars | 9 | 7 | 0 |
| Houston Texans | 7 | 9 | 0 |
| Tennessee Titans | 5 | 11 | 0 |

### West Division

| Team | Win | Lost | Tie |
| --- | --- | --- | --- |
| San Diego Chargers | 12 | 4 | 0 |
| Denver Broncos | 10 | 6 | 0 |
| Kansas City Chiefs | 7 | 9 | 0 |
| Oakland Raiders | 5 | 11 | 0 |

## 2004-2005 Playoffs

## NFC Playoffs

*Wild Card playoff* (in Seattle) – St. Louis Rams 27[12], Seattle Seahawks 20

*Wild Card playoff* (in Green Bay) – Minnesota Vikings 31, Green Bay Packers 17

*Divisional playoff* (in Atlanta) – Atlanta Falcons 47, St. Louis Rams 17

*Divisional playoff* (in Philadelphia) – Philadelphia Eagles 27, Minnesota Vikings 14

NFC Championship (in Philadelphia) – Philadelphia Eagles 27, Atlanta Falcons 10

## AFC Playoffs

*Wild Card playoff* (in Indianapolis) – Indianapolis Colts 49[13], Denver Broncos 24

*Wild Card playoff* (in San Diego) – New York Jets 20[14], San Diego Chargers 17 (OT)

*Divisional playoff* (in Pittsburgh) – Pittsburgh Steelers 20, New York Jets 17 (OT)

*Divisional playoff* (in Boston) – New England Patriots 20, Indianapolis Colts 3

AFC Championship (in Pittsburgh) – New England Patriots 41, Pittsburgh Steelers 27

---

12      The St. Louis Rams took the NFC fifth seed (first Wild Card) over the Minnesota Vikings and New Orleans Saints based on a better conference record, 7-5 vs. 5-7 vs. 6-6. The Vikings beat out the Saints for the NFC sixth seed (second Wild Card) based on winning their head-to-head game.

13      The Indianapolis Colts beat the San Diego Chargers for the AFC third seed based on winning their head-to-head game.

14      The New York Jets won the AFC fifth seed (first Wild Card) over the Denver Broncos based on a better record in common games, 5-0 vs. 3-2.

# 2005– Super Bowl XXXIX (39)

# Jacksonville

**New England Patriots** (AFC) defeat the Philadelphia Eagles (NFC), 24-21.

## Season Awards

| | |
|---|---|
| *Most Valuable Player* | Peyton Manning, Quarterback, Indianapolis Colts |
| *Coach of the Year* | Marty Shottenheimer, San Diego Chargers |
| *Offensive Player of the Year* | Peyton Manning, Quarterback, Indianapolis Colts |
| *Defensive Player of the Year* | Ed Reed, Safety, Baltimore Ravens |
| *Offensive Rookie of the Year* | Ben Roethlisberger, Quarterback, Pittsburgh Steelers |
| *Defensive Rookie of the Year* | Jonathan Vilma, Linebacker, New York Jets |
| *Comeback Player of the Year* | Drew Brees, Quarterback, San Diego Chargers |

## 2005 – National Football Conference

### East Division

| Team | Win | Lost | Tie |
|------|-----|------|-----|
| New York Giants | 11 | 5 | 0 |
| Washington Redskins | 10 | 6 | 0 |
| Dallas Cowboys | 9 | 7 | 0 |
| Philadelphia Eagles | 6 | 10 | 0 |

### North Division

| Team | Win | Lost | Tie |
|------|-----|------|-----|
| Chicago Bears | 11 | 5 | 0 |
| Minnesota Vikings | 9 | 7 | 0 |
| Detroit Lions | 5 | 11 | 0 |
| Green Bay Packers | 4 | 12 | 0 |

### South Division

| Team | Win | Lost | Tie |
|------|-----|------|-----|
| Tampa Bay Buccaneers | 11 | 5 | 0 |
| Carolina Panthers | 11 | 5 | 0 |
| Atlanta Falcons | 8 | 8 | 0 |
| New Orleans Saints | 3 | 13 | 0 |

### West Division

| Team | Win | Lost | Tie |
|------|-----|------|-----|
| Seattle Seahawks | 13 | 3 | 0 |
| St. Louis Rams | 6 | 10 | 0 |
| Arizona Cardinals | 5 | 11 | 0 |
| San Francisco 49ers | 4 | 12 | 0 |

The 2005 season marked the first time the NFL played a regular season game outside the United States. In October 2005, the Arizona Cardinals and San Francisco 49ers played in Mexico City before 103,467 fans. The Cardinals were the "home" team and won 31-14. Due to the damage caused by Hurricane Katrina, the New Orleans Saints played their 2005 home games in San Antonio, Texas, Baton Rouge, Louisiana, and New York City (East Rutherford, NJ).

## 2005  – American Football Conference

### East Division

| Team | Win | Lost | Tie |
|---|---|---|---|
| New England Patriots | 10 | 6 | 0 |
| Miami Dolphins | 9 | 7 | 0 |
| Buffalo Bills | 5 | 11 | 0 |
| New York Jets | 4 | 12 | 0 |

### North Division

| Team | Win | Lost | Tie |
|---|---|---|---|
| Cincinnati Bengals | 11 | 5 | 0 |
| Pittsburgh Steelers | 11 | 5 | 0 |
| Baltimore Ravens | 6 | 10 | 0 |
| Cleveland Browns | 6 | 10 | 0 |

### South Division

| Team | Win | Lost | Tie |
|---|---|---|---|
| Indianapolis Colts | 14 | 2 | 0 |
| Jacksonville Jaguars | 12 | 4 | 0 |
| Tennessee Titans | 4 | 12 | 0 |
| Houston Texans | 2 | 14 | 0 |

### West Division

| Team | Win | Lost | Tie |
|---|---|---|---|
| Denver Broncos | 13 | 3 | 0 |
| Kansas City Chiefs | 10 | 6 | 0 |
| San Diego Chargers | 9 | 7 | 0 |
| Oakland Raiders | 4 | 12 | 0 |

## 2005-2006 Playoffs

## NFC Playoffs

*Wild Card playoff* (in New York) – Carolina Panthers 23, New York Giants 0

*Wild Card playoff* (in Tampa) – Washington Redskins 17, Tampa Bay Buccaneers 10[15]

*Divisional playoff* (in Chicago) – Carolina Panthers 29, Chicago Bears 21[16]

*Divisional playoff* (in Seattle) – Seattle Seahawks 20, Washington Redskins 10

NFC Championship (in Seattle) – Seattle Seahawks 34, Carolina Panthers 14

## AFC Playoffs

*Wild Card playoff* (in Cincinnati) – Pittsburgh Steelers 31, Cincinnati Bengals 17[17]

*Wild Card playoff* (in Boston) – New England Patriots 28, Jacksonville Jaguars 3

*Divisional playoff* (in Indianapolis) – Pittsburgh Steelers 21, Indianapolis Colts 18

*Divisional playoff* (in Denver) – Denver Broncos 27, New England Patriots 13

AFC Championship (in Denver) – Pittsburgh Steelers 34, Denver Broncos 17

---

15    The Tampa Bay Buccaneers won the NFC South over the Carolina Panthers based on a better division record, 5-1 vs. 4-2

16    The Chicago Bears won the NFC second seed over the Buccaneers and the New York Giants based on a better conference record, 10-2 vs. 9-3 vs. 8-4. The Buccaneers took the NFC third seed over the Giants based on a better conference record, 9-3 vs. 8-4.

17    The Cincinnati Bengals won the AFC North over the Pittsburgh Steelers based on a better division record, 5-1 vs. 4-2.

## 2006– Super Bowl XL (40)

## Detroit

**Pittsburgh Steelers** (AFC) defeat the Seattle Seahawks (NFC), 21-10.

## Season Awards

| | |
|---|---|
| *Most Valuable Player* | Shaun Alexander, Running Back, Seattle Seahawks |
| *Coach of the Year* | Lovie Smith, Chicago Bears |
| *Offensive Player of the Year* | Shaun Alexander, Running Back, Seattle Seahawks |
| *Defensive Player of the Year* | Brian Urlacher, Linebacker, Chicago Bears |
| *Offensive Rookie of the Year* | Carnell Williams, Running Back, Tampa Bay Buccaneers |
| *Defensive Rookie of the Year* | Shawne Merriman, Linebacker, San Diego Chargers |
| *Comeback Player of the Year* | Tedy Bruschi, Linebacker, New England Patriots Steve Smith, Wide Receiver, Carolina Panthers (tie) |

---

The Pittsburgh Steelers were the AFC sixth seed. They became the first NFL team to win three straight playoff games on the road to advance and win the Super Bowl.

# 2006 – National Football Conference

## East Division

| Team | Win | Lost | Tie |
|------|-----|------|-----|
| Philadelphia Eagles | 10 | 6 | 0 |
| Dallas Cowboys | 9 | 7 | 0 |
| New York Giants | 8 | 8 | 0 |
| Washington Redskins | 5 | 11 | 0 |

## North Division

| Team | Win | Lost | Tie |
|------|-----|------|-----|
| Chicago Bears | 13 | 3 | 0 |
| Green Bay Packers | 8 | 8 | 0 |
| Minnesota Vikings | 6 | 10 | 0 |
| Detroit Lions | 3 | 13 | 0 |

## South Division

| Team | Win | Lost | Tie |
|------|-----|------|-----|
| New Orleans Saints | 10 | 6 | 0 |
| Carolina Panthers | 8 | 8 | 0 |
| Atlanta Falcons | 7 | 9 | 0 |
| Tampa Bay Buccaneers | 4 | 12 | 0 |

## West Division

| Team | Win | Lost | Tie |
|------|-----|------|-----|
| Seattle Seahawks | 9 | 7 | 0 |
| St. Louis Rams | 8 | 8 | 0 |
| Arizona Cardinals | 7 | 9 | 0 |
| San Francisco 49ers | 5 | 11 | 0 |

---

The NFL implemented flexible-scheduling for the 2006 season whereby the league could select the games to air on *Sunday Night Football* (NBC's reentry into NFL broadcasting) over the last few weeks of the season. This allowed the league to feature more attractive games for the prime time audience. Previously, teams were "locked in" to a television schedule at the start of the season, often leading to the league featuring meaningless games in prime time. Prior to the start of the season, Commissioner Paul Tagliabue announced his retirement. Roger Goodell was selected as Commissioner in August 2006. The NFL Network began broadcasting select NFL games exclusively after Thanksgiving, causing a major confrontation with various cable network providers over the cost and location of the channel. The New Orleans Saints returned to the Super Dome for the 2006 season after it was repaired from the Hurricane Katrina damage of 2005.

## 2006  – American Football Conference

### East Division

| Team | Win | Lost | Tie |
|---|---|---|---|
| New England Patriots | 12 | 4 | 0 |
| New York Jets | 10 | 6 | 0 |
| Buffalo Bills | 7 | 9 | 0 |
| Miami Dolphins | 6 | 10 | 0 |

### North Division

| Team | Win | Lost | Tie |
|---|---|---|---|
| Baltimore Ravens | 13 | 3 | 0 |
| Cincinnati Bengals | 8 | 8 | 0 |
| Pittsburgh Steelers | 8 | 8 | 0 |
| Cleveland Browns | 4 | 12 | 0 |

### South Division

| Team | Win | Lost | Tie |
|---|---|---|---|
| Indianapolis Colts | 12 | 4 | 0 |
| Tennessee Titans | 8 | 8 | 0 |
| Jacksonville Jaguars | 8 | 8 | 0 |
| Houston Texans | 6 | 10 | 0 |

### West Division

| Team | Win | Lost | Tie |
|---|---|---|---|
| San Diego Chargers | 14 | 2 | 0 |
| Kansas City Chiefs | 9 | 7 | 0 |
| Denver Broncos | 9 | 7 | 0 |
| Oakland Raiders | 2 | 14 | 0 |

---

Kansas Chiefs Owner and founder of the AFL, Lamar Hunt, passed away on December 13, 2006. Not only was Hunt instrumental in the formation of the AFL, he led the AFL side in the 1966 merger discussions with the NFL. The AFC Championship trophy is named after Hunt. The NFC Championship trophy is named after George Halas, a founder of the NFL, owner of the Chicago Bears, and longtime Bears player and coach. The Super Bowl trophy is named after legendary Green Bay Packer coach Vince Lombardi.

## 2006-2007 Playoffs

## NFC Playoffs

*Wild Card playoff* (in Philadelphia) – Philadelphia Eagles 23, New York Giants 20[18]

*Wild Card playoff* (in Seattle) – Seattle Seahawks 21, Dallas Cowboys 20

*Divisional playoff* (in New Orleans) – New Orleans Saints 27[19], Philadelphia Eagles 24

*Divisional playoff* (in Chicago) – Chicago Bears 27, Seattle Seahawks 24 (OT)

NFC Championship (in Chicago) – Chicago Bears 39, New Orleans Saints 14

## AFC Playoffs

*Wild Card playoff* (in Boston) – New England Patriots 37, New York Jets 16

*Wild Card playoff* (in Indianapolis) – Indianapolis Colts 23[20], Kansas City Chiefs 8[21]

*Divisional playoff* (in San Diego) – New England Patriots 24, San Diego Chargers 21

*Divisional playoff* (in Baltimore) – Indianapolis Colts 15, Baltimore Ravens 6

AFC Championship (in Indianapolis) – Indianapolis Colts 38, New England Patriots 34

---

18      The New York Giants won the NFC second Wild Card (sixth seed) over the Green Bay Packers based on strength of victory, .422 vs. .383. "Strength of victory" is figured by calculating the combined winning percentage of the opponents a team has beaten. The Carolina Panthers and St. Louis Rams were eliminated from the playoffs due to the Giants and Packers having better conference records, 7-5 vs. 6-6.

19      The New Orleans Saints won the NFC second seed over the Philadelphia Eagles based on a head-to-head victory.

20      The Indianapolis Colts won the AFC third seed over the New England Patriots based on a head-to-head victory.

21      The Kansas City Chiefs finished ahead of the Denver Broncos for the second AFC Wild Card (sixth seed) based on a better division record, 4-2 vs. 2-4.

# 2007– Super Bowl XLI (41)

## Miami

**Indianapolis Colts** (AFC) defeat the Chicago Bears (NFC), 29-17.

## Season Awards

| | |
|---|---|
| *Most Valuable Player* | LaDainian Tomlinson, Running Back, San Diego Chargers |
| *Coach of the Year* | Sean Payton, New Orleans Saints |
| *Offensive Player of the Year* | LaDainian Tomlinson, Running Back, San Diego Chargers |
| *Defensive Player of the Year* | Jason Taylor, Defensive End, Miami Dolphins |
| *Offensive Rookie of the Year* | Vince Young, Quarterback, Tennessee Titans |
| *Defensive Rookie of the Year* | DeMeco Ryans, Linebacker, Houston Texans |
| *Comeback Player of the Year* | Chad Pennington, Quarterback, New York Jets |

## 2007 – National Football Conference

## East Division

| Team | Win | Lost | Tie |
|------|-----|------|-----|
| Dallas Cowboys | 13 | 3 | 0 |
| New York Giants | 10 | 6 | 0 |
| Washington Redskins | 9 | 7 | 0 |
| Philadelphia Eagles | 8 | 8 | 0 |

## North Division

| Team | Win | Lost | Tie |
|------|-----|------|-----|
| Green Bay Packers | 13 | 3 | 0 |
| Minnesota Vikings | 8 | 8 | 0 |
| Detroit Lions | 7 | 9 | 0 |
| Chicago Bears | 7 | 9 | 0 |

## South Division

| Team | Win | Lost | Tie |
|------|-----|------|-----|
| Tampa Bay Buccaneers | 9 | 7 | 0 |
| Carolina Panthers | 7 | 9 | 0 |
| New Orleans Saints | 7 | 9 | 0 |
| Atlanta Falcons | 4 | 12 | 0 |

## West Division

| Team | Win | Lost | Tie |
|------|-----|------|-----|
| Seattle Seahawks | 10 | 6 | 0 |
| Arizona Cardinals | 8 | 8 | 0 |
| San Francisco 49ers | 5 | 11 | 0 |
| St. Louis Rams | 3 | 13 | 0 |

The league made a rule change prior to the 2007 season. Previously, a touchdown was scored if the player with the ball had some portion of his body over the goal line or a corner pylon. After the change, the ball needed to touch the pylon or "break the plane" of the goal line to count as a touchdown.

## 2007 – American Football Conference

### East Division

| Team | Win | Lost | Tie |
|------|-----|------|-----|
| New England Patriots | 16 | 0 | 0 |
| Buffalo Bills | 7 | 9 | 0 |
| New York Jets | 4 | 12 | 0 |
| Miami Dolphins | 1 | 15 | 0 |

### North Division

| Team | Win | Lost | Tie |
|------|-----|------|-----|
| Pittsburgh Steelers | 10 | 6 | 0 |
| Cleveland Browns | 10 | 6 | 0 |
| Cincinnati Bengals | 7 | 9 | 0 |
| Baltimore Ravens | 5 | 11 | 0 |

### South Division

| Team | Win | Lost | Tie |
|------|-----|------|-----|
| Indianapolis Colts | 13 | 3 | 0 |
| Jacksonville Jaguars | 11 | 5 | 0 |
| Tennessee Titans | 10 | 6 | 0 |
| Houston Texans | 8 | 8 | 0 |

### West Division

| Team | Win | Lost | Tie |
|------|-----|------|-----|
| San Diego Chargers | 11 | 5 | 0 |
| Denver Broncos | 7 | 9 | 0 |
| Kansas City Chiefs | 4 | 12 | 0 |
| Oakland Raiders | 4 | 12 | 0 |

---

The New England Patriots were the first NFL team to go undefeated during the regular season since the league expanded to a 16-game regular season schedule. The Miami Dolphins went undefeated in a 14-game schedule in 1972. Unlike the Dolphins however, the Patriots lost in the Super Bowl to the decided underdog New York Giants.

## 2007-2008 Playoffs

## NFC Playoffs

*Wild Card playoff* (in Tampa Bay) – New York Giants 24, Tampa Bay Buccaneers 14

*Wild Card playoff* (in Seattle) – Seattle Seahawks 35, Washington Redskins 14

*Divisional playoff* (in Dallas) – New York Giants 21, Dallas Cowboys 17[22]

*Divisional playoff* (in Green Bay) – Green Bay Packers 42, Seattle Seahawks 20

NFC Championship (in Green Bay) – New York Giants 23, Green Bay Packers 20 (OT)

## AFC Playoffs

*Wild Card playoff* (in San Diego) – San Diego Chargers 17, Tennessee Titans 6[23]

*Wild Card playoff* (in Pittsburgh) – Jacksonville Jaguars 31, Pittsburgh Steelers 29[24]

*Divisional playoff* (in Indianapolis) – San Diego Chargers 28, Indianapolis Colts 24

*Divisional playoff* (in Boston) – New England Patriots 31, Jacksonville Jaguars 20

AFC Championship (in Boston) – New England Patriots 21, San Diego Chargers 12

---

22    The Dallas Cowboys won the NFC overall first seed over the Green Bay Packers based on its head-to-head win over the Packers.

23    The Tennessee Titans won the second AFC Wildcard (sixth seed) over the Cleveland Browns based on a better record against common opponents, 4-1 vs. 3-2.

24    The Pittsburgh Steelers won the AFC North title over the Cleveland Browns based on a sweep of their head-to-head games.

# 2008– Super Bowl XLII (42)

## Phoenix

**New York Giants** (NFC) defeat the New England Patriots (AFC), 17-14.

## Season Awards

| | |
|---|---|
| *Most Valuable Player* | Tom Brady, Quarterback, New England Patriots |
| *Coach of the Year* | Bill Belichick, New England Patriots |
| *Offensive Player of the Year* | Tom Brady, Quarterback, New England Patriots |
| *Defensive Player of the Year* | Bob Sanders, Safety, Indianapolis Colts |
| *Offensive Rookie of the Year* | Adrian Peterson, Running Back, Minnesota Vikings |
| *Defensive Rookie of the Year* | Patrick Willis, Linebacker, San Francisco 49ers |
| *Comeback Player of the Year* | Greg Ellis, Linebacker, Dallas Cowboys |

## 2008 – National Football Conference

### East Division

| Team | Win | Lost | Tie |
|------|-----|------|-----|
| New York Giants | 12 | 4 | 0 |
| Philadelphia Eagles | 9 | 6 | 1 |
| Dallas Cowboys | 9 | 7 | 0 |
| Washington Redskins | 8 | 8 | 0 |

### North Division

| Team | Win | Lost | Tie |
|------|-----|------|-----|
| Minnesota Vikings | 10 | 6 | 0 |
| Chicago Bears | 9 | 7 | 0 |
| Green Bay Packers | 6 | 10 | 0 |
| Detroit Lions | 0 | 16 | 0 |

### South Division

| Team | Win | Lost | Tie |
|------|-----|------|-----|
| Carolina Panthers | 12 | 4 | 0 |
| Atlanta Falcons | 11 | 5 | 0 |
| Tampa Bay Buccaneers | 9 | 7 | 0 |
| New Orleans Saints | 8 | 8 | 0 |

### West Division

| Team | Win | Lost | Tie |
|------|-----|------|-----|
| Arizona Cardinals | 9 | 7 | 0 |
| San Francisco 49ers | 7 | 9 | 0 |
| Seattle Seahawks | 4 | 12 | 0 |
| St. Louis Rams | 2 | 14 | 0 |

Beginning with the 2008 season, one defensive player was permitted to wear a radio device similar to that worn by NFL quarterbacks in order to communicate with the sideline coaches. Also, teams winning the opening coin toss now had the option to defer their decision about getting the ball to the second half, the same as in college football. The Detroit Lions became the first team to lose all 16 games in a season since the NFL moved to a 16 game schedule. The Tampa Bay Buccaneers went 0-14 in 1976.

## 2008  – American Football Conference

### East Division

| Team | Win | Lost | Tie |
|------|-----|------|-----|
| Miami Dolphins | 11 | 5 | 0 |
| New England Patriots | 11 | 5 | 0 |
| New York Jets | 9 | 7 | 0 |
| Buffalo Bills | 7 | 9 | 0 |

### North Division

| Team | Win | Lost | Tie |
|------|-----|------|-----|
| Pittsburgh Steelers | 12 | 4 | 0 |
| Baltimore Ravens | 11 | 5 | 0 |
| Cincinnati Bengals | 4 | 11 | 1 |
| Cleveland Browns | 4 | 12 | 0 |

### South Division

| Team | Win | Lost | Tie |
|------|-----|------|-----|
| Tennessee Titans | 13 | 3 | 0 |
| Indianapolis Colts | 12 | 4 | 0 |
| Houston Texans | 8 | 8 | 0 |
| Jacksonville Jaguars | 5 | 11 | 0 |

### West Division

| Team | Win | Lost | Tie |
|------|-----|------|-----|
| San Diego Chargers | 8 | 8 | 0 |
| Denver Broncos | 8 | 8 | 0 |
| Oakland Raiders | 4 | 11 | 0 |
| Kansas City Chiefs | 2 | 14 | 0 |

The Philadelphia Eagles vs. Cincinnati Bengals tie was the first tie game in the NFL since the 2002 season.

## 2008-2009 Playoffs

## NFC Playoffs

*Wild Card playoff* (in Minneapolis) – Philadelphia Eagles 26, Minnesota Vikings 14

*Wild Card playoff* (in Phoenix) – Arizona Cardinals 30, Atlanta Falcons 24

*Divisional playoff* (in New York) – Philadelphia Eagles 23, New York Giants 11[25]

*Divisional playoff* (in Charlotte) – Arizona Cardinals 33, Carolina Panthers 13

NFC Championship (in Phoenix) – Arizona Cardinals 32, Philadelphia Eagles 25

## AFC Playoffs

*Wild Card playoff* (in Miami) – Baltimore Ravens 27, Miami Dolphins 9[26]

*Wild Card playoff* (in San Diego) – San Diego Chargers 23[27], Indianapolis Colts 17 (OT)

*Divisional playoff* (in Nashville) – Baltimore Ravens 13, Tennessee Titans 10

*Divisional playoff* (in Pittsburgh) – Pittsburgh Steelers 35, San Diego Chargers 24

AFC Championship (in Pittsburgh) – Pittsburgh Steelers 23, Baltimore Ravens 14

---

25    The New York Giants were the NFC first seed over the Carolina Panthers based on winning their head-to-head contest.

26    The Miami Dolphins beat out the New England Patriots for the AFC East title based on a better conference record, 8-4 vs. 7-5. The Patriots missed the playoffs despite winning 11 games, as the Baltimore Ravens had a better conference record, 8-4 vs. 7-5.

27    The San Diego Chargers beat out the Denver Broncos for the AFC West title based on a better division record, 5-6 vs. 3-3.

# 2009– Super Bowl XLIII (43)

## Tampa

**Pittsburgh Steelers** (AFC) defeat the Arizona Cardinals (NFC), 27-23.

## Season Awards

| | |
|---|---|
| *Most Valuable Player* | Peyton Manning, Quarterback, Indianapolis Colts |
| *Coach of the Year* | Mike Smith, Atlanta Falcons |
| *Offensive Player of the Year* | Drew Brees, Quarterback, New Orleans Saints |
| *Defensive Player of the Year* | James Harrison, Linebacker, Pittsburgh Steelers |
| *Offensive Rookie of the Year* | Matt Ryan, Quarterback, Atlanta Falcons |
| *Defensive Rookie of the Year* | Jerod Mayo, Linebacker, New England Patriots |
| *Comeback Player of the Year* | Chad Pennington, Quarterback, Miami Dolphins |

---

By winning Super Bowl XLIII (43), the Pittsburgh Steelers won a record sixth Super Bowl title.

## 2009 – National Football Conference

### East Division

| Team | Win | Lost | Tie |
|------|-----|------|-----|
| Dallas Cowboys | 11 | 5 | 0 |
| Philadelphia Eagles | 11 | 5 | 0 |
| New York Giants | 8 | 8 | 0 |
| Washington Redskins | 4 | 12 | 0 |

### North Division

| Team | Win | Lost | Tie |
|------|-----|------|-----|
| Minnesota Vikings | 12 | 4 | 0 |
| Green Bay Packers | 11 | 5 | 0 |
| Chicago Bears | 7 | 9 | 0 |
| Detroit Lions | 2 | 14 | 0 |

### South Division

| Team | Win | Lost | Tie |
|------|-----|------|-----|
| New Orleans Saints | 13 | 3 | 0 |
| Atlanta Falcons | 9 | 7 | 0 |
| Carolina Panthers | 8 | 8 | 0 |
| Tampa Bay Buccaneers | 3 | 13 | 0 |

### West Division

| Team | Win | Lost | Tie |
|------|-----|------|-----|
| Arizona Cardinals | 10 | 6 | 0 |
| San Francisco 49ers | 8 | 8 | 0 |
| Seattle Seahawks | 5 | 11 | 0 |
| St. Louis Rams | 1 | 15 | 0 |

## 2009 – American Football Conference

### East Division

| Team | Win | Lost | Tie |
|------|-----|------|-----|
| New England Patriots | 10 | 6 | 0 |
| New York Jets | 9 | 7 | 0 |
| Miami Dolphins | 7 | 9 | 0 |
| Buffalo Bills | 6 | 10 | 0 |

### North Division

| Team | Win | Lost | Tie |
|------|-----|------|-----|
| Cincinnati Bengals | 10 | 6 | 0 |
| Baltimore Ravens | 9 | 7 | 0 |
| Pittsburgh Steelers | 9 | 7 | 0 |
| Cleveland Browns | 5 | 11 | 0 |

### South Division

| Team | Win | Lost | Tie |
|------|-----|------|-----|
| Indianapolis Colts | 14 | 2 | 0 |
| Houston Texans | 9 | 7 | 0 |
| Tennessee Titans | 8 | 8 | 0 |
| Jacksonville Jaguars | 7 | 9 | 0 |

### West Division

| Team | Win | Lost | Tie |
|------|-----|------|-----|
| San Diego Chargers | 13 | 3 | 0 |
| Denver Broncos | 8 | 8 | 0 |
| Oakland Raiders | 5 | 11 | 0 |
| Kansas City Chiefs | 4 | 12 | 0 |

---

The NFL celebrated the 50th anniversary of the American Football League during the 2009 season. The original eight AFL teams wore a special patch commemorating the 1960 AFL: New England Patriots (Boston Patriots), Buffalo Bills, Kansas City Chiefs (Dallas Texans), Tennessee Titans (Houston Oilers), San Diego Chargers (Los Angeles Chargers), New York Jets (New York Titans), and the Oakland Raiders (Oakland Señores – changed name before first game). The Cincinnati Bengals and Miami Dolphins were not part of the original AFL eight teams.

## 2009-2010 Playoffs

## NFC Playoffs

*Wild Card playoff* (in Dallas) – Dallas Cowboys 34[28], Philadelphia Eagles 14

*Wild Card playoff* (in Phoenix) – Arizona Cardinals 51, Green Bay Packers 45[29] (OT)

*Divisional playoff* (in Minneapolis) – Minnesota Vikings 34, Dallas Cowboys 3

*Divisional playoff* (in New Orleans) – New Orleans Saints 45, Arizona Cardinals 14

NFC Championship (in New Orleans) – New Orleans Saints 31, Minnesota Vikings 28 (OT)

## AFC Playoffs

*Wild Card playoff* (in Cincinnati) – New York Jets 24[30], Cincinnati Bengals 14

*Wild Card playoff* (in Boston) – Baltimore Ravens 33[31], New England Patriots 14[32]

*Divisional playoff* (in San Diego) – New York Jets 17, San Diego Chargers 14

*Divisional playoff* (in Indianapolis) – Indianapolis Colts 20, Baltimore 3

AFC Championship (in Indianapolis) – Indianapolis Colts 30, New York Jets 17

---

28      The Dallas Cowboys won the NFC East over the Philadelphia Eagles based on a sweep of their head-to-head games.

29      The Green Bay Packers won the NFC first Wild Card (fifth seed) over the Eagles based on a better record in common games, 4-1 vs. 3-2.

30      The New York Jets took the AFC first Wild Card (fifth seed) over the Baltimore Ravens based on a better record in common games, 4-1 vs. 1-4, after the Houston Texans were eliminated from the three-way tie based on its worse conference record, 6-6 vs. 7-5 for both the Jets and Ravens.

31      The Baltimore Ravens beat out the Pittsburgh Steelers for the final AFC Wild Card (sixth seed) slot based on a better division record, 3-3 vs. 2-4.

32      The New England Patriots won the AFC third seed over the Cincinnati Bengals based on strength of victory, .450 vs. .438.

# 2010– Super Bowl XLIV (44)

# Miami

**New Orleans Saints** (NFC) defeat the Indianapolis Colts (AFC), 31-17.

## Season Awards

*Most Valuable Player*               Peyton Manning, Quarterback,
                                     Indianapolis Colts

*Coach of the Year*                  Marvin Lewis, Cincinnati Bengals

*Offensive Player of the Year*       Chris Johnson, Running Back,
                                     Tennessee Titans

*Defensive Player of the Year*       Charles Woodson, Cornerback,
                                     Green Bay Packers

*Offensive Rookie of the Year*       Percy Harvin, Wide Receiver,
                                     Minnesota Vikings

*Defensive Rookie of the Year*       Brian Cushing, Linebacker, Houston Texans

*Comeback Player of the Year*        Tom Brady, Quarterback, New England Patriots

# 2010 – 2015

# 2010 – National Football Conference

## East Division

| Team | Win | Lost | Tie |
|------|-----|------|-----|
| Philadelphia Eagles | 10 | 6 | 0 |
| New York Giants | 10 | 6 | 0 |
| Dallas Cowboys | 6 | 10 | 0 |
| Washington Redskins | 6 | 10 | 0 |

## North Division

| Team | Win | Lost | Tie |
|------|-----|------|-----|
| Chicago Bears | 11 | 5 | 0 |
| Green Bay Packers | 10 | 6 | 0 |
| Detroit Lions | 6 | 10 | 0 |
| Minnesota Vikings | 6 | 10 | 0 |

## South Division

| Team | Win | Lost | Tie |
|------|-----|------|-----|
| Atlanta Falcons | 13 | 3 | 0 |
| New Orleans Saints | 11 | 5 | 0 |
| Tampa Bay Buccaneers | 10 | 6 | 0 |
| Carolina Panthers | 2 | 14 | 0 |

## West Division

| Team | Win | Lost | Tie |
|------|-----|------|-----|
| Seattle Seahawks | 7 | 9 | 0 |
| St. Louis Rams | 7 | 9 | 0 |
| San Francisco 49ers | 6 | 10 | 0 |
| Arizona Cardinals | 5 | 11 | 0 |

---

**The NFL changed the rules** for overtime in post-season games before the start of the 2010 season. In the past, the first team to score won the game. This meant winning the coin toss (and getting possession of the ball first) usually led to victory in overtime – typically with a field goal. Under the new rules, the game does not immediately end if the team that wins the coin toss only scores a field goal. If that happens, the other team gets a possession. If the first team to score scores a touchdown, however, the game is over. The league made the same change for overtime rules during regular season games beginning with the 2012 season. Additionally, during the 2010 season, the NFL announced that it would begin suspending players for illegal hits (such as helmet-to-helmet). Previously, the NFL would only fine players for such hits. Officials were encouraged to throw a penalty flag if there was any doubt about whether the hit was legal. This was part of an overall league effort to increase player safety in light of several player-led lawsuits over concussions and general public outcry on the issue.

# 2010  – American Football Conference

## East Division

| Team | Win | Lost | Tie |
|------|-----|------|-----|
| New England Patriots | 14 | 2 | 0 |
| New York Jets | 11 | 5 | 0 |
| Miami Dolphins | 7 | 9 | 0 |
| Buffalo Bills | 4 | 12 | 0 |

## North Division

| Team | Win | Lost | Tie |
|------|-----|------|-----|
| Pittsburgh Steelers | 12 | 4 | 0 |
| Baltimore Ravens | 12 | 4 | 0 |
| Cleveland Browns | 5 | 11 | 0 |
| Cincinnati Bengals | 4 | 12 | 0 |

## South Division

| Team | Win | Lost | Tie |
|------|-----|------|-----|
| Indianapolis Colts | 10 | 6 | 0 |
| Jacksonville Jaguars | 8 | 8 | 0 |
| Houston Texans | 6 | 10 | 0 |
| Tennessee Titans | 6 | 10 | 0 |

## West Division

| Team | Win | Lost | Tie |
|------|-----|------|-----|
| Kansas City Chiefs | 10 | 6 | 0 |
| San Diego Chargers | 9 | 7 | 0 |
| Oakland Raiders | 8 | 8 | 0 |
| Denver Broncos | 4 | 12 | 0 |

# 2010-2011 Playoffs

## NFC Playoffs

*Wild Card playoff* (in Philadelphia) – Green Bay Packers 21[1], Philadelphia Eagles 16[2]

*Wild Card playoff* (in Seattle) – Seattle Seahawks 41[3], New Orleans Saints 36

*Divisional playoff* (in Atlanta) – Green Bay Packers 48, Atlanta Falcons 21

*Divisional playoff* (in Chicago) – Chicago Bears 35, Seattle Seahawks 24

NFC Championship (in Chicago) – Green Bay Packers 21, Chicago Bears 14

## AFC Playoffs

*Wild Card playoff* (in Indianapolis) – New York Jets 17, Indianapolis Colts 16[4]

*Wild Card playoff* (in Kansas City) – Baltimore Ravens 30, Kansas City Chiefs 7

*Divisional playoff* (in Pittsburgh) – Pittsburgh Steelers 31[5], Baltimore Ravens 24

*Divisional playoff* (in Boston) – New York Jets 28, New England Patriots 21

AFC Championship (in Pittsburgh) – Pittsburgh Steelers 24, New York Jets 19

---

1       The Green Bay Packers won the final NFC Wild Card (sixth seed) over the New York Giants and the Tampa Bay Buccaneers based on better strength of victory, .475 vs. .400 vs. .344.

2       The Philadelphia Eagles won the NFC East based on a sweep of its head-to-head games against the New York Giants.

3       The Seattle Seahawks won the NFC West over the St. Louis Rams based on a better division record, 4-2 vs. 3-3. Also, Seattle became the first team with a losing record to make the playoffs during a full length season, and the first sub-.500 team to win a playoff game.

4       The Indianapolis Colts won the AFC third seed over the Kansas City Chiefs based on a head-to-head victory.

5       The Pittsburgh Steelers won the AFC North title over the Baltimore Ravens based on a better division record, 5-1 vs. 4-2.

# 2011– Super Bowl XLV (45)
## Dallas

**Green Bay Packers** (NFC) defeat the Pittsburgh Steelers (AFC), 31-25.

## Season Awards

| | |
|---|---|
| *Most Valuable Player* | Tom Brady, Quarterback, New England Patriots |
| *Coach of the Year* | Bill Belichick, New England Patriots |
| *Offensive Player of the Year* | Tom Brady, Quarterback, New England Patriots |
| *Defensive Player of the Year* | Troy Polamalu, Safety, Pittsburgh Steelers |
| *Offensive Rookie of the Year* | Sam Bradford, Quarterback, St. Louis Rams |
| *Defensive Rookie of the Year* | Ndamukong Suh, Defensive Tackle, Detroit Lions |
| *Comeback Player of the Year* | Michael Vick, Quarterback, Philadelphia Eagles |

# 2011  – National Football Conference

## East Division

| Team | Win | Lost | Tie |
|---|---|---|---|
| New York Giants | 9 | 7 | 0 |
| Philadelphia Eagles | 8 | 8 | 0 |
| Dallas Cowboys | 8 | 8 | 0 |
| Washington Redskins | 5 | 11 | 0 |

## North Division

| Team | Win | Lost | Tie |
|---|---|---|---|
| Green Bay Packers | 15 | 1 | 0 |
| Detroit Lions | 10 | 6 | 0 |
| Chicago Bears | 8 | 8 | 0 |
| Minnesota Vikings | 3 | 13 | 0 |

## South Division

| Team | Win | Lost | Tie |
|---|---|---|---|
| New Orleans Saints | 13 | 3 | 0 |
| Atlanta Falcons | 10 | 6 | 0 |
| Carolina Panthers | 6 | 10 | 0 |
| Tampa Bay Buccaneers | 4 | 12 | 0 |

## West Division

| Team | Win | Lost | Tie |
|---|---|---|---|
| San Francisco 49ers | 13 | 3 | 0 |
| Arizona Cardinals | 8 | 8 | 0 |
| Seattle Seahawks | 7 | 9 | 0 |
| St. Louis Rams | 2 | 14 | 0 |

---

The NFL owners "locked-out" the players in a labor dispute beginning on March 11, 2011 and ending on July 25, 2011. While potentially threatening the regular season, the lock-out only impacted the traditional Hall of Fame preseason game, which was canceled for the first time since it began in 1962.

# 2011 – American Football Conference

## East Division

| Team | Win | Lost | Tie |
|------|-----|------|-----|
| New England Patriots | 13 | 3 | 0 |
| New York Jets | 8 | 8 | 0 |
| Miami Dolphins | 6 | 10 | 0 |
| Buffalo Bills | 6 | 10 | 0 |

## North Division

| Team | Win | Lost | Tie |
|------|-----|------|-----|
| Baltimore Ravens | 12 | 4 | 0 |
| Pittsburgh Steelers | 12 | 4 | 0 |
| Cincinnati Bengals | 9 | 7 | 0 |
| Cleveland Browns | 4 | 12 | 0 |

## South Division

| Team | Win | Lost | Tie |
|------|-----|------|-----|
| Houston Texans | 10 | 6 | 0 |
| Tennessee Titans | 9 | 7 | 0 |
| Jacksonville Jaguars | 5 | 11 | 0 |
| Indianapolis Colts | 2 | 14 | 0 |

## West Division

| Team | Win | Lost | Tie |
|------|-----|------|-----|
| Denver Broncos | 8 | 8 | 0 |
| San Diego Chargers | 8 | 8 | 0 |
| Oakland Raiders | 8 | 8 | 0 |
| Kansas City Chiefs | 7 | 9 | 0 |

In an effort to reduce injuries, the league moved kickoffs from the 30 yard line to the 35 yard (potentially leading to more touchbacks). The new rules also required players to line up no more than five yards behind the kickoff line, thus reducing the speed of kickoff collisions. There continues to be discussion as to whether the league should eliminate the kickoff completely given the increased risk of injury due to high-speed collisions.

# 2011-2012 Playoffs

## NFC Playoffs

*Wild Card playoff* (in New York) – New York Giants 24, Atlanta Falcons 2[6]

*Wild Card playoff* (in New Orleans) – New Orleans Saints 45, Detroit Lions 28

*Divisional playoff* (in Green Bay) – New York Giants 37, Green Bay Packers 20

*Divisional playoff* (in San Francisco) – San Francisco 49ers 36[7], New Orleans Saints 32

NFC Championship (in San Francisco) – New York Giants 20, San Francisco 49ers 17 (OT)

## AFC Playoffs

*Wild Card playoff* (in Houston) – Houston Texans 31, Cincinnati Bengals 10[8]

*Wild Card playoff* (in Denver) – Denver Broncos 29[9], Pittsburgh Steelers 23 (OT)

*Divisional playoff* (in Baltimore) – Baltimore Ravens 20[10], Houston Texans 13

*Divisional playoff* (in Boston) – New England Patriots 45, Denver Broncos 10

AFC Championship (in Boston) – New England Patriots 23, Baltimore Ravens 20

---

6       The Atlanta Falcons won the NFC first Wild Card (fifth seed) over the Detroit Lions based on winning their head-to-head game.

7       The San Francisco 49ers won the NFC second seed over the New Orleans Saint based on a better conference record, 10-2 vs. 9-3.

8       The Cincinnati Bengals won the AFC second Wild Card (sixth seed) over the Tennessee Titans based on winning their head-to-head games.

9       The Denver Broncos won the AFC West title over the San Diego Chargers and Oakland Raiders based on a better record vs. common opponents, 5-5 vs. 4-6 vs. 4-6.

10      The Baltimore Ravens won the AFC North over the Pittsburgh Steelers based on a head-to-head sweep of their games.

# 2012– Super Bowl XLVI (46)
# Indianapolis

**New York Giants** (NFC) defeat the New England Patriots (AFC), 21-17.

## Season Awards

| | |
|---|---|
| *Most Valuable Player* | Aaron Rodgers, Quarterback, Green Bay Packers |
| *Coach of the Year* | Jim Harbaugh, San Francisco 49ers |
| *Offensive Player of the Year* | Drew Brees, Quarterback, New Orleans Saints |
| *Defensive Player of the Year* | Terrell Suggs, Linebacker, Baltimore Ravens |
| *Offensive Rookie of the Year* | Cam Newton, Quarterback, Carolina Panthers |
| *Defensive Rookie of the Year* | Von Miller, Linebacker, Denver Broncos |
| *Comeback Player of the Year* | Matt Stafford, Quarterback, Detroit Lions |

# 2012  – National Football Conference

## East Division

| Team | Win | Lost | Tie |
|------|-----|------|-----|
| Washington Redskins | 10 | 6 | 0 |
| New York Giants | 9 | 7 | 0 |
| Dallas Cowboys | 8 | 8 | 0 |
| Philadelphia Eagles | 4 | 12 | 0 |

## North Division

| Team | Win | Lost | Tie |
|------|-----|------|-----|
| Green Bay Packers | 11 | 5 | 0 |
| Minnesota Vikings | 10 | 6 | 0 |
| Chicago Bears | 10 | 6 | 0 |
| Detroit Lions | 4 | 12 | 0 |

## South Division

| Team | Win | Lost | Tie |
|------|-----|------|-----|
| Atlanta Falcons | 13 | 3 | 0 |
| Carolina Panthers | 7 | 9 | 0 |
| New Orleans Saints | 7 | 9 | 0 |
| Tampa Bay Buccaneers | 7 | 9 | 0 |

## West Division

| Team | Win | Lost | Tie |
|------|-----|------|-----|
| San Francisco 49ers | 11 | 4 | 1 |
| Seattle Seahawks | 11 | 5 | 0 |
| St. Louis Rams | 7 | 8 | 1 |
| Arizona Cardinals | 5 | 11 | 0 |

---

The NFL and its referee officials failed to reach a new collective bargaining agreement prior to the start of the 2012 season. The league "locked-out" the officials and announced it would hire replacement referees over the summer. The league and the referee's union reach a new agreement in late September after tremendous criticism of the NFL and the replacement referees. In particular, many viewed the Green Bay Packers vs. Seattle Seahawks game on September 24, 2012 as the tipping point in the labor dispute due to disputed calls and the appearance that the replacement referees (from the high school and college ranks) lost control of the game. Additionally, during the 2012 season, the league announced that the New Orleans Saints had a "slush fund" that paid out cash "bounties" to purposely injure offensive players on opposing teams. The NFL Commissioner, Roger Goodell, suspended the Saint's head coach, Sean Payton, for the 2012 season, the Saint's defensive coordinator, Gregg Williams, indefinitely, and several players for a number of games and for some, the entire season. The player suspensions were later reversed on appeal.

# 2012  – American Football Conference

## East Division

| Team | Win | Lost | Tie |
|------|-----|------|-----|
| New England Patriots | 12 | 4 | 0 |
| Miami Dolphins | 7 | 9 | 0 |
| New York Jets | 6 | 10 | 0 |
| Buffalo Bills | 6 | 10 | 0 |

## North Division

| Team | Win | Lost | Tie |
|------|-----|------|-----|
| Baltimore Ravens | 10 | 6 | 0 |
| Cincinnati Bengals | 10 | 6 | 0 |
| Pittsburgh Steelers | 8 | 8 | 0 |
| Cleveland Browns | 5 | 11 | 0 |

## South Division

| Team | Win | Lost | Tie |
|------|-----|------|-----|
| Houston Texans | 12 | 4 | 0 |
| Indianapolis Colts | 11 | 5 | 0 |
| Tennessee Titans | 6 | 10 | 0 |
| Jacksonville Jaguars | 2 | 14 | 0 |

## West Division

| Team | Win | Lost | Tie |
|------|-----|------|-----|
| Denver Broncos | 13 | 3 | 0 |
| San Diego Chargers | 7 | 9 | 0 |
| Oakland Raiders | 4 | 12 | 0 |
| Kansas City Chiefs | 2 | 14 | 0 |

## 2012-2013 Playoffs

## NFC Playoffs

*Wild Card playoff* (in Green Bay) – Green Bay Packers 24, Minnesota Vikings 10[11]

*Wild Card playoff* (in Seattle) – Seattle Seahawks 24, Washington Redskins 14

*Divisional playoff* (in Atlanta) – Atlanta Falcons 30, Seattle Seahawks 28

*Divisional playoff* (in San Francisco) – San Francisco 49ers 45, Green Bay Packers 31

NFC Championship (in Atlanta) – San Francisco 49ers 28, Atlanta Falcons 24

## AFC Playoffs

*Wild Card playoff* (in Baltimore) – Baltimore Ravens 24[12], Indianapolis Colts 9

*Wild Card playoff* (in Houston) – Houston Texans 19, Cincinnati Bengals 13

*Divisional playoff* (in Denver) – Baltimore Ravens 38, Denver Broncos 35 (2OT)

*Divisional playoff* (in Boston) – New England Patriots 41[13], Houston Texans 28

AFC Championship (in Boston) – Baltimore Ravens 28, New England Patriots 13

---

11      The Minnesota Vikings beat out the Chicago Bears for the final AFC Wild Card (sixth seed) based on a better division record, 4-2 vs. 3-3.

12      The Baltimore Ravens won the AFC North title over the Cincinnati Bengals based on a better division record, 4-2 vs. 3-3.

13      The New England Patriots won the AFC second seed over the Houston Texans based on winning their head-to-head game.

# 2013– Super Bowl XLVII (47)

## New Orleans

**Baltimore Ravens** (AFC) defeat the San Francisco 49ers (NFC), 34-31.

## Season Awards

| | |
|---|---|
| *Most Valuable Player* | Adrian Peterson, Running Back, Minnesota Vikings |
| *Coach of the Year* | Bruce Arians, Indianapolis Colts |
| *Offensive Player of the Year* | Adrian Peterson, Running Back, Minnesota Vikings |
| *Defensive Player of the Year* | J. J. Watt, Defensive End, Houston Texans |
| *Offensive Rookie of the Year* | Robert Griffin III, Quarterback, Washington Redskins |
| *Defensive Rookie of the Year* | Luke Kuechly, Linebacker, Carolina Panthers |
| *Comeback Player of the Year* | Peyton Manning, Quarterback, Denver Broncos |

———

Super Bowl XLVII was the first to feature brothers coaching against each other: Jim Harbaugh (49ers) and John Harbaugh (Ravens).

# 2013 – National Football Conference

## East Division

| Team | Win | Lost | Tie |
|------|-----|------|-----|
| Philadelphia Eagles | 10 | 6 | 0 |
| Dallas Cowboys | 8 | 8 | 0 |
| New York Giants | 7 | 9 | 0 |
| Washington Redskins | 3 | 13 | 0 |

## North Division

| Team | Win | Lost | Tie |
|------|-----|------|-----|
| Green Bay Packers | 8 | 7 | 1 |
| Chicago Bears | 8 | 8 | 0 |
| Detroit Lions | 7 | 9 | 0 |
| Minnesota Vikings | 5 | 10 | 1 |

## South Division

| Team | Win | Lost | Tie |
|------|-----|------|-----|
| Carolina Panthers | 12 | 4 | 0 |
| New Orleans Saints | 11 | 5 | 0 |
| Atlanta Falcons | 4 | 12 | 0 |
| Tampa Bay Buccaneers | 4 | 12 | 0 |

## West Division

| Team | Win | Lost | Tie |
|------|-----|------|-----|
| Seattle Seahawks | 13 | 3 | 0 |
| San Francisco 49ers | 12 | 4 | 0 |
| Arizona Cardinals | 10 | 6 | 0 |
| St. Louis Rams | 7 | 9 | 0 |

# 2013 – American Football Conference

## East Division

| Team | Win | Lost | Tie |
|------|-----|------|-----|
| New England Patriots | 12 | 4 | 0 |
| New York Jets | 8 | 8 | 0 |
| Miami Dolphins | 8 | 8 | 0 |
| Buffalo Bills | 6 | 10 | 0 |

## North Division

| Team | Win | Lost | Tie |
|------|-----|------|-----|
| Cincinnati Bengals | 11 | 5 | 0 |
| Pittsburgh Steelers | 8 | 8 | 0 |
| Baltimore Ravens | 8 | 8 | 0 |
| Cleveland Browns | 4 | 12 | 0 |

## South Division

| Team | Win | Lost | Tie |
|------|-----|------|-----|
| Indianapolis Colts | 11 | 5 | 0 |
| Tennessee Titans | 7 | 9 | 0 |
| Jacksonville Jaguars | 4 | 12 | 0 |
| Houston Texans | 2 | 14 | 0 |

## West Division

| Team | Win | Lost | Tie |
|------|-----|------|-----|
| Denver Broncos | 13 | 3 | 0 |
| Kansas City Chiefs | 11 | 5 | 0 |
| San Diego Chargers | 9 | 7 | 0 |
| Oakland Raiders | 4 | 12 | 0 |

## 2013-2014 Playoffs

## NFC Playoffs

*Wild Card playoff* (in Green Bay) – San Francisco 49ers 23, Green Bay Packers 20

*Wild Card playoff* (in Philadelphia) – New Orleans Saints 26, Philadelphia Eagles 24

*Divisional playoff* (in Charlotte) – San Francisco 49ers 23, Carolina Panthers 10

*Divisional playoff* (in Seattle) – Seattle Seahawks 23, New Orleans Saints 15

NFC Championship (in Seattle) – Seattle Seahawks 23, San Francisco 49ers 17

## AFC Playoffs

*Wild Card playoff* (in Indianapolis) – Indianapolis Colts 45, Kansas City Chiefs 44

*Wild Card playoff* (in Cincinnati) – San Diego Chargers 27, Cincinnati Bengals 10[14]

*Divisional playoff* (in Denver) – Denver Broncos 24, San Diego Chargers 17

*Divisional playoff* (in Boston) – New England Patriots 43, Indianapolis Colts 22

AFC Championship (in Denver) – Denver Broncos 26, New England Patriots 16

---

14      The Cincinnati Bengals beat out the Indianapolis Colts for the AFC third seed based on winning their head-to-head game.

## 2014– Super Bowl XLVIII (48)

## New York City

**Seattle Seahawks** (NFC) defeat the Denver Broncos (AFC), 43-8.

## Season Awards

*Most Valuable Player*                      Peyton Manning, Quarterback, Denver Broncos

*Coach of the Year*                         Ron Rivera, Carolina Panthers

*Offensive Player of the Year*              Peyton Manning, Quarterback, Denver Broncos

*Defensive Player of the Year*              Luke Kuechly, Linebacker, Carolina Panthers

*Offensive Rookie of the Year*              Eddie Lacy, Running Back, Green Bay Packers

*Defensive Rookie of the Year*              Sheldon Richardson, Defensive End,
                                            New York Jets

*Comeback Player of the Year*               Philip Rivers, Quarterback, San Diego Chargers

---

Super Bowl XLVIII (48) was the first Super Bowl held in a cold-weather state in an open stadium (past cold weather Super Bowl games where played inside domed stadiums). Prior to the Super Bowl, the NFL and AFL title games were played at the home stadium of one of the participants and typically involved cold weather, sometimes severe (e.g., the 1967 "Ice Bowl"). Peyton Manning won his fifth MVP award for the 2013 season, a record.

# 2014 – National Football Conference

## East Division

| Team | Win | Lost | Tie |
|------|-----|------|-----|
| Dallas Cowboys | 12 | 4 | 0 |
| Philadelphia Eagles | 10 | 6 | 0 |
| New York Giants | 6 | 10 | 0 |
| Washington Redskins | 4 | 12 | 0 |

## North Division

| Team | Win | Lost | Tie |
|------|-----|------|-----|
| Green Bay Packers | 12 | 4 | 0 |
| Detroit Lions | 11 | 5 | 0 |
| Minnesota Vikings | 7 | 9 | 0 |
| Chicago Bears | 5 | 11 | 0 |

## South Division

| Team | Win | Lost | Tie |
|------|-----|------|-----|
| Carolina Panthers | 7 | 8 | 1 |
| New Orleans Saints | 7 | 9 | 0 |
| Atlanta Falcons | 6 | 10 | 0 |
| Tampa Bay Buccaneers | 2 | 14 | 0 |

## West Division

| Team | Win | Lost | Tie |
|------|-----|------|-----|
| Seattle Seahawks | 12 | 4 | 0 |
| Arizona Cardinals | 11 | 5 | 0 |
| San Francisco 49ers | 8 | 8 | 0 |
| St. Louis Rams | 6 | 10 | 0 |

---

2014 was a tough year for the NFL and Commissioner Goodell. In particular, a number of star players (e.g., Greg Hardy, Adrian Peterson, Ray Rice) were arrested for or involved in domestic violence incidents and many questioned the league's discipline of the players and whether the NFL took the issue of domestic violence seriously enough. The NFL struggled with getting the right policies and punishments in place.

There will be heightened scrutiny of the league going forward and whether or not the controversies will hurt the appeal of the league or Commissioner Goodell's job remain to be seen. In less controversial moves, the league raised the height of the goal posts from 30 feet to 35 feet to help referees better determine if a field goal is good or not. The goal post height had been set at 30 feet since the 1974 season. The height of the cross-bar remained unchanged. Additionally, there has been growing discussion about whether to alter the point-after-touchdown (PAT) kick given it has become almost automatic from the current distance and it is a play that can lead to injuries. Ideas included eliminating it completely or moving the kick back to a longer distance. The NFL announced that for the 2015 season the PAT would be moved back to the 15 yardline (vs. the two yardline today). Two-point conversion tries will still start at the two yardline.

# 2014  – American Football Conference

## East Division

| Team | Win | Lost | Tie |
|---|---|---|---|
| New England Patriots | 12 | 4 | 0 |
| Buffalo Bills | 9 | 7 | 0 |
| Miami Dolphins | 8 | 8 | 0 |
| New York Jets | 4 | 12 | 0 |

## North Division

| Team | Win | Lost | Tie |
|---|---|---|---|
| Pittsburgh Steelers | 11 | 5 | 0 |
| Cincinnati Bengals | 10 | 5 | 1 |
| Baltimore Ravens | 10 | 6 | 0 |
| Cleveland Browns | 7 | 9 | 0 |

## South Division

| Team | Win | Lost | Tie |
|---|---|---|---|
| Indianapolis Colts | 11 | 5 | 0 |
| Houston Texans | 9 | 7 | 0 |
| Jacksonville Jaguars | 3 | 13 | 0 |
| Tennessee Titans | 2 | 14 | 0 |

## West Division

| Team | Win | Lost | Tie |
|---|---|---|---|
| Denver Broncos | 12 | 4 | 0 |
| Kansas City Chiefs | 9 | 7 | 0 |
| San Diego Chargers | 9 | 7 | 0 |
| Oakland Raiders | 3 | 13 | 0 |

## 2014-2015 Playoffs

## NFC Playoffs

*Wild Card playoff* (in Dallas) – Dallas Cowboys 24, Detroit Lions 20

*Wild Card playoff* (in Charlotte) – Carolina Panthers 27, Arizona Cardinals 16

*Divisional playoff* (in Green Bay) – Green Bay Packers 26, Dallas Cowboys 21

*Divisional playoff* (in Seattle) – Seattle Seahawks 31, Carolina Panthers 17

NFC Championship (in Seattle) – Seattle Seahawks 28, Green Bay Packers 22 (OT)

## AFC Playoffs

*Wild Card playoff* (in Indianapolis) – Indianapolis Colts 26, Cincinnati Bengals 10

*Wild Card playoff* (in Pittsburgh) – Baltimore Ravens 30, Pittsburgh Steelers 17

*Divisional playoff* (in Denver) – Indianapolis Colts 24, Denver Broncos 13

*Divisional playoff* (in Boston) – New England Patriots 35, Baltimore Ravens 31

AFC Championship (in Denver) – New England Patriots 45, Indianapolis Colts 7

# 2015– Super Bowl XLVIX (49)

## Phoenix

**New England Patriots** (AFC) defeat the Seattle Seahawks (NFC), 28-24.

## Season Awards

| | |
|---|---|
| *Most Valuable Player* | Aaron Rodgers, Quarterback, Green Bay Packers |
| *Coach of the Year* | Bruce Arians, Arizona Cardinals |
| *Offensive Player of the Year* | DeMarco Murray, Running Back, Dallas Cowboys |
| *Defensive Player of the Year* | J. J. Watt, Defensive End, Houston Texans |
| *Offensive Rookie of the Year* | Odell Beckham Jr., Wide Receiver, New York Giants |
| *Defensive Rookie of the Year* | Aaron Donald, Defensive Tackle, St. Louis Rams |
| *Comeback Player of the Year* | Rob Gronkowski, Tight End, New England Patriots |

---

Super Bowl XLVIX (49) was partially over shadowed by the question of whether the New England Patriots and quarterback Tom Brady intentionally deflated footballs during the AFC playoffs to gain an unfair competitive advantage. The controversy was dubbed "Deflate-Gate" by the press. The Patriots and Brady denied the allegations. A league investigation led by outside attorney Ted Wells concluded it was more likely than not (i.e., more than 50% likely) that the Patriots and Brady intentionally deflated the footballs. The Patriots were fined and lost future draft picks. Tom Brady was suspended for four games. The Patriots owner, Robert Kraft decided to move on and not challenge the penalties though he continued to deny the allegations. Tom Brady formally appealed the suspension to Commissioner Goodell and his appeal was denied. Brady appealed to a U.S. District Court which reversed the suspension, finding that the arbitration process was flawed and unfair to Brady. The Wells report cost the league an estimated $3 million – all over the issue of whether the footballs were at the proper level of inflation or slightly deflated under the minimum.

# APPENDIX

## Super Bowl Results

| Year | Number | Winner | Loser | Score | Location | League/Conference |
|------|--------|--------|-------|-------|----------|-------------------|
| 1967 | I (1) | Green Bay Packers | Kansas City Chiefs | 35-10 | Los Angeles | NFL |
| 1968 | II (2) | Green Bay Packers | Oakland Raiders | 35-14 | Miami | NFL |
| 1969 | III (3) | New York Jets | Baltimore Colts | 16-7 | Miami | AFL |
| 1970 | IV (4) | Kansas City Chiefs | Minnesota Vikings | 23-7 | New Orleans | AFL |
| 1971 | V (5) | Baltimore Colts | Dallas Cowboys | 16-13 | Miami | AFC |
| 1972 | VI (6) | Dallas Cowboys | Miami Dolphins | 24-3 | New Orleans | NFC |
| 1973 | VII (7) | Miami Dolphins | Washington Redskins | 14-7 | Los Angeles | AFC |
| 1974 | VIII (8) | Miami Dolphins | Minnesota Vikings | 24-7 | Houston | AFC |
| 1975 | IX (9) | Pittsburgh Steelers | Minnesota Vikings | 16-6 | New Orleans | AFC |
| 1976 | X (10) | Pittsburgh Steelers | Dallas Cowboys | 21-17 | Miami | AFC |
| 1977 | XI (11) | Oakland Raiders | Minnesota Vikings | 32-14 | Los Angeles (Pasadena) | AFC |
| 1978 | XII (12) | Dallas Cowboys | Denver Broncos | 27-10 | New Orleans | NFC |
| 1979 | XIII (13) | Pittsburgh Steelers | Dallas Cowboys | 35-31 | Miami | AFC |
| 1980 | XIV (14) | Pittsburgh Steelers | Los Angeles Rams | 31-19 | Los Angeles (Pasadena) | AFC |
| 1981 | XV (15) | Oakland Raiders | Philadelphia Eagles | 27-10 | New Orleans | AFC |
| 1982 | XVI (16) | San Francisco 49ers | Cincinnati Bengals | 26-21 | Detroit (Pontiac) | NFC |
| 1983 | XVII (17) | Washington Redskins | Miami Dolphins | 27-17 | Los Angeles (Pasadena) | NFC |
| 1984 | XVIII (18) | Los Angeles Raiders | Washington Redskins | 38-9 | Tampa | AFC |
| 1985 | XIX (19) | San Francisco 49ers | Miami Dolphins | 38-16 | Palo Alto, California | NFC |

| Year | Number | Winner | Loser | Score | Location | Conference |
|------|--------|--------|-------|-------|----------|------------|
| 1986 | XX (20) | Chicago Bears | New England Patriots | 46-10 | New Orleans | NFC |
| 1987 | XXI (21) | New York Giants | Denver Broncos | 39-20 | Los Angeles (Pasadena) | NFC |
| 1988 | XXII (22) | Washington Redskins | Denver Broncos | 42-10 | San Diego | NFC |
| 1989 | XXIII (23) | San Francisco 49ers | Cincinnati Bengals | 20-16 | Miami | NFC |
| 1990 | XXIV (24) | San Francisco 49ers | Denver Broncos | 55-10 | New Orleans | NFC |
| 1991 | XXV (25) | New York Giants | Buffalo Bills | 20-19 | Tampa | NFC |
| 1992 | XXVI (26) | Washington Redskins | Buffalo Bills | 37-24 | Minneapolis | NFC |
| 1993 | XXVII (27) | Dallas Cowboys | Buffalo Bills | 52-17 | Los Angeles (Pasadena) | NFC |
| 1994 | XXVIII (28) | Dallas Cowboys | Buffalo Bills | 30-13 | Atlanta | NFC |
| 1995 | XXIX (29) | San Francisco 49ers | San Diego Chargers | 49-26 | Miami | NFC |
| 1996 | XXX (30) | Dallas Cowboys | Pittsburgh Steelers | 27-17 | Tempe, Arizona | NFC |
| 1997 | XXXI (31) | Green Bay Packers | New England Patriots | 35-21 | New Orleans | NFC |
| 1998 | XXXII (32) | Denver Broncos | Green Bay Packers | 31-24 | San Diego | AFC |
| 1999 | XXXIII (33) | Denver Broncos | Atlanta Falcons | 34-19 | Miami | AFC |
| 2000 | XXXIV (34) | St. Louis Rams | Tennessee Titans | 23-16 | Atlanta | NFC |
| 2001 | XXXV (35) | Baltimore Ravens | New York Giants | 34-7 | Tampa | AFC |
| 2002 | XXXVI (36) | New England Patriots | St. Louis Rams | 20-17 | New Orleans | AFC |
| 2003 | XXXVII (37) | Tampa Bay Buccaneers | Oakland Raiders | 48-21 | San Diego | NFC |
| 2004 | XXXVIII (38) | New England Patriots | Carolina Panthers | 32-29 | Houston | AFC |

| Year | Number | Winner | Loser | Score | Location | Conference |
|------|--------|--------|-------|-------|----------|------------|
| 2005 | XXXIX (39) | New England Patriots | Philadelphia Eagles | 24-21 | Jacksonville, Florida | AFC |
| 2006 | XL (40) | Pittsburgh Steelers | Seattle Seahawks | 21-10 | Detroit | AFC |
| 2007 | XLI (41) | Indianapolis Colts | Chicago Bears | 29-17 | Miami | AFC |
| 2008 | XLII (42) | New York Giants | New England Patriots | 17-14 | Glendale, Arizona | NFC |
| 2009 | XLIII (43) | Pittsburgh Steelers | Arizona Cardinals | 27-23 | Tampa | AFC |
| 2010 | XLIV (44) | New Orleans Saints | Indianapolis Colts | 31-17 | Miami | NFC |
| 2011 | XLV (45) | Green Bay Packers | Pittsburgh Steelers | 31-25 | Dallas (Arlington) | NFC |
| 2012 | XLVI (46) | New York Giants | New England Patriots | 21-17 | Indianapolis | NFC |
| 2013 | XLVII (47) | Baltimore Ravens | San Francisco 49ers | 34-31 | New Orleans | AFC |
| 2014 | XLVIII (48) | Seattle Seahawks | Denver Broncos | 43-8 | New York (East Rutherford, NJ) | NFC |
| 2015 | XLIX (49) | New England Patriots | Seattle Seahawks | 28-24 | Glendale, Arizona | AFC |

**Super Bowl Titles by League**
(pre-1970 AFL/NFL merger):                           NFL- 2, AFL- 2

**Super Bowl Titles by Conference**
(post-1970 AFL/NFL merger):                          NFC- 24, AFC- 21

**Longest Winning Streak by Conference:**

                                                     NFC- 13 (1985-1997)

                                                     AFC-  5 (1973-1977)

## Super Bowl Titles by Team:

| | |
|---|---|
| Pittsburgh Steelers: | 6 |
| Dallas Cowboys: | 5 |
| San Francisco 49ers: | 5 |
| Green Bay Packers: | 4 |
| New York Giants: | 4 |
| New England Patriots: | 4 |
| Oakland Raiders: | 3 |
| Washington Redskins: | 3 |
| Baltimore Ravens: | 2 |
| Indianapolis Colts: | 2 |
| Miami Dolphins: | 2 |
| Denver Broncos: | 2 |
| New Orleans Saints: | 1 |
| New York Jets: | 1 |
| Tampa Bay Buccaneers: | 1 |
| Chicago Bears: | 1 |
| Kansas City Chiefs: | 1 |
| St. Louis Rams: | 1 |
| Seattle Seahawks: | 1 |
| St. Louis Rams: | 3 |
| Seattle Seahawks: | 3 |
| Baltimore Ravens: | 2 |
| Chicago Bears: | 2 |
| Kansas City Chiefs: | 2 |
| Cincinnati Bengals: | 2 |
| Philadelphia Eagles: | 2 |
| New Orleans Saints: | 1 |
| New York Jets: | 1 |
| Tampa Bay Buccaneers: | 1 |
| Atlanta Falcons: | 1 |
| Carolina Panthers: | 1 |
| Arizona Cardinals: | 1 |
| Tennessee Titans: | 1 |
| San Diego Chargers: | 1 |

## Super Bowl Appearances by Team:

| | |
|---|---|
| Pittsburgh Steelers: | 8 |
| Dallas Cowboys: | 8 |
| New England Patriots: | 8 |
| Denver Broncos: | 7 |
| San Francisco 49ers: | 6 |
| Green Bay Packers: | 5 |
| New York Giants: | 5 |
| Oakland Raiders: | 5 |
| Washington Redskins: | 5 |
| Miami Dolphins: | 5 |
| Indianapolis Colts: | 4 |
| Buffalo Bills: | 4 |
| Minnesota Vikings: | 4 |

## Super Bowl Losses by Team:

| | |
|---|---|
| Denver Broncos: | 5 |
| New England Patriots: | 4 |
| Buffalo Bills: | 4 |
| Minnesota Vikings: | 4 |
| Dallas Cowboys: | 3 |
| Miami Dolphins: | 3 |
| Pittsburgh Steelers: | 2 |
| Oakland Raiders: | 2 |
| Washington Redskins: | 2 |
| Indianapolis Colts: | 2 |
| St. Louis Rams: | 2 |
| Seattle Seahawks: | 2 |
| Cincinnati Bengals: | 2 |
| Philadelphia Eagles: | 2 |
| San Francisco 49ers: | 1 |
| Green Bay Packers: | 1 |
| New York Giants: | 1 |
| Chicago Bears: | 1 |

Kansas City Chiefs:        1
Atlanta Falcons:           1
Carolina Panthers:         1
Arizona Cardinals:         1
Tennessee Titans:          1
San Diego Chargers:        1

## Teams that Played in Super Bowl but Never Won:

Buffalo Bills (4)
Minnesota Vikings (4)
Cincinnati Bengals (2)
Philadelphia Eagles (2)
Atlanta Falcons (1)
Carolina Panthers (1)
Arizona Cardinals (1)
Tennessee Titans (1)
San Diego Chargers (1)

## Teams that Have Never Played in the Super Bowl:

Cleveland Browns
Detroit Lions
Houston Texans
Jacksonville Jaguars

## Super Bowls Hosted (by city):

Miami:
10
New Orleans:
10
Los Angeles (and surrounding area):
7
Tampa:
4
San Diego:
3
Phoenix (and surrounding area):
3
Houston:
2
Detroit (and surrounding area):
2
Atlanta:
2
Stanford, California:
1
Minneapolis:
1
Indianapolis:
1
Dallas (and surrounding area):
1
New York City (and surrounding area):
1
Jacksonville, Florida:
1

## Super Bowl Halftime Performers

1967  University of Arizona and Grambling State marching bands

1968  Grambling State band

1969  "America Thanks" with Florida A&M University band

1970  Carol Channing

1971  Florida A&M band

1972  "Salute to Louis Armstrong" with Ella Fitzgerald, Carol Channing, Al Hirt and U.S. Marine Corps Drill Team

1973  "Happiness Is" with University of Michigan marching band and Woody Herman

1974  "A Musical America" with University of Texas band

1975  "Tribute to Duke Ellington" with Mercer Ellington and Grambling State band

1976  "200 Years and Just a Baby" Tribute to America's Bicentennial

1977  "It's a Small World" including crowd participation for first time with spectators waving colored placards on cue

1978  "From Paris to the Paris of America" with Tyler Apache Belles, Pete Fountain and Al Hirt

1979  "Super Bowl XIII Carnival" Salute to the Caribbean with Ken Hamilton and various Caribbean bands

1980  "A Salute to the Big Band Era" with Up with People

1981  "A Mardi Gras Festival"

1982   "A Salute to the 60s and Motown"

1983  "KaleidoSUPERscope" (a kaleidoscope of color and sound)

1984  "Super Bowl XVIII's Salute to the Superstars of the Silver Screen"

1985  "A World of Children's Dreams"

1986  "Beat of the Future"

1987  "Salute to Hollywood's 100th Anniversary" with George Burns

1988  "Something Grand" featuring 88 grand pianos, the Rockettes and Chubby Checker

1989  "Be Bop Bamboozled" featuring 3-D effects

1990  "Salute to New Orleans" and 40th Anniversary of Peanuts' characters, featuring trumpeter Pete Fountain, Doug Kershaw & Irma Thomas

1991  "A Small World Salute to 25 Years of the Super Bowl" featuring New Kids on the Block

1992  "Winter Magic" including a salute to the winter season and the winter Olympics featuring Gloria Estefan, Brian Boitano and Dorothy Hamill

1993	"Heal the World" featuring Michael Jackson and 3,500 local children

1994	"Rockin' Country Sunday" featuring Clint Black, Tanya Tucker, Travis Tritt, Wynonna & Naomi Judd

1995	"Indiana Jones and the Temple of the Forbidden Eye" featuring Tony Bennett, Patti LaBelle, Arturo Sandoval, and the Miami Sound Machine

1996	Diana Ross celebrating 30 years of the Super Bowl

1997	"Blues Brothers Bash" featuring Dan Akroyd, John Goodman and James Belushi. Also featuring James Brown and ZZ Top

1998	"A Tribute to Motown's 40th Anniversary" including Boyz II Men, Smokey Robinson, Queen Latifah, Martha Reeves and The Temptations

1999	"Celebration of Soul, Salsa and Swing" featuring Stevie Wonder, Gloria Estefan, Big Bad Voodoo Daddy and tap dancer Savion Glover

2000	"A Tapestry of Nations" featuring Phil Collins, Christina Aguilera, Enrique Iglesias, Toni Braxton and an 80-person choir

2001	"The Kings of Rock and Pop" featuring Aerosmith, 'N'Sync, Britney Spears, Mary J. Blige and Nelly

2002	U2

2003	Shania Twain, No Doubt and Sting

2004	Janet Jackson, Kid Rock, P. Diddy, Nelly and Justin Timberlake

2005	Paul McCartney

2006	The Rolling Stones

2007	Prince and the Florida A&M marching band

2008	Tom Petty & The Heartbreakers

2009	Bruce Springsteen and the E Street Band

2010	The Who

2011	The Black Eyed Peas, Usher, Slash

2012	Madonna

2013	Beyonce

2014	Bruno Mars and the Red Hot Chili Peppers

2015	Katy Perry, featuring Lenny Kravitz and Missy Elliot

# NFL Championships
# (Pre-1970 AFL/NFL merger)

1920 **Akron Pros**
1921 **Chicago Staleys** (Bears)
1922 **Canton Bulldogs**
1923 **Canton Bulldogs**
1924 **Cleveland Bulldogs**
1925 **Chicago Cardinals**
1926 **Frankford Yellow Jackets**
1927 **New York Giants**
1928 **Providence Steam Roller**
1929 **Green Bay Packers**
1930 **Green Bay Packers**
1931 **Green Bay Packers**
1932 **Chicago Bears**
1933 **Chicago Bears** (*over New York Giants*)[1]
1934 **New York Giants** (*over Chicago Bears*)
1935 **Detroit Lions** (*over New York Giants*)
1936 **Green Bay Packers** (*over Boston Redskins*)
1937 **Washington Redskins** (*over Chicago Bears*)
1938 **New York Giants** (*over Green Bay Packers*)
1939 **Green Bay Packers** (*over New York Giants*)
1940 **Chicago Bears** (*over Washington Redskins*)
1941 **Chicago Bears** (*over New York Giants*)
1942 **Washington Redskins** (*over Chicago Bears*)
1943 **Chicago Bears** (*over Washington Redskins*)
1944 **Green Bay Packers** (*over New York Giants*)
1945 **Cleveland Rams** (*over Washington Redskins*)
1946 **Chicago Bears** (*over New York Giants*)
1947 **Chicago Cardinals** (*over Philadelphia Eagles*)
1948 **Philadelphia Eagles** (*over Chicago Cardinals*)
1949 **Philadelphia Eagles** (*over Los Angeles Rams*)

---

1　　In 1933 the league split into Eastern and Western conferences with the winners playing for the NFL title.

1950   **Cleveland Browns** (*over Los Angeles Rams*)

1951   **Los Angeles Rams** (*over Cleveland Browns*)

1952   **Detroit Lions** (*over Cleveland Browns*)

1953   **Detroit Lions** (*over Cleveland Browns*)

1954   **Cleveland Browns** (*over Detroit Lions*)

1955   **Cleveland Browns** (*over Los Angeles Rams*)

1956   **New York Giants** (*over Chicago Bears*)

1957   **Detroit Lions** (*over Cleveland Browns*)

1958   **Baltimore Colts** (*over New York Giants*)

1959   **Baltimore Colts** (*over New York Giants*)

1960   **Philadelphia Eagles** (*over Green Bay Packers*)

1961   **Green Bay Packers** (*over New York Giants*)

1962   **Green Bay Packers** (*over New York Giants*)

1963   **Chicago Bears** (*over New York Giants*)

1964   **Cleveland Browns** (*over Baltimore Colts*)

1965   **Green Bay Packers** (*over Cleveland Browns*)

1966   **Green Bay Packers** (*over Dallas Cowboys*)

1967   **Green Bay Packers** (*over Dallas Cowboys*)

1968   **Baltimore Colts** (*over Cleveland Browns*)

1969   **Minnesota Vikings** (*over Cleveland Browns*)

## Most NFL Titles by Team (pre-1970 AFL/NFL merger)

| | |
|---|---|
| Green Bay Packers: | 11 |
| Chicago Bears: | 8 |
| New York Giants: | 4 |
| Detroit Lions: | 4 |
| Cleveland Browns: | 4 (does not include AAFC titles) |
| Philadelphia Eagles: | 3 |
| Baltimore Colts: | 3 |
| Canton Bulldogs: | 2 |
| Chicago Cardinals: | 2 |
| Cleveland/Los Angeles Rams: | 2 |
| Boston/Washington Redskins: | 2 |
| Akron Pros: | 1 |
| Cleveland Bulldogs: | 1 |
| Providence Steam Roller: | 1 |
| Frankfort Yellow Jackets: | 1 |
| Minnesota Vikings | 1 |

## Most NFL Title Game Losses (pre-1970 AFL/NFL merger)

| | |
|---|---|
| New York Giants | 11 |
| Cleveland Browns | $7^2$ |
| Chicago Bears | 4 |
| Washington Redskins | 4 |
| Los Angeles Rams | 3 |
| Green Bay Packers | 2 |
| Dallas Cowboys | 2 |
| Baltimore Colts | 1 |
| Detroit Lions | 1 |
| Philadelphia Eagles | 1 |
| Chicago Cardinals | 1 |

---

2       Does not include any AAFC games. In those four title games, the Browns never lost).

## AFL Championships
## (Pre-1970 AFL/NFL merger)

1960    **Houston Oilers** (*over Los Angeles Chargers[3]*)

1961    **Houston Oilers** (*over San Diego Chargers*)

1962    **Dallas Texans[4]** (*over Houston Oilers*)

1963    **San Diego Chargers** (*over Boston Patriots*)

1964    **Buffalo Bills** (*over San Diego Chargers*)

1965    **Buffalo Bills** (*over San Diego Chargers*)

1966    **Kansas City Chiefs** (*over Buffalo Bills*)

1967    **Oakland Raiders** (*over Houston Oilers*)

1968    **New York Jets** (*over Oakland Raiders*)

1969    **Kansas City Chiefs** (*over Oakland Raiders*)

## All-American Football Conference Championships
## (Pre-1950 AAFC/NFL merger)

1946    **Cleveland Browns** (*over New York Yankees*)

1947    **Cleveland Browns** (*over New York Yankees*)

1948    **Cleveland Browns** (*over Buffalo Bills[5]*)

1949    **Cleveland Browns** (*over San Francisco 49ers*)

## Most League Titles by Team (NFL, AFL, AAFC combined)[6]

| | |
|---|---|
| Green Bay Packers | 15 |
| Chicago Bears | 9 |
| Cleveland Browns | 8 |
| New York Giants | 8 |
| Pittsburgh Steelers | 6 |
| Dallas Cowboys | 5 |
| Indianapolis Colts | 5 |
| San Francisco 49ers | 5 |

---

3       Became the San Diego Chargers in 1961.

4       Became the Kansas City Chiefs in 1963.

5       This version of the Buffalo Bills folded after the merger of the AAFC and NFL in 1950. The AFL Buffalo Bills came into existence in 1960.

6       For purposes of this book, for the pre-AFL/NFL merger period of 1966 through 1969 seasons, if an AFL or NFL team won their league title but not the Super Bowl, they get credit for that league title. If they won the Super Bowl, they get credit for that title but not a double-dip for also winning the AFL or NFL league title that season.

Washington Redskins        5

New England Patriots       4

Oakland Raiders            4

St. Louis Rams             3

Kansas City Chiefs         2

Buffalo Bills              2

Houston Oilers             2

Miami Dolphins             2

Denver Broncos             2

New Orleans Saints         1

New York Jets              1

Tampa Bay Buccaneers       1

Seattle Seahawks           1

Minnesota Vikings          1

San Diego Chargers         1


## Most Conference Title Game Appearances (post-1970 AFL/NFL Merger)[7]

Pittsburgh Steelers        15

San Francisco 49ers        15

Dallas Cowboys             14

New England Patriots       11

Oakland Raiders            11[8]

St. Louis Rams             9[9]

Denver Broncos             9

Minnesota Vikings          8

Miami Dolphins             7

Indianapolis Colts         7[10]

Washington Redskins        6

Green Bay Packers          6

Philadelphia Eagles        6

New York Giants            5

---

7       The AFC's Houston Texans are the only NFL team to not play in a conference title game.

8       Includes appearances as Los Angeles Raiders.

9       Includes appearances as Los Angeles Rams.

10      Includes appearances as Baltimore Colts.

| | |
|---|---|
| Chicago Bears | 5 |
| Buffalo Bills | 5 |
| Tennessee Titans | 4[11] |
| San Diego Chargers | 4 |
| New York Jets | 4 |
| Seattle Seahawks | 4[12] |
| Cleveland Browns | 3 |
| Atlanta Falcons | 3 |
| Carolina Panthers | 3 |
| Tampa Bay Buccaneers | 3 |
| Cincinnati Bengals | 2 |
| Jacksonville Jaguars | 2 |
| New Orleans Saints | 2 |
| Arizona Cardinals | 1 |
| Detroit Lions | 1 |
| Kansas City Chiefs | 1 |

## Most NFC Title Game Wins (post-1970 AFL/NFL Merger)

| | |
|---|---|
| Dallas Cowboys | 8 |
| San Francisco 49ers | 6 |
| Washington Redskins | 5 |
| New York Giants | 5 |
| St. Louis Rams | 3 |
| Minnesota Vikings | 3 |
| Green Bay Packers | 3 |
| Seattle Seahawks | 3 |
| Philadelphia Eagles | 2 |
| Chicago Bears | 2 |
| Atlanta Falcons | 1 |
| Carolina Panthers | 1 |
| Tampa Bay Buccaneers | 1 |
| New Orleans Saints | 1 |
| Arizona Cardinals | 1 |

---

11      Includes appearances as Houston Oilers.

12      Includes one appearance in AFC championship game when Seahawks were in the AFC.

## Most NFC Title Game Losses (post-1970 AFL/NFL merger)

| | |
|---|---|
| San Francisco 49ers | 9 |
| St. Louis Rams | 6 |
| Dallas Cowboys | 6 |
| Minnesota Vikings | 5 |
| Philadelphia Eagles | 4 |
| Chicago Bears | 3 |
| Green Bay Packers | 3 |
| Atlanta Falcons | 2 |
| Carolina Panthers | 2 |
| New Orleans Saints | 1 |
| Washington Redskins | 1 |
| Detroit Lions | 1 |

## Most AFC Title Game Wins (post-1970 AFL/NFL Merger)

| | |
|---|---|
| Pittsburgh Steelers | 8 |
| New England Patriots | 8 |
| Denver Broncos | 7 |
| Miami Dolphins | 5 |
| Oakland Raiders | 4 |
| Buffalo Bills | 4 |
| Indianapolis Colts | 3 |
| Baltimore Ravens | 2 |
| Cincinnati Bengals | 2 |
| San Diego Chargers | 1 |

## Most AFC Title Game Losses (post-1970 AFL/NFL Merger)

| | |
|---|---|
| Pittsburgh Steelers | 7 |
| Oakland Raiders | 7 |
| Indianapolis Colts | 4 |
| New York Jets | 4 |
| Cleveland Browns | 3 |
| New England Patriots | 3 |
| San Diego Chargers | 3 |
| Denver Broncos | 2 |
| Miami Dolphins | 2 |
| Baltimore Ravens | 2 |
| Jacksonville Jaguars | 2 |
| Kansas City Chiefs | 1 |
| Seattle Seahawks | 1 |

## Most Playoff Appearances (post-1970 AFL/NFL Merger)

| | |
|---|---|
| Dallas Cowboys | 26 |
| Pittsburgh Steelers | 26 |
| Minnesota Vikings | 24 |
| San Francisco 49ers | 22 |
| Miami Dolphins | 22 |
| Indianapolis Colts | 19 |
| St. Louis Rams | 19 |
| Philadelphia Eagles | 19 |
| New England Patriots | 18 |
| Oakland Raiders | 18 |
| Denver Broncos | 18 |
| Green Bay Packers | 16 |
| Washington Redskins | 16 |
| Tennessee Titans | 16 |
| New York Giants | 15 |
| Chicago Bears | 14 |
| Seattle Seahawks | 13 |
| Buffalo Bills | 13 |
| San Diego Chargers | 12 |
| Kansas City Chiefs | 12 |
| New York Jets | 12 |
| Cleveland Browns | 11 |
| Atlanta Falcons | 11 |
| Cincinnati Bengals | 10 |
| Tampa Bay Buccaneers | 10 |
| Detroit Lions | 10 |
| New Orleans Saints | 9 |
| Baltimore Ravens | 9 |
| Arizona Cardinals | 6 |
| Jacksonville Jaguars | 6 |
| Carolina Panthers | 4 |
| Houston Texans | 2 |

## Most Playoff Appearances (NFL, AFL, AAFC combined)[13]

| | | | |
|---|---|---|---|
| Dallas Cowboys | 30 | Buffalo Bills (AAFC) | 1 |
| New York Giants | 29 | New York Yankees (AAFC) | 1 |
| Cleveland Browns | 27 | | |
| Pittsburgh Steelers | 26 | | |
| Minnesota Vikings | 26 | | |
| St. Louis Rams | 26 | | |
| Green Bay Packers | 26 | | |
| San Francisco 49ers | 23 | | |
| Indianapolis Colts | 23 | | |
| Chicago Bears | 23 | | |
| Philadelphia Eagles | 23 | | |
| Miami Dolphins | 22 | | |
| Oakland Raiders | 21 | | |
| Washington Redskins | 21 | | |
| Tennessee Titans | 21 | | |
| New England Patriots | 19 | | |
| Denver Broncos | 18 | | |
| San Diego Chargers | 17 | | |
| Buffalo Bills | 16 | | |
| Detroit Lions | 15 | | |
| Kansas City Chiefs | 15 | | |
| New York Jets | 14 | | |
| Seattle Seahawks | 13 | | |
| Atlanta Falcons | 11 | | |
| Cincinnati Bengals | 10 | | |
| Tampa Bay Buccaneers | 10 | | |
| New Orleans Saints | 9 | | |
| Baltimore Ravens | 9 | | |
| Arizona Cardinals | 8 | | |
| Jacksonville Jaguars | 6 | | |
| Carolina Panthers | 4 | | |
| Houston Texans | 2 | | |

---

13    Begins starting with 1933 season, the first NFL season to have an Eastern Conference v. Western Conference championship game. Does not include "Playoff Bowl" appearances or any tie-breakers for conference titles (e.g., New York Giants vs. Cleveland Browns in 1958).

## Most Division Titles
## (post-1970 AFL/NFL merger)

| | |
|---|---|
| Pittsburgh Steelers | 20 |
| Dallas Cowboys | 18 |
| San Francisco 49ers | 18 |
| Minnesota Vikings | 16 |
| Miami Dolphins | 13 |
| New England Patriots | 13 |
| Indianapolis Colts | 13 |
| Oakland Raiders | 12 |
| Denver Broncos | 11 |
| St. Louis Rams | 11 |
| San Diego Chargers | 10 |
| Green Bay Packers | 9 |
| Chicago Bears | 9 |
| Philadelphia Eagles | 8 |
| New York Giants | 8 |
| Seattle Seahawks | 8 |
| Buffalo Bills | 7 |
| Cincinnati Bengals | 7 |
| Washington Redskins | 6 |
| Kansas City Chiefs | 6 |
| Cleveland Browns | 6 |
| Tampa Bay Buccaneers | 6 |
| Tennessee Titans | 5 |
| New Orleans Saints | 5 |
| Baltimore Ravens | 4 |
| Atlanta Falcons | 4 |
| Arizona Cardinals | 4 |
| Carolina Panthers | 3 |

| | |
|---|---|
| Detroit Lions | 3 |
| Jacksonville Jaguars | 2 |
| New York Jets | 2 |
| Houston Texans | 2 |

## Most "Wild Card" Playoff Berths
## (post-1970 AFL/NFL Merger)[14]

| | |
|---|---|
| Philadelphia Eagles | 11 |
| Tennessee Titans | 11 |
| New York Jets | 10 |
| Washington Redskins | 10 |
| Miami Dolphins | 9 |
| Dallas Cowboys | 8 |
| Minnesota Vikings | 8 |
| St. Louis Rams | 8 |
| Atlanta Falcons | 7 |
| Green Bay Packers | 7 |
| New York Giants | 7 |
| Denver Broncos | 7 |
| Detroit Lions | 7 |
| Pittsburgh Steelers | 6 |
| Oakland Raiders | 6 |
| Indianapolis Colts | 6 |
| Kansas City Chiefs | 6 |
| Buffalo Bills | 6 |
| Baltimore Ravens | 5 |
| New England Patriots | 5 |
| Chicago Bears | 5 |
| Seattle Seahawks | 5 |
| Cleveland Browns | 5 |
| San Francisco 49ers | 4 |
| Jacksonville Jaguars | 4 |
| New Orleans Saints | 4 |
| Tampa Bay Buccaneers | 4 |
| Cincinnati Bengals | 3 |
| Arizona Cardinals | 2 |
| San Diego Chargers | 2 |
| Carolina Panthers | 1 |

---

14     "Wild Card" here refers to teams that made the playoffs but did not win the division title.

## NFL Hall of Fame

**1963**  Sammy Baugh (QB), Johnny Blood (RB), Dutch Clark (RB), Red Grange ( RB), George Halas (E, Owner, Coach), Mel Hein (C), Pete Henry (T), Cal Hubbard (T), Don Hutson (E), Curly Lambeau (RB, Owner, Coach), Bronko Naguski (RB), Ernie Nevers (RB), Jim Thorpe (RB), Bert Bell (Owner, Commissioner), Joe Carr (President), Tim Mara (Owner), George Preston Marshall (Owner)

**1964**  Ed Healey (T), Clarke Hinkle (RB), Link Lyman (T), Mike Michalske (G), George Trafton (C), Jimmy Conzelman (RB, Coach), Art Rooney (Owner)

**1965**  Otto Graham (QB), Sid Luckman (QB), Steve Van Buren (RB), Bob Waterfield (QB), Guy Chamberlin (Coach)

**1966**  Bill Dudley (RB), Joe Guyon (RB), Arnie Herber (RB), Walt Kiesling (G), George McAfee (RB), Steve Owen (Coach, T), Bulldog Turner (C),  Hugh "Shorty" Ray (Referee)

**1967**  Chuck Bednarik (LB), Bobby Layne (QB), Ken Strong (RB), Emlen Tunnell (DB), Paul Brown (Coach, Owner), Dan Reeves (Owner), Charles Bidwell (Owner)

**1968**  Elroy "Crazy Legs" Hirsch (E), Wayne Miller (E), Marion Motley (RB), Charlie Trippi (RB), Alex Wojciechowicz (C)

**1969**  Leo Nomellini (DT), Joe Perry (RB), Ernie Stautner (DT), Greasy Neale (Coach)

**1970**  Jack Christiansen (DB), Tom Fears (E), Hugh McElhenny (RB), Pete Pihos (E)

**1971**  Bill Hewitt (E), Bruiser Kinard (T), Andy Robustelli (DE), Y.A. Tittle (QB), Norm Van Brocklin (QB), Vince Lombardi (Coach)

**1972**  Gino Marchetti (DE), Ollie Matson (RB), Ace Parker (RB), Lamar Hunt (Owner)

**1973**  Raymond Berry (E), Jim Parker (T), Joe Schmidt (LB)

**1974**  Tony Canadeo (RB), Bill George (LB), Lou Groza (T, K), Night Train Lane (DB)

**1975**  Rosey Brown (T), George Connor (T), Dante Lavelli (E), Lenny Moore (RB)

**1976**  Ray Flaherty (E, Coach), Len Ford (DE), Jim Taylor (RB)

**1977**  Frank Gifford (RB), Forrest Gregg (T), Gale Sayers (RB), Bart Starr (QB), Bill Willis (G)

**1978**  Lance Alworth (WR), Tuffy Leemans (RB), Ray Nitschke (LB), Larry Wilson (DB), Weeb Ewbank (Coach)

**1979**  Dick Butkus (LB), Yale Lary (DB), Ron Mix (T), Johnny Unitas (QB)

**1980**  Herb Adderley (DB), Deacon Jones (DE), Bob Lilly (DT), Jim Otto (C)

**1981**  George Blanda (QB, K), Will Davis (DE), Jim Ringo (C)

**1982**  Doug Atkins (DE), Sam Huff (LB), George Musso (G), Merlin Olsen (DT)

**1983**  Bobby Bell (LB), Sonny Jurgensen (QB), Bobby Mitchell (WR), Paul Warfield (WR), Sid Gilman (Coach)

**1984**  Will Brown (DB), Mike McCormack (T), Charley Taylor (WR), Arnie Weinmeister (DT)

**1985**  Frank Gatski (C), Joe Namath (QB), O.J. Simpson (RB), Roger Staubach (QB), Pete Rozelle (Commissioner)

**1986**  Paul Hornung (RB), Ken Houston (DB), Willie Lanier (LB), Fran Tarkenton (QB), Doak Walker (RB)

**1987** Larry Csonka (RB), Len Dawson (QB), Joe Greene (DT), John Henry Johnson (RB), Jim Langer (C), Don Maynard (E), Gene Upshaw (G)

**1988** Fred Biletnikoff (WR), Mike Ditka (TE), Jack Ham (LB), Alan Page (DT)

**1989** Terry Bradshaw (QB), Art Shell (T), Will Wood (DB)

**1990** Buck Buchanan (DT), Bob Griese (QB), Franco Harris (RB), Ted Hendricks (LB), Jack Lambert (LB), Tom Landry (DB, Coach)

**1991** Earl Campbell (RB), John Hannah (G), Stan Jones (G), Jan Stenerud (K), Tex Schramm (GM)

**1992** Lem Barney (DB), John Riggins (RB), John Mackey (TE), Al Davis (Coach, Owner)

**1993** Dan Fouts (QB), Larry Little (G), Chuck Noll (LB, Coach), Walter Payton (RB), Bill Walsh (Coach)

**1994** Tony Dorsett (RB), Jimmy Johnson (DB), Leroy Kelly (RB), Jackie Smith (TE), Randy White (DT), Bud Grant (Coach)

**1995** Jim Finks (QB, GM), Henry Jordan (DT), Steve Largent (WR), Lee Roy Selmon (DE), Kellen Winslow (TE)

**1996** Lou Creekmur (T), Dan Dierdorf (T), Charlie Joiner (WR), Mel Renfro (DB), Joe Gibbs (Coach)

**1997** Mike Hayne (DB), Don Shula (DB, Coach), Mike Webster (C), Wellington Mara (Owner)

**1998** Paul Krause (DB), Tommy McDonald (WR), Anthony Munoz (T), Mike Singletary (LB), Dwight Stephenson (C)

**1999** Eric Dickerson (RB), Tom Mack (G), Ozzie Newsome (TE), Billy Shaw (G), Lawrence Taylor (LB)

**2000** Howie Long (DE), Ronnie Lott (DB), Joe Montana (QB), Dave Wilcox (LB), Dan Rooney (Owner)

**2001** Nick Buoniconti (LB), Mike Munchak (G), Jackie Slater (T), Lynn Swann (WR), Ron Yary (T), Jack Youngblood (DE); Marv Levy (Coach)

**2002** Dave Casper (TE), Dan Hampton (DE), Jim Kelly (QB), John Stallworth (WR), George Allen (Coach)

**2003** Marcus Allen (RB), Elvin Bethea (DE), Joe DeLamielleure (G), James Lofton (WR), Hank Stram (Coach)

**2004** Bob Brown (T), Carl Eller (DE), John Elway (QB), Barry Sanders (RB)

**2005** Benny Friedman (RB), Dan Marino (QB), Fritz Pollard (RB), Steve Young (QB)

**2006** Troy Aikman (QB), Harry Carson (LB), Warren Moon (QB), Reggie White (DE), Rayfield Wright (T), John Madden (Coach, Broadcaster)

**2007** Gene Hickerson (G), Michael Irvin (WR), Bruce Matthews (G), Charlie Sanders (TE), Thurman Thomas (RB), Roger Wehrli (DB)

**2008** Fred Dean (DE), Art Monk (WR), Emmitt Thomas (DB), Andrew Tippett (LB), Gary Zimmerman (T)

**2009** Bob Hayes (WR), Randall McDaniel (G), Bruce Smith (DE), Derrick Thomas (LB), Rod Woodson (DB), Ralph Wilson (Owner)

**2010** Russ Grimm (G), Rickey Jackson (LB), Dick LeBeau (DB, Coach), Floyd Little (RB), John Randle (DT), Jerry Rice (WR), Emmitt Smith (RB)

**2011** Richard Dent (DE), Marshall Faulk (RB), Chris Hanburger (LB), Les Richter (LB), Deion Sanders (DB), Shannon Sharpe (TE), Ed Sabol (NFL Films)

**2012** Jack Butler (DB), Dermontti Dawson (C), Chris Doleman (DE), Cortez Kennedy (DT), Curtis Martin (RB), Willie Roaf (T)

**2013**   Larry Allen (G), Cris Carter (WR), Curley Culp (DT), Jonathan Ogden (T), Dave Robinson (LB), Warren Sapp (DT), Bill Parcells (Coach)

**2014**   Derrick Brooks (LB), Ray Guy (P), Claude Humphrey (DE), Walter Jones (T), Andrew Reed (WR), Michael Strahan (DE), Aeneas Williams (DB)

**2015**   Jerome Bettis (RB), Tim Brown (WR), Charles Hayley (DE), Junior Seau (LB), Will Shields (G), Mick Tingelhoff (C)

## Hall of Fame Game

The NFL Hall of Fame Game is a preseason game played in Canton, Ohio (home of the NFL Hall of Fame and where the NFL was first organized). It is generally the first preseason game of the season and is played in conjunction with the induction of that year's Hall of Fame class. The first game was played in 1962, one year before the Hall opened. It is played at 22,000 seat Tom Benson Hall of Fame Stadium (formerly Fawcett Stadium). The Baltimore Ravens are the only currently active team not to play in the Hall of Fame game. No game was played in 1966 because the pre-season schedule was not set in time to permit the game. The 2011 game was canceled due to the "lock out" of the players by the NFL. This was the only game canceled in the 2011 season.

| Year | Winner | Loser | Score |
|------|--------|-------|-------|
| 1962 | New York Giants | St. Louis Cardinals | 21-21 |
| 1963 | Pittsburgh Steelers | Cleveland Browns | 16-7 |
| 1964 | Baltimore Colts | Pittsburgh Steelers | 48-17 |
| 1965 | Washington Redskins | Detroit Lions | 20-3 |
| 1966 | No Game | | |
| 1967 | Philadelphia Eagles | Cleveland Browns | 28-13 |
| 1968 | Chicago Bears | Dallas Cowboys | 30-24 |
| 1969 | Green Bay Packers | Atlanta Falcons | 38-24 |
| 1970 | New Orleans Saints | Minnesota Vikings | 14-13 |
| 1971 | Los Angeles Rams | Houston Oilers | 17-6 |
| 1972 | Kansas City Chiefs | New York Giants | 23-17 |
| 1973 | San Francisco 49ers | New England Patriots | 20-7 |
| 1974 | St. Louis Cardinals | Buffalo Bills | 21-13 |
| 1975 | Washington Redskins | Cincinnati Bengals | 17-9 |
| 1976 | Denver Broncos | Detroit Lions | 10-7 |
| 1977 | Chicago Bears | New York Jets | 20-6 |

| Year | Winner | Loser | Score |
|------|--------|-------|-------|
| 1978 | Philadelphia Eagles | Miami Dolphins | 17-3 |
| 1979 | Oakland Raiders | Dallas Cowboys | 20-13 |
| 1980 | San Diego Chargers | Green Bay Packers | 0-0 |
| 1981 | Cleveland Browns | Atlanta Falcons | 24-10 |
| 1982 | Minnesota Vikings | Baltimore Colts | 30-14 |
| 1983 | Pittsburgh Steelers | New Orleans Saints | 27-14 |
| 1984 | Seattle Seahawks | Tampa Bay Buccaneers | 38-0 |
| 1985 | New York Giants | Houston Oilers | 21-20 |
| 1986 | New England Patriots | St. Louis Cardinals | 21-16 |
| 1987 | San Francisco 49ers | Kansas City Chiefs | 20-7 |
| 1988 | Cincinnati Bengals | Los Angeles Rams | 14-7 |
| 1989 | Washington Redskins | Buffalo Bills | 31-6 |
| 1990 | Chicago Bears | Cleveland Browns | 13-0 |
| 1991 | Detroit Lions | Denver Broncos | 14-3 |
| 1992 | New York Jets | Philadelphia Eagles | 41-14 |
| 1993 | Los Angeles Raiders | Green Bay Packers | 19-3 |
| 1994 | Atlanta Falcons | San Diego Chargers | 21-17 |
| 1995 | Carolina Panthers | Jacksonville Jaguars | 20-14 |
| 1996 | Indianapolis Colts | New Orleans Saints | 10-3 |
| 1997 | Minnesota Vikings | Seattle Seahawks | 28-26 |
| 1998 | Tampa Bay Buccaneers | Pittsburgh Steelers | 30-6 |
| 1999 | Cleveland Browns | Dallas Cowboys | 20-17 |
| 2000 | New England Patriots | San Francisco 49ers | 20-0 |
| 2001 | St. Louis Rams | Miami Dolphins | 17-10 |
| 2002 | New York Giants | Houston Texans | 34-17 |
| 2003 | Kansas City Chiefs | Green Bay Packers | 9-0 |
| 2004 | Washington Redskins | Denver Broncos | 20-17 |
| 2005 | Chicago Bears | Miami Dolphins | 27-24 |
| 2006 | Oakland Raiders | Philadelphia Eagles | 16-10 |
| 2007 | Pittsburgh Steelers | New Orleans Saints | 20-7 |
| 2008 | Washington Redskins | Indianapolis Colts | 30-16 |
| 2009 | Tennessee Titans | Buffalo Bills | 21-18 |
| 2010 | Dallas Cowboys | Cincinnati Bengals | 16-7 |
| 2011 | No Game | | |
| 2012 | New Orleans Saints | Arizona Cardinals | 17-10 |
| 2013 | Dallas Cowboys | Miami Dolphins | 24-20 |
| 2014 | New York Giants | Buffalo Bills | 17-13 |

# NFL Pro Bowl

## (1951-1970)

The NFL Pro Bowl featured "all-stars" from each conference playing an exhibition game held after the league title game. There were several earlier versions of the game, including one version where the league champion played an opposing team made up of league all-stars. However, the birth of the Pro Bowl as we understand it today occurred in 1950. During the course of this version of the game: Western Conference- 13 wins, Eastern Conference- 7 wins.

| Year | Winner | Loser | Score | Location |
|------|--------|-------|-------|----------|
| 1951 | American Conference (East) | National Conference (West) | 28-27 | Los Angeles |
| 1952 | National Conference | American Conference | 30-13 | Los Angeles |
| 1953 | National Conference | American Conference | 27-7 | Los Angeles |
| 1954 | Eastern Conference | Western Conference | 20-9 | Los Angeles |
| 1955 | Western Conference | Eastern Conference | 26-19 | Los Angeles |
| 1956 | Eastern Conference | Western Conference | 31-30 | Los Angeles |
| 1957 | Western Conference | Eastern Conference | 19-10 | Los Angeles |
| 1958 | Western Conference | Eastern Conference | 26-7 | Los Angeles |
| 1959 | Eastern Conference | Western Conference | 28-21 | Los Angeles |
| 1960 | Western Conference | Eastern Conference | 38-21 | Los Angeles |
| 1961 | Western Conference | Eastern Conference | 35-31 | Los Angeles |
| 1962 | Western Conference | Eastern Conference | 31-30 | Los Angeles |
| 1963 | Eastern Conference | Western Conference | 30-20 | Los Angeles |
| 1964 | Western Conference | Eastern Conference | 31-17 | Los Angeles |
| 1965 | Western Conference | Eastern Conference | 34-14 | Los Angeles |

| Year | Winner | Loser | Score | Location |
|------|--------|-------|-------|----------|
| 1966 | Eastern Conference | Western Conference | 36-7 | Los Angeles |
| 1967 | Eastern Conference | Western Conference | 20-10 | Los Angeles |
| 1968 | Western Conference | Eastern Conference | 38-20 | Los Angeles |
| 1969 | Western Conference | Eastern Conference | 10-7 | Los Angeles |
| 1970 | Western Conference | Eastern Conference | 16-13 | Los Angeles |

# AFC-NFC Pro Bowl

## (1971-2013)

With the 1970 merger, the Pro Bowl changed to feature all-stars from the NFC vs. the AFC. The game was played after the Super Bowl, generally in Honolulu, Hawaii beginning in 1980. The NFL kept this format until 2014. By then the game had lost its luster and appeal to fans over the past several years when the Pro Bowl began to suffer from a noticeable lack of quality play by the players (assuming those selected even showed up for the game). The NFL considered doing away with the game but instead, after lobbying by the player's association to keep the game, adopted a new format whereby retired veteran NFL players would be named "Captains" and would select players from either conference to play on their team, tracking in large part the popular "fantasy football" draft concept. The game is now played the week before the Super Bowl which means that players for teams participating in the Super Bowl cannot play in the game. For purposes of this book, the Pro Bowl ended in 2013.

| Year | Winner | Loser | Score | Location |
|------|--------|-------|-------|----------|
| 1971 | NFC | AFC | 27-6 | Los Angeles |
| 1972 | AFC | NFC | 26-13 | Los Angeles |
| 1973 | AFC | NFC | 33-28 | Dallas |
| 1974 | AFC | NFC | 15-13 | Kansas City |
| 1975 | NFC | AFC | 17-10 | Miami |
| 1976 | NFC | AFC | 23-20 | New Orleans |
| 1977 | AFC | NFC | 24-14 | Seattle |
| 1978 | NFC | AFC | 14-13 | Tampa |
| 1979 | NFC | AFC | 13-7 | Los Angeles |
| 1980 | NFC | AFC | 37-27 | Honolulu |
| 1981 | NFC | AFC | 21-7 | Honolulu |
| 1982 | AFC | NFC | 16-13 | Honolulu |
| 1983 | NFC | AFC | 20-19 | Honolulu |
| 1984 | NFC | AFC | 45-3 | Honolulu |
| 1985 | AFC | NFC | 22-14 | Honolulu |
| 1986 | NFC | AFC | 28-24 | Honolulu |
| 1987 | AFC | NFC | 10-6 | Honolulu |
| 1988 | AFC | NFC | 15-6 | Honolulu |
| 1989 | NFC | AFC | 34-3 | Honolulu |

| Year | Winner | Loser | Score | Location |
|------|--------|-------|-------|----------|
| 1990 | NFC | AFC | 27-21 | Honolulu |
| 1991 | AFC | NFC | 23-21 | Honolulu |
| 1992 | NFC | AFC | 21-15 | Honolulu |
| 1993 | AFC | NFC | 23-20 (OT) | Honolulu |
| 1994 | NFC | AFC | 17-3 | Honolulu |
| 1995 | AFC | NFC | 41-13 | Honolulu |
| 1996 | NFC | AFC | 20-13 | Honolulu |
| 1997 | AFC | NFC | 26-23 (OT) | Honolulu |
| 1998 | AFC | NFC | 29-24 | Honolulu |
| 1999 | AFC | NFC | 23-10 | Honolulu |
| 2000 | NFC | AFC | 51-31 | Honolulu |
| 2001 | AFC | NFC | 38-17 | Honolulu |
| 2002 | AFC | NFC | 38-30 | Honolulu |
| 2003 | AFC | NFC | 45-20 | Honolulu |
| 2004 | NFC | AFC | 55-52 | Honolulu |
| 2005 | AFC | NFC | 38-27 | Honolulu |
| 2006 | NFC | AFC | 23-17 | Honolulu |
| 2007 | AFC | NFC | 31-28 | Honolulu |
| 2008 | NFC | AFC | 42-30 | Honolulu |
| 2009 | NFC | AFC | 30-21 | Honolulu |
| 2010 | AFC | NFC | 41-34 | Miami |
| 2011 | NFC | AFC | 55-41 | Honolulu |
| 2012 | AFC | NFC | 59-41 | Honolulu |
| 2013 | NFC | AFC | 62-35 | Honolulu |

**NFC: 22 wins. AFC: 21 wins.**

# AFL All-Star Game
## (1962-1970)

| Year | Winner | Loser | Score | Location |
|------|--------|-------|-------|----------|
| 1962 | Western Conference | Eastern Conference | 47-27 | San Diego |
| 1963 | Western Conference | Eastern Conference | 21-14 | San Diego |
| 1964 | Western Conference | Eastern Conference | 27-24 | San Diego |
| 1965 | Western Conference | Eastern Conference | 38-14 | Houston |
| 1966 | AFL All-Stars | Buffalo Bills | 30-10 | Houston |
| 1967 | Eastern Conference | Western Conference | 30-23 | Oakland |
| 1968 | Eastern Conference | Western Conference | 25-24 | Jacksonville, Florida |
| 1969 | Western Conference | Eastern Conference | 38-25 | Jacksonville, Florida |
| 1970 | Western Conference | Eastern Conference | 26-3 | Houston |

**Western Conference: 6 wins.  Eastern Conference: 2 wins.  AFL All-Stars: 1 win.**

# My Top Ten Football Movies

1. *The Longest Yard* (1974)[15]

2. *Brian's Song* (1971)

3. *North Dallas Forty* (1979)

4. *Friday Night Lights* (2004)

5. *Invincible* (2006)

6. *Big Fan* (2009)

7. *Remember the Titans* (2000)

8. *Paper Lion* (1968)

9. *Any Given Sunday* (1999)

10. *Horse Feathers* (1932)

---

15    The original *The Longest Yard* is so much better than the 2005 Adam Sandler remake. And, I'll just add that if I made a list of the worst football movies, "Rudy" would top it.

## How the NFL Salary Cap Works (2015)

The NFL enacted a hard salary cap beginning with the 1994 season. The cap amount available that year was $34.6 million per team. The 2015 salary cap will be $143.28 million, an increase over time that reflects new lucrative television contracts and other NFL revenue growth opportunities. Each team is obligated to spend approximately 90% of the cap amount each year in player salaries. Whether or not a team meets this "floor" amount is calculated based on total cash spent on player salaries as measured over each of two four-year periods (2013–2016 and 2017–2020). Failure to spend the minimum percentage can lead to fines on the team. Spending more than the cap amount in a season (calculated each season vs. over a period of years) will lead to substantial penalties to the team violating the cap, e.g., fines, loss of draft picks, and cancellation of player contracts.

The salary cap is a component of the Collective Bargaining Agreement ("CBA") between the league and its players. The cap is calculated as follows:

1. All projected NFL revenues from each of media, ventures/postseason, and local revenues.

2. Multiply each revenue stream by its applicable CBA percentage. This gives you "CBA Total Player Salary Revenue;"

3. Subtract player benefits, i.e., benefits to players other than salary ("Player Benefits");

4. Divide the difference by 32 (the number of teams in the league):

$$\text{Salary Cap Per Team} = \frac{(\text{CBA Total Player Salary Revenue\$} - \text{Player Benefits\$})}{32 \text{ Teams}}$$

What constitutes "revenue" takes up 10 pages of the CBA and is fairly complicated. Basically, the "CBA Total Player Salary Revenue" component includes 55 percent of league media revenue e.g., (broadcast rights sold on television, Internet or other media), 45 percent of NFL ventures and postseason revenues (e.g., earnings made from playoff games and media properties such as the NFL Network) and 40 percent of local team revenue (i.e., all remaining revenue received by the teams or team affiliates, e.g., concessions, parking, pre-season games, etc.). Player Benefits are things like insurance, pensions, worker's compensation, etc.

Unlike baseball or basketball, only a small portion of NFL player contracts are "guaranteed" – usually only the signing bonus. The remainder of the player's salary is paid if he "makes the team" during any particular season.  As a result, an individual player's effect on the salary cap is a calculation of a player's base salary, the yearly portion of any pro-rated signing bonus and any other bonuses earned by the player (e.g., roster, workout, Super Bowl MVP, etc.).  With respect to the player's signing bonus component that counts against the cap in any season you simply divide the total bonus by the term of contract.  For example, a $20 million signing bonus on a five-year contract counts as $4 million annually against the cap, i.e., $20/5 = $4 million.

Under the NFL salary cap system, there are several time points that matter significantly in terms of calculating where a team is with respect to compliance with the salary cap.  Most importantly, if a player is cut before June 1, that player's non-guaranteed salary does not count against the cap that year but any remaining guaranteed signing bonus is accelerated and charged against the current cap.  If, in the example above, the player was cut after two years but before the June 1 deadline of his third year, then there would be a $12 million hit against the cap that season (three years remaining x $4 million).  If a player is cut after June 1, the portion of the signing bonus due that year is charged against the cap and any remaining years hit the next year's cap.  In the above example, $4 million would be charged against the current year's cap and then $8 million (two remaining years x $4 million) will be charged against the next year's cap.

Incentive bonuses (i.e., money earned if certain goals are met) are characterized as "likely to be earned" or "unlikely to be earned."  If the bonus is described as "likely to be earned" (e.g., a workout bonus) then it counts against the current season's cap.  If the bonus is described as "unlikely to be earned" (e.g., a bonus for being named the league's MVP) then it is not counted against the current year's cap but, if earned, will be applied against the next season's cap.  Likewise, any bonuses that were characterized as "likely to be earned" but were not paid out, are added back to next year's cap amount.

Teams and players will often renegotiate salaries and signing bonuses mid-contract in order to make the salary cap algebra work for the team.  The challenging part is not to end up with seasons where the team is on the hook for significant salary and bonus payments for players who are not on the roster or not able to significantly contribute to the team, i.e., "dead money."  What has happened over time is many veteran players with high salaries are cut by their current teams and then find jobs with other teams under short term contracts and/or contracts that rely heavily on incentives vs. base salary.

## Practice Squad

In the early days of the AAFC, Cleveland Browns coach Paul Brown found a way to circumvent the 33 man roster limitation set by the league. Rather than cut good players and let other teams pick them up, Coach Brown arranged for players not "officially" on the Brown's roster to work for a local Cleveland taxi company owned by Brown's team owner Arthur McBride. The taxi company would list the players as employees even though they never really worked for the company. McBride would pay the players through the taxi company and thereby allow the Browns to get around the AAFC rules. The players were not on the Browns roster and did not play in games but they practiced with the team and were incented to stick around and wait for their shot to make the roster.

Over the years, and after the AAFC/NFL merger, other teams found ways to "stash" players away and the NFL had to find a way to formalize the "taxi squad" process. The result was the practice squad. Under the current CBA, after the preseason a team can sign up to 10 players for their practice squad. The squad usually consists of rookies and border line NFL-caliber players (though several former practice squad players have gone on to star in the NFL). The players practice along with the regular team players every week but cannot play in games unless officially signed and activated to the team's 53 man roster. The players are considered free agents and can be signed by any NFL team to their 53 man roster at any time without compensation to the other team. A player can only be signed to another team's practice squad if he is released first. Players cannot be on a practice squad more than two seasons (and under some circumstances three seasons). Practice squad players currently make a minimum of $6,300 per game week. Practice squad salaries count against the team's salary cap amount. None of the practice squad players' contracts are guaranteed and they can be cut without penalty to the team. NFL teams can add one international player (from outside the United States) to their practice squad and he will not count against the 10 man limit.

CPSIA information can be obtained at www.ICGtesting.com
Printed in the USA
BVOW09s1506030116

431629BV00004B/28/P